# TRAVELS
AMONGST
# THE TODAS

# TRAVELS

AMONGST

# THE TODAS:

OR

THE STUDY OF A PRIMITIVE TRIBE IN

# SOUTH INDIA,

THEIR HISTORY, CHARACTER, CUSTOMS,
RELIGION, INFANTICIDE, POLYANDRY, LANGUAGE;
WITH OUTLINES OF THE TUDA GRAMMAR

WILLIAM E. MARSHALL

GYAN

*Published by*

Gyan Publishing House
5, Ansari Road
Daryaganj, New Delhi-110002
Phone: 011-47034999, 9811692060
E-mail: books@gyanbooks.com

*Distribution Network*
gyanbooks.com
India, USA, Canada, UK, Australia



ISBN: 978-93-6780-273-1 (HB)

First Published, 1873

2nd Impression 2024

*Printed at:* Gyan Press, Delhi.



**TRAVELS AMONGST THE TODAS**
Author: WILLIAM E. MARSHALL

# THE TODAS

N°. 1

AUTOTYPE, LONDON.

REDUCED FROM A PHOTOGRAPH BY MESSRS BOURNE & SHEPHERD. SIMLA.

A TODA MAND.

# TRAVELS

AMONGST

# THE TODAS

OR

THE STUDY OF A PRIMITIVE TRIBE IN

## SOUTH INDIA,

THEIR HISTORY, CHARACTER, CUSTOMS, RELIGION, INFANTICIDE, POLYANDRY, LANGUAGE;

WITH OUTLINES OF THE TUDA GRAMMAR.

BY

WILLIAM E. MARSHALL,

LIEUTENANT-COLONEL OF HER MAJESTY'S BENGAL STAFF CORPS.

*PERMANENT ILLUSTRATIONS BY THE AUTOTYPE PROCESS.*

LONDON:
LONGMANS, GREEN, AND CO.
1873.

# PREFACE.

In the course of a furlough I took in the year 1870 to the Madras sanatarium of Utacamand, in the Nilagiri mountains,[1] I heard much of an 'aboriginal race' living in the neighbourhood; which, infanticidal and polyandrous, was said to be fast dying out.

I had long been curious to understand the mysterious process by which, as appears inevitable, savage tribes melt away when forced into prolonged contact with a superior civilisation. But, ignorant of all the languages of South India, I should have relinquished attempt to study the Todas, had I not the great good fortune to make the acquaintance of the Reverend Friedrich Metz, of the Basel Missionary Society, who had spent upwards of twenty years in labours amongst the primitive tribes forming the inhabitants of the Nilagiris; and who, in addition to being skilled in several Drâvidian dialects, was exceptionally practised in High Kanarese and Tamil. Above all, he was the only European able to speak the obscure Toda tongue.

Mr. Metz most readily agreed to co-operate with me in strict enquiry into the condition of the Todas, and

[1] Commonly called 'Ootacamund, in the Nilgherry hills'; it being the peculiar Anglo-Indian custom to style all mountains, hills. Thus the Himalayas are only hills, whilst in England, Ben Nevis and Snowdon are mountains.

henceforth became my sole associate in all expeditions amongst them—save one or two.

It is the more proper and just that I should in this place render Mr. METZ the warmest acknowledgment of the very disinterested and important share he had in the undertaking, that there is so little in what I have written in these pages to recall his name. It was not only that his knowledge of Toda dialect was invaluable for minute and truthful investigation, but the personal respect in which he was held by the people, and the confidence they placed in his fidelity to them, obtained for us a more friendly welcome and complete exposure of their minds than would have been accorded had we been mere strangers. I must state, however, that my friend is not, even in the slightest degree, responsible for any opinions I have expressed.

A small Vocabulary, compiled and carefully revised by Mr. METZ, will be found as the groundwork of the last Chapter. It may be said, more entirely to consist of actual Toda words than any other existing.

Our operations began with a census of a portion of the tribe, combined with an examination of each of the families that came before us. But in proportion as our work advanced, so did interest in the subject develop, until the scheme was entertained of enlarging the topic from its original design, so as to embrace 'a study of the manners and customs of a primitive race of man.'

With this evolution grew also the desire so to describe what I had seen, as to enable readers who could never have an opportunity of witnessing life amongst untutored races, to realise justly and without exaggeration, what it really is, and—by analogy—what it must have been in the pre-historic era, long ere 'Adam delved and Eve spun,' *before man had much developed in manly qualities.*

I have actually witnessed most of the scenes here described. Such of the remainder as are not otherwise authorised, I have compiled from direct narrative of the most reliable Todas.

Whilst hoping, though not without some misgivings, that the ugly statistics collected with so much care, and the speculations advanced to account physiologically for the origin of obscure customs, may have some slight value, even to the savant, I am sanguine that the antique practices now brought to light, and the illustrations I have attempted of every-day life, may render the book acceptable to the general reader. I may say, that great and especial pains have been taken to render as large a portion of the work as the subject permits, attractive, and suited for ladies' reading.

A few words of explanation are perhaps called for; to account for my having devoted an entire chapter to the description of some of the first principles of phrenology—a subject which is fully treated in standard works by acknowledged authorities. I wished primarily, to show the premises forming the basis for many conjectures which otherwise would have borne too much the appearance of dogmatism, or that might have been misunderstood. Secondly, I desired to show for phrenology, a marked practical value for ethnological purposes: and no single work containing, with clearness and brevity combined, so much information calculated to be serviceable to enquirers disposed to pursue the phrenologic mode of enquiry into the nature of barbarous races, which I have here faintly attempted; I trusted that the chapter might be useful, in some sort, as a manual for ethnographers so circumstanced.

But in this matter, as indeed throughout the book, I must trust very much to the lenient judgment of my readers; if, as a solitary Indian, far away from contact with men of science, but fresh from the actual and impressive presence of 'nature's children,' in attempting to work out for myself some of the vastly interesting unsolved problems of our day, I air some seemingly quaint ideas. *The public is concerned simply in their truth.*

The publication of these results of investigations made two years ago, has been delayed through the impossibility of finding in a very hot climate, and in the intervals of official duties, leisure sufficient for completing a subject demanding much thought and care.

I beg to invite especial attention to the important contributions made by the eminent philologist and great Tamil scholar, the Rev. G. U. Pope, D.D., at present Head Master of the 'Bishop Cotton' School at Bangalore. These will be found both in the form of foot-notes throughout this little work, and forming a distinct chapter at the end. The interesting and often most valuable derivations of Toda words given in these notes, have enabled me, in the absence of other evidence, to explain several customs and to work out some speculations that otherwise seemed quite incomprehensible.

But for the linguist, I trust Chapter XXIX. will have especial attractions.

To the Honorable Sir A. ARBUTHNOT, C.S., K.C.S.I., Secretary to the Government of Madras, I am greatly indebted, for having placed at my disposal, the records existing in the Revenue Department, on the subject of Toda infanticide.

I am beholden to the skill of the distinguished artists, Messrs. BOURNE and SHEPHERD, of Simla, and to Messrs. NICHOLAS and CURTHS, of Madras, for the photographs which decorate the book. These have been printed in carbon, by the Autotype Fine Art Company, 36 Rathbone Place, London.

W. E. MARSHALL.

FAIZABAD:
*2nd October*, 1872.

# CONTENTS.

## CHAPTER I.

### HISTORICAL OUTLINE.



## CHAPTER II.

### PHRENOLOGICAL BASIS.



## CHAPTER III.

### PHYSIOLOGY OF THE TODAS.

## CHAPTER IV.

### CHARACTERISTICS.



## CHAPTER V.

### THE LAND HE LIVES IN.



## CHAPTER VI.

### THE MAND.



## CHAPTER VII.

### THE FAMILY.



## CHAPTER VIII.

### FOOD.

## CHAPTER IX.

### SAVAGE ANTITYPE.



## CHAPTER X.

### CENSUS.



## CHAPTER XI.

### FAMILY STATISTICS.



## CHAPTER XII.

### RELIGION.

## CHAPTER XIII.

### THE BELL-GODS.



## CHAPTER XIV.

### TIRIÊRI PRIESTS.



## CHAPTER XV.

### PRIESTLY DUTIES.



## CHAPTER XVI.

### THE TIRIÊRI.

## CHAPTER XVII.

### THE ÊTUD MAND.



## CHAPTER XVIII.

### THE FUTURE STATE.



## CHAPTER XIX.

### THE BOATH.



## CHAPTER XX.

### THE GREEN FUNERAL.



## CHAPTER XXI.

### THE DRY FUNERAL.

## CHAPTER XXII.

### RELIGIOUS CULTURE.



## CHAPTER XXIII.

### INFANTICIDE.



## CHAPTER XXIV.

### POLYANDRY.



## CHAPTER XXV.

### POLYANDRY—MARRIAGE.



## CHAPTER XXVI.

### POLYANDRY—MORALITY.

## TABLES.

## ILLUSTRATIONS.

# SCHEME OF TRANSLITERATION

FOR

# THE TODA LANGUAGE.

| | | | | | | | | |
|---|---|---|---|---|---|---|---|---|
| **a** | = u | in | 'cut' | | **e** | = e | in | 'pen' |
| **â** | = au | „ | 'caught' | | **ê** | = a | „ | 'sale' |
| **i** | = i | „ | 'pin' | | **ei** | = i | „ | 'pile' |
| **í** | = ee | „ | 'thee' | | **o** | = o | „ | 'potato' |
| **u** | = oo | „ | 'cook' | | **ô** | = o | „ | 'dote' |
| **û** | = oo | „ | 'booth' | | **au** | = ou | „ | 'out' |

**oi** = oi in 'oil'

**ch** = ch in 'niche' **kh** = kh in 'khan

Erratum.—Page 129, line 19, *for* No. 15, *read* No. 14.

# A PHRENOLOGIST

AMONGST

# THE TODAS.

## CHAPTER I.

### HISTORICAL OUTLINE.

*Meaning of the Name Toda—Names of Clans—Kôls, the Aborigines of India—Todas are Drâvidians—Drâvidians penetrate India, and dispossess the Kôl Race—Affinities of the Drâvidians—Âryan Conquest; its Effects on the Kôl and Drâvidian Races—The mutual Influence of the Kôl, Drâvidian, and Âryan Races on one another—Positions in India now held by the three Races—Positions in the Dekkan of the Drâvidian Tribes—Affinities of the Toda Dialect—Last Migration of the Todas—Kairns and Kromlechs on the Nilagiris—Are the Kairn-builders allied to the Todas?*



THE PEOPLE whose ancient customs and primitive habits form the topic of these pages are called by the English Todas; but in their own language an individual of the tribe is Todan,[1] the plural being Todaru.

The Badagas—of whom more hereafter—who for centuries past have lived in close proximity to the Todas, style them in the singular Todawanu,[2] and in the plural Todawaru: from which, by abbreviation, Todawan or Todawar. Hence

[1] Todan. Tamil, Toṛavam and Tôṛam = *a herd.* And thus Toṛavan or Tôṛan = *herdsman.* [POPE.]

On this note, Mr. Metz remarks: 'As the d in Toda is not a lingual ḍ, but dental, I do not believe the word means *herdsman*, as Toḍa in Old Tamil. I do not know the meaning of Toda with the dental d.'

[2] Todawanu. Tora = *a herd,* Wanu = *a person.* Drâvidian. [POPE.]

CHAP. I.

also have arisen other corruptions in English; as Torawar, Thautawars, Todars, Todies, &c. Dr. Hunter gives, in his Dictionary,[3] a Toḍuva variety of the Toḍu language; which is an error.

The Toda tribe is divided into five clans, called Pēiki, Pekkan, Tôdi, Kuttan, and Kenna.[4] The two first are very closely related, although they do not now intermarry; the former having become what might be termed a Levitical clan. All of the remaining four freely marry amongst one another.

We have very little positive information of the earliest inhabitants of India; but, so far as the existing condition of evidence enables us to determine, they were of a race whose speech, having analogies to the extensive Hô or Kôl group of languages, 'derived from a source common both to themselves and the Chinese,'[5] gives grounds for the belief that, at some extremely early prehistoric period, a migration of barbarians into India took place from over its north-eastern confines 'from the northern shores of the Indian Ocean and the Chinese Sea;'[6] thus *seemingly* earning for themselves the title of children of the soil, the aboriginal inhabitants of at least the central and north-eastern tracts of India.

The physical type of this race, judging from the many distinct tribes of the family still to be found in various hill ranges, partook of the main features of the Mongol—in the hairless face, broad and short, the spreading unshapely nose, small eyes and high cheek-bones: and evidences of the people exist even in the southern portion of the Indian peninsula, both in the presence of this peculiar stamp of countenance, and apparently in the names of places and of natural features of the country.

The Toda tongue is entirely apart from that of the Kôl

[3] Hunter, 'Comparative Dictionary of the Non-Aryan Languages of India and High Asia.'

[4] Mr. Metz writes me that he believes he has found a sixth clan, called Târâl; but the statement needs confirmation.

[5] Hunter. [6] Hunter.

family. It is, indeed, now known with absolute certainty to be a dialect of the development of Turanian speech styled Drâvidian;[7] the language of a group of primitive, illiterate, and perhaps warlike tribes who, between three thousand and four thousand years ago, migrated from tracts of Western Asia, and penetrating India, probably through Beluchistan and the natural water lines[8] of the country, filled all its western and southern districts, pushing before them, in some period of their advance, the various tribes of the Kôl aborigines, some of whom, in slavery or menial conditions of life, survived as subjects of their conquerors.



The Rev. Dr. Caldwell[9] has drawn attention to the remarkable circumstance that the closest and most distinct affinities to the speech of this race are those which have been discovered in the languages of the Finns and Lapps of Northern Europe and of the Ostiaks and other Ugrians of Siberia: and consequently that the Drâvidian is proved, by 'language alone, in the silence of history, in the absence of all ordinary probabilities, to be allied to tribes that appear to have overspread Europe before the arrival of the Goths and the Pelasgi, and even before the arrival of the Celts.'

The characteristics of the Toda branch of this race, form the burden of the following pages. In the process of writing

[7] A term which, applied by the Brahmans apparently in supercilious envy and contempt of the people they could not conquer—the word Drâvida implying the condition of being beyond the pale of the castes—is now used ethnologically, to designate that which has grown to be a distinct race of man.

[8] It would seem an absolute necessity, that primitive tribes should maintain the water-lines of the country they penetrated. If such be the case, noticing the geographical peculiarities of the west frontier of India, this Turanian race would have divided at the Desert of Scinde; one branch following the course of the Indus and its tributaries to the Land of the Five Rivers: the other, turning south, would have both crossed and followed the many watercourses which drain into the Arabian Sea, on their way towards the Dekkan.

[9] Caldwell, 'Comparative Grammar of the Drâvidian Languages.'

I beg here to acknowledge my debt to the above valuable work for much of the information I have incorporated in this chapter.

CHAP. I.

of them, I have grown to the very strong conviction that the people are a surviving sample of some portion of the Turanian race when in its very primitive stage. Without much exercise of the imagination, I can picture them the cotemporaries and neighbours, even perhaps the ancestors, of races of South-Western Asia which have made a figure in early history. There is much of the 'blameless Ethiopian' about them: something of the Jew and of the Chaldean in their appearance. I do not venture to hazard an opinion as to their cradle-land. It is safer to draw attention to what, judging by appearances and customs, are their possible ethnic affinities.[10]

At a period which historians have placed 300 or 400 years subsequent to this Turanian inroad, a branch of the Âryas—an Indo-European race of the Caucasian mould, speaking Sanskrit—burst in on India from the north-west. At first occupying that part of the country now known as the Punjab, these warlike colonists grew in the course of centuries into a conquering power, establishing empires on the Indus and Ganges after the fashion of lawless times, on the ruins of the Kôl aborigines and Drâvidians, holding possession of the soil of various parts. And with a success so complete, that we find the Âryas ultimately occupying the whole of the arable tracts which in the main follow the course of those rivers, and form the northern base of the Indian Peninsula. As a consequence of this crushing conquest in the north-west, we recognise Drâvidian tribes in the inferior strata of the resident populace, and their blood mixed with that of even the highest Âryan castes. The Sikh bears a considerable though refined likeness to the Toda. And the province of Oudh has manifestly a large Drâvidian substratum.

Warlike and gifted though this branch of the Indo-European family has shown itself to have been, it does not appear

[10] On the eve of sending this work to the press, I would beg again to urge my belief in the connection between the Drâvidian Toda and the Ethiop. Dr. Pritchard's 'Natural History of Man' might be compared.

to have subjugated those Drâvidians which colonised the Dekkan; but rather obtained sacerdotal influence amongst them through the means of a superior religious culture and civilisation, of which ambitious and wily Pundits, like monks in the barbarous days of Europe, were the exponents and pioneers.

As might be expected, the three main races of India could not be located in the close contiguity which resulted of repeated conquest and subsequent expanding numbers, before their various religious customs, their languages, and even their blood, began to show their influence in reaction on one another. Perhaps the most striking effect of all these operations, was that which the barbarous rites and beliefs of the inferior races exercised on the purer and more spiritual religious faith which originally distinguished the Âryas.

In their desire to absorb all the subject and utterly savage tribes of the conquered inhabitants, the Brahmans opened the portals of their religion, and incorporated the many gods of the aborigines with the ancient deities of their Vedic pantheon.

The pure Hindu religion, although thus actually debased in the process, probably became an instrument of even greater efficiency, when wielded by clever priests, for the purpose of obtaining an ascendancy over races in an extremely low stage of culture. And we recognise this truth in the great influence which Hinduism and the Sanskrit tongue, have obtained over the entire Indian Continent.

In the case of the Drâvidians; it seems to me, on reviewing Toda religious practice, an extremely probable event. that a possible early contact with the Âryas, long before either race entered India, rendered Sanskrit, especially in regard to all pious notions and reverent observance, influential amongst them, even then. This is a very interesting consideration; one which must render it difficult to determine at what early period this Drâvidian branch of the

CHAP. I.

Turanian tree had first been biassed through the superior religious instinct of the Ârya.

If we consider that the many tribes of these three dominant races, brought into India the various habits, religious observances, and dialects of the diverse tracts of Asia whence they emigrated. When we further reflect on the different results which must have ensued during their residence in the country of their adoption, from the contiguity of certain of them to the progressive Brahmanical race, with its refined and copious vocabulary, its elevated moral code, with idealised pantheon of heroes and heroines; and the proximity of others to the carnivorous Kôl, his tutelary deities and bloody rites. Further, bearing in mind the isolation of tribes kept asunder by the lawlessness of the times, the pathless nature of the country, and the conservative nature of tribal barbarians;—we can readily comprehend why Drâvidian tribes have now concreted into separate nationalities, whose dialects are 'distinct though affiliated languages,'[11] and whose religion varies in every shade, from the simple but senseless, or perhaps cruel, observances introduced by original immigrants, to the complex rites of corrupted Hinduism.

The accompanying sketch map of the Indian peninsula describes the position in the country which the Drâvidians hold at the present day; when, after their wanderings and their wars, the various tribes of which the race is composed had settled down, then expanded into important nations, speaking distinct dialects, of which the following are now highly cultivated:—

i. Tamil. iii. Kanarese.
ii. Telugu. iv. Malayâlam.
v. Tuluva.

Three others, viz.,

vi. Toda. vii. Gônd. viii. Ku or Khond,

[11] Caldwell.

No. 2

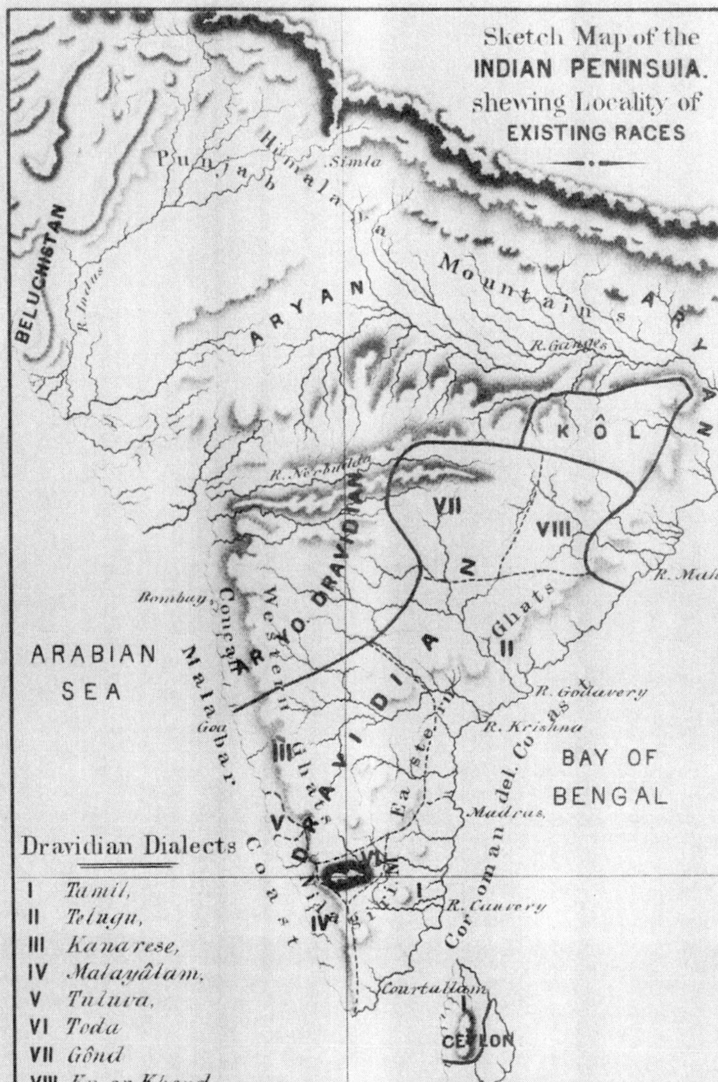


Drawn by Sheick Amir-oo-din. AUTOTYPE, LONDON.

remain in their pristine barbarous state; innocent even of written characters; and there are said to be several other minor dialects or corruptions belonging to small sylvan families holding unimportant geographical positions in the Drâvidian area.

Remnants of the ejected Kôls are shown on the eastern limits, and Âryanised peoples are closed in on the entire northern boundary.

The Rev. Dr. Pope, in his contribution to this book,[12] gives it as his opinion that the Toda language was originally old Kanarese, and not a distinct dialect. He thinks that the language has dwindled to a mere skeleton, as a result of isolation and consequent degeneration of the people.

The early Indian history of the Todas has been as completely lost as that of the long protracted period which preceded their migration to the Dekkan.

We know, indeed, with a tolerable degree of certainty, both from their own legends and from those of neighbouring tribes, that until the last few hundred years they inhabited a jungle tract of inferior hills situated between the Kanarese and Tamilian districts, in the direction of Hâsanûr; which, on E. longitude 77° 20′ and N. latitude 11° 45′ form portion of the Eastern Ghats. And that they then divided into two or more parts, of which one settled in a northerly direction, near Kôlegâll, and the other migrated or was driven in the direction of the Nilagiri Mountain;[13] the greater number

[12] Vide Chapter XXIX., 'Outlines of the Tuḍa Grammar.'

At the time of recording this opinion, Dr. Pope had not had opportunity of perusing any portion of my descriptions of Toda life. Had he done so, it is possible he might have modified his views. I, who judge the Todas physically and through their antique customs and practices, fail to discover any degeneracy in the people; rather regarding them as not only without evidence of having been better, but with little appearance of having been materially different from what they now are, within any period whose length may be fixed or even approximated.

[13] Mr. Metz, who obtained this information from the Todas, is my authority for this paragraph.

CHAP. I.

settling on its very topmost plateau, where we now find them, whilst a small remnant, winding behind its north-western slopes, remained on one of the lower plateaus, called the Wynâd.

This modern place of Toda residence is an isolated mountain, upwards of seven thousand feet above sea level, upreared on E. longitude 76° 45′ and N. latitude 11° 20′, amidst the plains of South India—the gigantic and sudden culmination of the minor mountain-chain system, called the Eastern and Western Ghats, which there meet.

These, their last movements, having been very small and of minor importance, I have included their past and their present places of residence in one area, marked VI. on the map.

Not only the summit of the Nilagiris, but the tops of the minor rounded eminences thereon, are studded with kairns, raised for the reception of ashes of the dead, by a race whose history has been so completely lost that not a tradition even of it remains. On the same plateau are also a few kromlechs, also many deserted circles of stones, situated near streams of running water; some manifestly constructed for pounding cattle, others, with equal certainty, not made for that purpose —being in exposed situations and having rocky beds.

These erections undoubtedly do not belong to the Todas, who not only do not regard them with reverence, but assert that they were of a people antecedent to themselves on the mountain. Moreover they are found in many parts of the Indian peninsula and of Western India. But I may do service in drawing attention to points in which the cremation customs of this unknown race are those of the Todas, and to those in which they differ from them.

In brief, we find, from relics exhumed from kairns, that their owners made use of the horse: that they practised agriculture, holding the buffalo in high esteem, and burying its bell with the manes of the deceased. We learn that they were acquainted with the use of the spear, bow and arrow:

that their women wore simple jewelry, and that all their implements, weapons and ornaments, whilst of a very primitive nature, were of designs extant, not only in India, but in this part of the country.

We may safely deduce from the evidences of care manifest in the solidity of these stone receptacles, as well as from the positions in which we find them, both that these people held the memory of the dead in great respect, and their property alive to be their property when dead, and that their religious belief, as regards the future state, was connected by some line of thought with prominent natural features of the country.

In many respects, viz. in the custom of cremation, the regard shown to buffaloes, the especial notice of its bell, the practice of burying weapons and personal ornaments, we shall find in due course, almost an identity with the obsequies and modes of thought now displayed by the Todas; and Mr. Metz writes, concerning the Toda faith: 'Their idea is that the spirits of deceased Todas, together with the souls of the buffaloes killed by their friends to accompany them to heaven and supply them with milk there, *take a leap from Makurti Peak,* as the nearest way to the celestial regions.'[14]

The chief points of variance between the two peoples, consist in the evidences in the Kairn-builders, of a civilisation —implied in the practice of agriculture, and in raising stone constructions to contain their dead—somewhat superior to that of the Todas. Regarding the matter of husbandry, the Todas could not be more backward in respect to these unknown Kairn-builders than they are behind all the tribes of Drâvidians which at this very day surround and isolate them. A certain small degree only of civilisation is of necessity implied in the presence of simple implements of cultivation.

The evidence of stone cemeteries, probably does not imply

[14] Metz, 'The Tribes of the Nilgherry Hills.'

the exercise of so much labour as would at first appear; for what more likely—indeed, almost certain—than that each village or family erected one once for all for itself, and that it was filled in by degrees? But it would express a method of disposing of the ashes, somewhat superior in completeness, refinement, and perhaps in depth of religious feeling, to that practised by the Todas, nothing more. No essential difference in race, but merely a tribal custom.

I would advance, therefore, the great likelihood of these Kairn-builders having been members of certain Turanian tribes of a similar stage of culture to our early Drâvidians; each of which would have brought with it the custom of the particular portion of Western Asia from which it migrated—this tribe, apparently, from a rocky and hilly region.

It does not seem too much to insist that, in grand migrations of primitive races, not merely families of one spirited tribe would move together, but they would be attended or followed at intervals of time by other tribes dependent on or patronised by them; not necessarily closely related, though perhaps near neighbours. All, however, moved by the same impetus: continued pressure from without, a succession of famines at the door, or a vacuum to be filled up.

Had the Todas died out a hundred years ago, but little remembrance of them would survive at this day. Similarly, these defunct races live solely in their imperishable monuments.

In Chapter XIX., on the Boath, will be found the suggestion that that eccentric building may have belonged to the Kairn-builders. I do not wish to press the theory with undue vigour; yet, if form is in a degree, a sort of index or expression of the mind that adopts it, I think that, in the unusual shape of roof (pointing upwards) in the Boath, may lurk a mental impulse in co-ordination with that which prompted them to place kairns on the top of hills; some superior religious development of the tribe; the root, I may term it, of some such conception as leads us to the words: 

Nearer, my God, to Thee, nearer to Thee.

Certain it is that the Todas, who grovel to the earth, show in their cremation custom, as in the architecture of their most holy place, a parity in lowliness as much marked as this prominence of individuality which we note in the Kairn-builders.

I have apparently stepped out of my way to speculate on the remains of an unknown people, but my object has been to show a possible connection between the Kairn-builders and the Todas.

# CHAPTER II.

## PHRENOLOGICAL BASIS.

*Contrast between simple and complex Races—Advantages in noting Groups of Organs—Necessity for studying individual Organs—The Properties and Positions of Groups and of the Organs in each Group—Effects of Size and Quality in Brain—Power—Two Varieties of Energy—Mutual Influence of the Organs—Correlation between Organology, Temperament, and Bodily Structure—Description of the main Temperaments amongst Oriental Races.*

CHAP. II.

IN the practice of phrenology amongst a civilised people, more especially in one which is—like the English for example—the resultant breed of several distinct races, which though intimately mixed have never completely amalgamated and fused into a single type; an apparently endless variety of combinations of organs and temperaments is met with, sufficient to tax the utmost sensitiveness to perception of varieties and experience of character, to decipher and analyse. In such circumstances, amongst such races, ability to estimate the exact size of each separate faculty, and its value relative to the whole mass of the cranium: to understand the influence of each mixed-temperament upon that complicated headpiece, and to take into just consideration each one of the many circumstances that would influence its activity, is absolutely essential to success.

But in the examination of primitive tribes, particularly *one which having long practised endogamy*—or the habit of uniting in wedlock solely within its own community—*is uniform in appearance*, we escape most of these difficulties. Nothing perhaps marks the difference in cranial appearance, between savage and civilised races, more than the complexity in variety of temperament, the numerous shades of capacity and shape of brain, and the many degrees of sizes in organs amongst the latter, as compared with the extreme simplicity and uniformity of the former.

Visit one of these very primitive endogamous tribes, and we at once find ourselves in the presence of a crowd of individuals all of the same type, whose temperaments are in their least complex forms, the general size and configuration of whose skulls is very uniform and easy to read, whose figure, voice, and carriage, are similar, and whose circumstances of daily life, whether they be the cause or the effect, or the joint-cause and effect of this similarity, are throughout alike ; who in fact differ in outward appearance only in modifications—generally slight—of a few single organs.

They present scarcely more differences in appearance and character than any one dog does from any other of the same kennel of hounds.

For general ethnographic purposes therefore, in which research would probably be limited in its aim to determining a certain few specific points ; as for instance the relation of a given tribe to any other rude stock of man, or the acquisition of such knowledge of tribal idiosyncrasy as would afford the key to its management and education, a study of the physiognomy and powers of the main *groups* of cognate faculties, by which the elementary cranium of the savage acquires its distinguishing form, combined with observation of other external evidences—as size in mass of head, simple national temperament, as illustrated by physique: with voice and habits of life—will, whilst affording us much of the evidence obtainable during lifetime, also give the information necessary for learning early conditions of the human race, before the brain has acquired the great diversity in development and the amplitude in convolution which must accompany advance from absolute savagery—or extreme primitiveness—towards the superior stage, that of barbarism.[1] At this point of progress, the study of character growing involved and complicated, by reason of the subtle influences which fine nervous conditions exert on the form of the brain, a more minute record of the sizes of *single organs* becomes essential, more particularly if one desires to utilise phrenology to the more advanced ethnographic study, for which the science is peculiarly adapted, viz. to tracing the *correlation between the progressive growth of races, and the development of their skulls* at corresponding æras of advance.

If one wished to ascertain the true type of the English character—supposing there to be a type, and that it could be found—it certainly could not be even approximated, except by the analysis in character of a vast number of individuals of the race. But an average of ten of each sex would give us all we should care to know of the simple Toda.

With the view of enabling such of my readers as are willing, to follow me into the phrenologic mode of studying traits and customs of early races, I here give[2] briefly and concisely the attributes of each single organ and of each of the groups into which the faculties have been collected, as they would be exhibited, not so much in the conduct of civilised man, as in that of the same creature when acting under the inferior impulses of his primitive organisation.

The capacity of the following organs and groups being described as if they were each large, *their action when small* must be judged by supposing a *proportionate absence* of manifestation.

[1] Yet all barbarians have not been savages. The savage state is an energetic stage of barbarism, through which all races—especially so those who are natives of the torrid zones—do not pass.

This subject is further prosecuted in the Chapter on 'Savage Antitype.'

[2] I beg to acknowledge the advantages I have acquired in the compilation of the following pages from the perusal of Professor Bain's 'The Study of Character,' and Mr. Fowler's 'Synopsis of Phrenology,' in addition to the standard works of Mr. George Combe and others.

## GROUP A.—CONCENTRATIVE.

*Constituent organ.*

1. *Concentrativeness.*

This group has but one organ. Centripetal; it affects every faculty in the head by imparting to it continuity of thought and feeling, enabling it to concentrate the attention on one object, as contrasted with a desultory tendency. Thus it is an important element in steadiness of character, presence of mind, and good memory. It gives powers of self-abstraction. It impels to conservativism, abhorring change. It adds to the power of the will, by prolonging the sensations. Combined with Group B, it probably originated the belief in a future state, and suggested the desire for pyramids and mummies.

A steady voice marks this Group.

*Position and form.* Creates a fulness in the back of the head, between Groups B and D.

## GROUP B.—DOMESTIC.

*Constituent organs.*

2. *Amativeness.* Gives desire for the companionship of the opposite sex. An element in gallantry. Tends to general indecency.

3. *Philoprogenitiveness.* Is the faculty which primarily gives the love of a parent for its young whilst in the weak and defenceless state. Thence general fondness for the young and weak of all ages.

4. *Adhesiveness.* Creates a desire for friendship apart from considerations of sex. Hence gregariousness and clannishness.

Group B. Composed of the domestic and gregarious propensities. It impels to marriage; and in its love of children, fondness for the opposite sex, desire for friendship, regard for

CHAP. II. the dead, and love for the family or home, imparts the constituents of a warm-hearted disposition.

Low and tender notes are the expression of this Group.

*Position and form.* Causes elongation and fulness in the middle and lower portion of the back of the head.

### GROUP C. INVIGORATING.

*Constituent organs.*

5. *Combativeness.* Occasions opposiveness and willingness to meet physical danger; is therefore a main element in active courage and fortitude. Likes close fighting.

6. *Destructiveness.* Prompts to overcome difficulties by exertion, and gives the energy required. Tends to acts of revenge and cruelty, to suicide, sanguinary rites and cannibalism. Suggested the idea of perpetual punishment. Is accompanied by violence of temper. Believed to give fortitude to bear physical pain.

7. *Secretiveness.* Enjoins secrecy and silence. Gives the main element of tact, finesse, cunning, and capacity to hide one's own feelings, with skill to penetrate the designs of others. Tends to distrust, duplicity, and treachery. Combined with Destructiveness, enjoys the act of torture and refinements of cruelty. In war would be partial to ambushes and perhaps night attacks; in religion would practise mystic rites.

8. *Acquisitiveness.* Occasions desire generally. Gives talent for accumulation. Tenacious, it is opposed to communism. Tends to rapacity and theft.

9. *Alimentativeness.* Is the organ which gives discrimination in the flavour of food, and fondness for variety in diet; tends to gluttony. Combined with Destructiveness, demands flesh and stimulants; and, under exciting circumstances, prompts to cannibalism. When combined with a high coronal region, is also very partial to sweets.

10. *Constructiveness.* Creates talent for building and contrivance. Gave men houses, implements, forts and weapons.

Group C. Gives impulses to overcome difficulty of every nature, and to subdue. To provide by *action* for the daily animal wants of self and—in combination with Group B—of family. Hence it imparts vigour, skilful efficiency, and impetus to the whole character, by stimulating the other faculties. When in excess, the character tends to treachery, avarice, gluttony, and general ferocious habit.

Harsh low tones express the activity of this Group.

*Position and form.* Gives breadth and fulness to the sides of the head, immediately around and in front of the ears. When Destructiveness is very large, the holes of the ears are placed low with reference to the line of the eyebrows.

### GROUP D. PERSONAL.

*Constituent organs.*

11. *Self-esteem.* Gives self-regard and pride. Tends to self-reliance. Is fond of power. Sensitive to personal position. Enamoured of freedom.

12. *Love of approbation.* Desires to please. Vain. Fond of ornament. Sensitive to outside opinion. Tends to courtesy and the use of flattery.

13. *Firmness.* Gives capacity for pursuing a line of conduct, when unopposed. Is the main element in decision of character. Apt to decide too soon. Tends to obstinacy.

Group D supplies will and self-confidence, and gives personal motives, as pride, vanity, and perseverance, tending to action on account of self or—in combination with Group B—of family interests. Connected with Group E, it assumes an elevating and ennobling character, with a hatred of tyranny and desire to protect. Combined with Groups A and E, gave mainly the conception of Jehovah to the Jews.

The voice of this Group is firm and measured.

*Position and form.* Creates an elongation and fulness of and around the pole of the head, whence the hair radiates.

CHAP. II.

## Group E. Moral.

*Constituent organs.*

14. *Conscientiousness.* Gives love of truth, and of what is honest, just, right or faithful. Gives earnestness and simplicity to character. Gives the appearance of truth even to falsehood. Is apt to be harsh and exacting. Tends to austerities, asceticism, and general self-sacrifice.

15. *Veneration.* Desires to pay respect; raises and multiplies objects of worship; prompts to religious service, the nature of rites and sacrifices being dependent on the combinations made with other organs, as Amativeness, Destructiveness, Hope, Conscientiousness. Tends to slavishness.

16. *Hope.* Gives sanguine feelings, supporting and encouraging the belief in a future state, and inciting to acts by which it may be attained. Leads to idleness. Is a great element in the gambling spirit.

17. *Benevolence.* Leads to kindness, liberality, and mercy. Its impulse is, to give; thus tending to prodigality.

18. *Cautiousness.* Affords the desire to act with care and circumspection, and to provide for dangerous contingencies. If not coupled with Combativeness, tends to cowardice.

Group E. Creates virtuous sentiments, emotions, and duties of a sincere, generous, hopeful, and reverential nature. Combined with Amativeness and with Group C, religious action degenerates into the performance of sensual and cruel rites. In combination with Group D, it partakes of a personal nature; Group F supplying it with an element of romance, poetry, or superstition; and Groups G, H, and I with system and logic.

Soft and rich tones are the natural expression of this group.

*Position and form.* Gives fulness, height, and an arched appearance to the whole crown or roof of the head.

## Group F. Refining.

*Constituent organs.*

19. *Imitation.* Copies sounds, actions, forms, thoughts. By perpetuating usage, preserves results of progress. An element in all arts. Induces men to follow a lead.

20. *Wonder.* Is interested in the unseen or unusual. Tends to superstition. Gives credence in gods, spirits, ghosts, and witchcraft. Is a source of myths and legends. Exaggerates. Leads to investigation and to gossip.

21. *Ideality.* Loves the beautiful. Gives grace to all conceptions. Partial to ornament. Is a bardic element, and gave gods to the Âryas.

Group F. The refinement of the human race, or its progress beyond the material, owes its growth to the impulse given both to morals and the intellect by the imaginative, inquiring, speculative, inventive qualities of this group.

*Position and form.* Causes breadth and fulness of the head, from the top of the temples to the forepart of the crown.

## Group G. Reflective.

*Constituent organs.*

22. *Wit.* Notices incongruity. Is a main element in the sense of the ludicrous. Gives suppleness, discrimination, and resource to the intellect by presenting various sides of a question. Assists in caricaturing.

23. *Causality.* Observes the just relation between cause and effect. Acts with reason and judgment. Tends to excessive refinement in logical conception.

24. *Comparison.* Notices resemblances. Reasons by analogy. Is a source of parables and proverbs. Assists in

CHAP. II.

creating gods, and fashioning idols and symbols generally. Gives nicknames.

Group G. By its evolutionary powers of thought and reason, by its capacity for perceiving the connection between cause and effect, and for dividing truth from absurdity, is rendered not only competent to superintend the operations of all the other groups—leading them to act with judgment—but places them in a position to realise the true connection of all the parts of the universe. When this group is well developed, man has long left the savage stage.

*Position and form.* Gives height, fulness, and breadth to the upper part of the forehead.

GROUP H. { PERCEPTIVE. DYNAMICAL. }

*Constituent organs.*

25. *Language.* Gives to every faculty, power of expressing itself by signs or words. Articulates. Tends to garrulity.

26. *Eventuality.* Observes movements, events, and muscular expressions. Gives an inquiring nature, with much of intuition. Impulsive. An element in all dances. Gesticulates.

27. *Time.* Notices lapse of time. Gives cadence in song or dance. Tends to periodic celebrations.

28. *Tune.* Observes quality, succession, and harmony in tones of sound. Is an element in singing, and chief organ in musical composition. Prompts to invention of musical instruments.

Group H. Contains such faculties as obtain practical knowledge through observation of movement. Has great power of expressing ideas.

*Position and form.* Creates fulness, breadth, and squareness to the middle-horizontal zone of the forehead, and gives prominence to the eyes.

GROUP I. { PERCEPTIVE. STATICAL.

*Constituent organs.*

29. *Number.* Gives conception of numbers, and power to calculate and compute values. Is an important element in the talent for commerce and barter. Tends to economy and to love of money.

30. *Order.* Notes method in the relative position and succession of things. Gives neatness, and fondness for dress.

31. *Colour.* Perceives colours, the quality and harmony of their shades. Renders the sight of flowers pleasing. Gives colour in dress.

32. *Weight.* Gives sensibility in matters of weight and lightness, stability and resistance; as in the balance or poise, the touch, degree of force to be used. Gives dexterity in mental processes. Is fond of glitter. Is a source of skill in many games, as riding, and throwing weapons. Suggested the shape of the Pyramids.

33. *Locality.* Takes cognisance of the relative position of objects. Gives *coup d'œil.* Is fond of travelling; combined with large Eventuality, and deficient Concentrativeness, Acquisitiveness, and Order, tends to a vagrant life.

34. *Individuality.* Notes the existence of objects, without regard to their properties or modes of action.

35. *Form.* Judges of form; aids in making idols, hieroglyphs, and weapons. Joined with Size, Weight, and Comparison, gives judgment in the useful qualities of animals.

36. *Size.* Estimates size. Takes cognisance of space. Geometric. Is necessary in projecting missiles at unknown distances.

Group I. Is constituted of such faculties as obtain practical knowledge through noting statistics; as material objects,

CHAP. II.

facts, places, and numbers, with their physical properties and mutual relations.

*Position and form.* Causes protrusion, breadth and squareness of the whole ridge of the forehead on which the eyebrows grow; forming what is termed 'deep-set eyes.' The distance from the hole of the ear to the forehead is long.

It is not to be expected that the precise same collection of organs as I have included in each group will meet with universal approval. It must remain a matter of opinion whether certain faculties included in one cluster should not more properly belong to another, owing to the circumstance that organs often possess qualities partaking somewhat of the nature of one or more of those immediately adjoining them. Thus, Wit may by some be held a reflective faculty; by others, to be more imaginative. And with much appearance of truth, Cautiousness, whilst acknowledged to be eminently conducive to morality, may yet be esteemed a propensity.

Whilst adopting from Mr. Fowler[3] the idea of grouping organs together, I have yet been induced to make certain modifications from the groups he formed, guided by personal observation of the forms which—as I think I notice—the skulls of simple races actually assume. Prolonged study alone of such people, in various stages of their early culture, will demonstrate with any degree of certainty, the exact mode and succession by which man's cranium expands, unfolds, or blooms; but assuredly that study will well repay all trouble that can be bestowed upon it.

It is now universally admitted that, other conditions being equal, size of brain—the organ of the mind—is a measure of power in its manifestation, as in that of all other organs of the body. Professor Bain writes, 'Just as largeness of muscle gives greater strength of body as a general rule, so largeness

[3] Fowler, 'Synopsis of Phrenology.'

of brain gives greater vigour of mental impulse.'[4] 'The causes which modify the effects of size, are constitution, or quality, health, exercise, excitement from external objects, and in some cases the mutual influence of the organs.'[5] In fact, 'quality is as important as quantity, whether in nerve, muscle, or any other portion of the animal structure.'[6] What holds true of the whole is equally applicable as regards its component parts; hence, size of any organ, or of any group of organs, is, *cæteris paribus*, a measure of its or their capacity to act.

Power is the product of size and quality. Energy and rapidity being results of size and quality, combined in different proportions.

In studying the subject of energy in character, we should be careful to make a marked difference between that nature of vigour which arises from a brilliant temperament combined with well-developed Destructiveness and Combativeness, and that which is the result of the fine temperament acting with those organs small. The former works full power; actively, energetically, and with strength rising in proportion to the obstacles it meets, and lasting into advanced years. The latter shows the greatest brilliancy in positions where least opposition is met with; and its energy being very largely dependent on the state of the nervous system, the vigour of youth and health is often early supplanted by indolence.

It must be remembered, when judging of the joint action of two or more organs, that they habitually exert a mutual influence, tending to modify the mode in which both operate. But that at times they may act individually or separately according as one or other may be under the influence of exciting causes. Thus, Benevolence and Destructiveness when in unison, may give either active energy in doing a kind act, and in overcoming obstacles that may intervene between its

[4] Bain, 'The Senses and the Intellect.'
[5] G. Combe, 'Elements of Phrenology.'
[6] Bain, 'The Senses and the Intellect.'

CHAP. II.

performance; or they may operate to modify desire for revenge. On the other hand, if acting apart, the head would at one time be influenced by bloodthirsty desires, and at another by kindly motives.

Important constitutional qualities are to a certain extent indicated by Temperament; regarding which, although we have very much to learn as to its origin, modes of action, and precise effects in the economy of our system: yet, judging from the analogies nature continually presents to our consideration, in which—as an illustration—we observe the concord between the habits of birds of prey and the shape of their skull, beak, talons, and general configuration as contrasted with the inoffensive character and forms of the pigeon; I hold the belief—which can become illusionary only when hawk's talons are met allied with pigeon's brains—that an intimate connection, more close than we perhaps generally apprehend, will be shown with the advance of morphology and physiology, to exist through links of simple cause and effect, between the shapes which portions of the brain assume, and the temperament which results from certain conditions and relative proportions of our physical structure.

The study of temperament has hitherto been mainly conducted by examination of its effects in complex civilised life: but much advantage might accrue to our stock of knowledge, if the subject was prosecuted amongst isolated wild tribes. The conditions of their lives would afford many opportunities of watching the effects on negative as well as on positive developments of mind, of temperaments in various simple and healthy forms. 'There may be one' organ of the body 'vigorous and all the rest weak; one vigorous, the rest average; two vigorous and all the others weak; none preponderating, and all good, all middling, or all bad; and so on through endless combinations.'[7]

At present there is a seeming antagonism between organ-

[7] Bain, 'The Senses and the Intellect.'

ology and temperament, which further information might perhaps dissipate. For instance, the Fibrous combined with a brain deficient in the propensities and power of Will, or the Sanguine with small Hope and desire for motion, would seem to be anomalies. In both instances, the desire for action which the temperament brought, would not find correlation with harmonious mental desires. CHAP. II.

The following extracts from Mr. George Combe's interesting work, 'Phrenology applied to Painting and Sculpture,' affords some examples of his opinion as to the relation between size in particular regions of the brain and particular characteristics of the body. 'There is a correspondence between the thorax and abdomen and brain. It is rarely that a large anterior lobe and narrow base are combined with large lungs and a large abdomen. And equally seldom that a large base and small anterior lobe are combined with small lungs and a small abdomen.' Again, 'There is, generally speaking, a decided character pervading the whole corporeal frame of man, which bears a relation to the size, form, and condition of the brain. And every part of the visible surface expresses the quantity as well as the quality of the mental power which animates it.'[8]

I have observed a marked connection between the brachycephalous head—so termed by ethnographers—and broad shoulders. Although from exceptional causes the rule will not always hold good amongst individuals of a *mixed* race, yet an inspection of masses of men of the dolichocephalic type of nation, will convince most people that they cannot campare in width of shoulder with the brachycephali.[9]

A correlation may be noted between the high coronal region and sloping shoulders.

A connection between Alimentativeness and the organs of digestion is evident. When the faculty is small, the abdomi-

[8] G. Combe, 'Phrenology applied to Painting and Sculpture.'

[9] This subject is continued in Chapter IX.

nal region will be small also; and be generally accompanied by tendency to the maladies which arise from weak powers in that region. When large, the converse may with equal certainty be looked for.

The following are the outward indications by means of which the four main temperaments may be recognised amongst *dark races*, and their effects on the working qualities of body and brain.

## THE TEMPERAMENTS.

### *Fibrous.*

*Physiognomy.* A large lean frame of compact bone and hard spare muscles. Thorax broad rather than deep. Abdomen moderate.

Feet and hands broad and thick. Strong fingers and stout nails.

Teeth strong, broad, yellow, and blunt-edged.

Bold features: nose a coarse aquiline.

Eyes bright and dark; the whites not clear.

Skin coarse and hairy.

Hair coarse and curly.

*Brain.* The mind energetic, but not vivid: with power of long continued action, conspicuously so when 'mental exertion involves the muscles, which happens in such avocations as military command, teaching, speaking.'[10]

This temperament, from the excess of muscular energy over nerve, forms an excellent combination with the nervous; the amalgam, where the brain is large, giving great intellectual activity joined with powers of mental and bodily endurance. Where uncombined with the nervous temperament, and the brain is small, the energies show best when employed in operations requiring physical strength and moderate intelligence.

*Muscular action.* Sedate.

[10] Bain, 'On the Study of Character.'

### *Nervous.*[11]

*Physiognomy.* A slight frame, with small bones and muscles. Small thorax and abdomen.

Feet and hands narrow. Taper fingers and thin, often paper nails.

Teeth very white, and frequently sharp-edged. Apt to be crowded together, and to decay early.

Refined features: nostrils long, narrow, and thin.

Eyes bright and often brilliant. Whites very clear.

Skin thin, delicate. Body nearly free from hair.

Hair on the scalp, close, silky, and nearly straight, but often very long.

*Brain.* All the senses very acute. The mind impressible, clear, active, vivid or intense, but fatigues easily. Expression eminently intelligent and sensitive. Great definition of organs, arising from leanness of the skull.

This temperament, from the excess of nerve, 'delights in mental emotion and intellectual pursuits.'[12] But where the brain is intrinsically small, the energies waste themselves in excitement about trifles. It gives what is termed 'blood,' and tends to degenerate into 'want of bone,' with its concomitant, deficient strength.

*Muscular action.* Rapid and sharp, often confused and hurried.

### *Sanguine.*

*Physiognomy.* A well developed handsome form, with full rounded, rather than hard muscles. Thorax deep rather than broad. Abdomen full. Sternum protruding.

Hands and feet well shaped, with high instep. Healthy looking, pink, rounded nails.

[11] Perhaps the inhabitant of Bengal Proper, in the neighbourhood of Calcutta, affords the best *national* example of this temperament.

[12] G. Combe, 'Elements of Phrenology.'

CHAP. II.

Teeth long, strong, rather yellow, blunt-edged.

Nostrils broad and rather open.

Eyes open, ardent. Whites often blood-shot. Pupils blue amongst some races. More generally hazel.

Skin moderately fine, warm, often rich coloured and ruddy.

Hair: plenty of beard and whisker, of moderate firmness, wavy and flowing.

*Brain.* Vigorous, vivacious, ardent, enthusiastic, where the interests, emotions, or passions are engaged; otherwise apt to be indolent. Works best when business and physical pleasure combine. This temperament, with its vigorous circulatory system, combines well with the nervous and fibrous temperaments; the three together giving activity, strength, and buoyancy both of mind and body. But 'combined with much of the lymphatic, it is unfavourable to mental manifestations, and requires almost constant exercise in the open air.'[13]

*Muscular action.* Buoyant and active.

### *Lymphatic.*

This temperament is rarely to be met with amongst dark races. But Mr. Combe describes its appearance in western nations as follows:—'The lymphatic temperament is distinguishable by a round form of body, softness of the muscular system, repletion of the cellular tissue, fair hair, a pale clear skin, and a hazy sleepy eye. It is accompanied by languid vital actions, and weakness and slowness in the circulation. The brain, as a part of the system, is also slow, languid, and feeble in its action, and the mental manifestations are proportionally sluggish and weak.'[14]

[13] Fowler, 'Synopsis of Phrenology.'

[14] G. Combe, 'Elements of Phrenology.'

# CHAPTER III.

## PHYSIOLOGY OF THE TODAS.

*Table of Relative Proportions in the Toda Head—Scheme of numbering Organs—No Skulls procurable—Individual Organs frequently assume abnormal Proportions—Difference between the Sexes—Calliper Measurements—Amativeness of moderate Size—Why should Form be singularly small?—Physical Appearance of the Todas—Their Temperament—Largest and smallest Groups.*

CHAP. III.

THE Table No. 1, which represents the relative *proportions* in size of organs and groups of organs in the Toda head, is the recorded result of thirty-six manipulations in each of eighteen nearly unselected adults of both sexes. In inviting some degree of confidence in these investigations, it is necessary for me to disclaim pretensions to their absolute accuracy; for many circumstances which need scarcely be here enumerated, including the actual difficulty in obtaining satisfactory results in investigations amongst very thick tangled hair, oppose themselves to the practical attainment of such a result, however desirable. Yet, confident in my desire to obtain a correct record of the form of the savage skull, by maintaining as far as possible, freedom from bias or preference, I think that the *averages* at least, both of organs and of groups, may be recommended as containing as much of truth as may be obtained under like circumstances by any process of analysis with which science is at present acquainted.

The unvarying type of the Toda head, and the extraordinary uniformity of its general size, suggested to me both the possibility and the advantage of the principle adopted in recording these measurements; of referring them all to one

CHAP III.

## TABLE I.

*Relative Proportions in Size of Organs and Groups of Organs in the Toda Head.*

| Groups | | | Organs | | | | | | | | | | | | | | | | | | | | | | | | |
|---|---|---|---|---|---|---|---|---|---|---|---|---|---|---|---|---|---|---|---|---|---|---|---|---|---|---|---|
| Letters | Proportionate sizes | | Names | Average sizes | | Largest sizes | | Smallest sizes | | Proportionate sizes in Individuals | | | | | | | | | | | | | | | | | |
| | | | | | | | | | | Males | | | | | | | | | | Females | | | | | | | |
| | M | F | | M | F | M | F | M | F | 1 | 2 | 3 | 4 | 5 | 6 | 7 | 8 | 9 | 10 | 1 | 2 | 3 | 4 | 5 | 6 | 7 | 8 |
| A | 7 | 7 | Concentrativeness | 5·6 | 5·4 | 7 | 6 | 6 | 4 | 5 | 6 | 7 | 6 | 6 | 5 | 6 | 5 | 5 | 5 | 5 | 6 | 5 | 6 | 5 | 6 | 4 | 6 |
| | | | Amativeness | 4·0 | 3·3 | 5 | 4 | 3 | 3 | 4 | 3 | 4 | 4 | 4 | 4 | 4 | 4 | 4 | 5 | 3 | 3 | 3 | 4 | 3 | 4 | 3 | 3 |
| B | 7 | 7 | Philoprogenitiveness | 5·9 | 6·4 | 7 | 7 | 5 | 6 | 5 | 7 | 6 | 7 | 6 | 6 | 6 | 5 | 5 | 6 | 6 | 7 | 6 | 7 | 7 | 6 | 6 | 6 |
| | | | Adhesiveness | 6·6 | 6·3 | 7 | 7 | 5 | 6 | 6 | 5 | 6 | 5 | 6 | 6 | 7 | 5 | 7 | 7 | 6 | 6 | 6 | 6 | 7 | 6 | 6 | 7 |
| | | | Combativeness | 3·3 | 3·3 | 4 | 5 | 2 | 2 | 2 | 2 | 4 | 4 | 3 | 4 | 3 | 3 | 4 | 4 | 2 | 3 | 3 | 4 | 3 | 4 | 2 | 5 |
| | | | Destructiveness | 2·7 | 2·8 | 4 | 4 | 1 | 2 | 1 | 2 | 3 | 4 | 3 | 3 | 2 | 3 | 4 | 2 | 2 | 3 | 3 | 3 | 3 | 4 | 2 | 2 |
| C | 1 | 1 | Secretiveness | 2·9 | 2·8 | 4 | 4 | 1 | 1 | 2 | 4 | 3 | 4 | 3 | 3 | 2 | 4 | 3 | 1 | 2 | 3 | 3 | 4 | 3 | 4 | 1 | 2 |
| | | | Acquisitiveness | 2·5 | 2·6 | 3 | 3 | 1 | 2 | 2 | 3 | 3 | 3 | 3 | 3 | 2 | 2 | 3 | 1 | 2 | 3 | 3 | 3 | 3 | 3 | 2 | 2 |
| | | | Alimentativeness | 1·9 | 1·9 | 3 | 3 | 1 | 1 | 1 | 2 | 3 | 1 | 2 | 2 | 2 | 1 | 3 | 2 | 2 | 2 | 3 | 2 | 3 | 1 | 1 | 1 |
| | | | Constructiveness | 2·8 | 3·0 | 3 | 4 | 1 | 2 | 3 | 3 | 3 | 3 | 3 | 3 | 3 | 3 | 3 | 1 | 2 | 4 | 3 | 4 | 3 | 3 | 2 | 3 |
| | | | Self-esteem | 3·6 | 4·3 | 6 | 6 | 1 | 2 | 3 | 6 | 4 | 5 | 2 | 3 | 1 | 5 | 4 | 3 | 4 | 5 | 2 | 3 | 6 | 5 | 4 | 5 |
| D | 4 | 4 | Love of approbation | 3·9 | 4·4 | 6 | 6 | 2 | 2 | 2 | 4 | 5 | 6 | 3 | 5 | 3 | 4 | 5 | 2 | 4 | 6 | 2 | 3 | 5 | 5 | 4 | 6 |
| | | | Firmness | 5·0 | 5·0 | 6 | 6 | 4 | 4 | 6 | 6 | 5 | 6 | 4 | 5 | 4 | 6 | 4 | 4 | 4 | 6 | 4 | 4 | 6 | 6 | 5 | 5 |

CHAP. III.

| | | | | | | | | | | | | | | | | | | | | | | | | | | | | | |
|---|---|---|---|---|---|---|---|---|---|---|---|---|---|---|---|---|---|---|---|---|---|---|---|---|---|---|---|---|---|
| E | 4 | 5 | Conscientiousness | 3·8 | 3·8 | 6 | 5 | 2 | 2 | 6 | 5 | 5 | 5 | 2 | 4 | 2 | 4 | 2 | 3 | 2 | 5 | 2 | 4 | 3 | 5 | 4 | 5 |
| | | | Veneration | 4·5 | 5·4 | 6 | 6 | 3 | 4 | 6 | 6 | 5 | 5 | 4 | 4 | 3 | 5 | 4 | 3 | 6 | 5 | 6 | 4 | 6 | 6 | 5 | 5 |
| | | | Hope | 3·3 | 3·9 | 5 | 5 | 2 | 3 | 3 | 5 | 5 | 4 | 2 | 4 | 2 | 3 | 3 | 2 | 5 | 4 | 3 | 3 | 4 | 5 | 3 | 4 |
| | | | Benevolence | 4·4 | 4·8 | 6 | 6 | 2 | 4 | 5 | 6 | 5 | 5 | 5 | 4 | 2 | 3 | 6 | 3 | 5 | 5 | 6 | 4 | 5 | 5 | 4 | 4 |
| | | | Cautiousness | 3·7 | 2·9 | 4 | 4 | 3 | 2 | 3 | 4 | 4 | 4 | 3 | 4 | 3 | 4 | 4 | 4 | 2 | 3 | 3 | 3 | 3 | 3 | 2 | 4 |
| F | 1 | 1 | Imitation | 3·6 | 3·4 | 6 | 5 | 2 | 2 | 3 | 5 | 4 | 5 | 3 | 3 | 2 | 3 | 6 | 2 | 2 | 3 | 4 | 3 | 5 | 4 | 3 | 3 |
| | | | Wonder | 2·3 | 2·5 | 4 | 4 | 1 | 1 | 1 | 3 | 3 | 3 | 4 | 2 | 1 | 2 | 3 | 1 | 2 | 3 | 1 | 3 | 4 | 3 | 1 | 3 |
| | | | Ideality | 2·6 | 2·6 | 4 | 4 | 1 | 1 | 1 | 4 | 3 | 4 | 3 | 3 | 2 | 3 | 2 | 1 | 2 | 4 | 1 | 4 | 2 | 3 | 2 | 3 |
| G | 2 | 1 | Wit | 2·3 | 2·0 | 4 | 3 | 1 | 1 | 1 | 2 | 3 | 3 | 3 | 3 | 1 | 2 | 4 | 1 | 1 | 2 | 2 | 2 | 2 | 3 | 1 | 3 |
| | | | Causality | 3·1 | 2·9 | 4 | 4 | 1 | 2 | 3 | 3 | 4 | 4 | 3 | 4 | 1 | 3 | 4 | 2 | 2 | 3 | 3 | 3 | 2 | 4 | 2 | 4 |
| | | | Comparison | 4·1 | 3·6 | 6 | 5 | 2 | 1 | 4 | 4 | 6 | 5 | 4 | 5 | 2 | 5 | 3 | 3 | 2 | 4 | 5 | 4 | 4 | 4 | 1 | 5 |
| H | 3 | 2 | Language | 4·0 | 3·0 | 6 | 4 | 2 | 2 | 3 | 5 | 3 | 6 | 6 | 5 | 3 | 4 | 2 | 3 | 2 | 4 | 2 | 4 | 2 | 3 | 4 | 3 |
| | | | Eventuality | 5·4 | 3·9 | 6 | 5 | 4 | 1 | 5 | 4 | 6 | 6 | 5 | 6 | 6 | 5 | 5 | 6 | 1 | 5 | 5 | 5 | 5 | 4 | 2 | 4 |
| | | | Time | 4·5 | 3·0 | 6 | 4 | 2 | 1 | 2 | 4 | 4 | 6 | 5 | 6 | 5 | 4 | 4 | 5 | 1 | 4 | 4 | 4 | 4 | 3 | 1 | 3 |
| | | | Tune | 1·4 | 1·9 | 3 | 4 | 1 | 1 | 1 | 1 | 2 | 1 | 1 | 1 | 1 | 1 | 2 | 3 | 1 | 3 | 1 | 4 | 1 | 2 | 1 | 2 |
| $I_1$ | 1 | 1 | Number | 2·4 | 2·3 | 4 | 3 | 1 | 1 | 1 | 4 | 2 | 2 | 3 | 2 | 3 | 2 | 2 | 3 | 3 | 2 | 2 | 3 | 3 | 2 | 1 | 2 |
| | | | Order | 2·6 | 2·3 | 4 | 3 | 2 | 1 | 3 | 4 | 2 | 2 | 2 | 3 | 2 | 3 | 2 | 3 | 3 | 1 | 2 | 3 | 2 | 3 | 1 | 3 |
| $I_2$ | 6 | 3 | Colour | 3·8 | 3·3 | 6 | 4 | 2 | 2 | 4 | 4 | 4 | 6 | 3 | 4 | 3 | 4 | 2 | 4 | 3 | 2 | 4 | 4 | 4 | 3 | 2 | 4 |
| | | | Weight | 5·5 | 3·9 | 7 | 5 | 4 | 2 | 6 | 4 | 6 | 6 | 4 | 7 | 5 | 6 | 5 | 6 | 3 | 3 | 4 | 5 | 5 | 4 | 2 | 5 |
| | | | Locality | 6·5 | 4·0 | 7 | 6 | 5 | 3 | 7 | 5 | 7 | 6 | 7 | 7 | 6 | 7 | 6 | 7 | 3 | 4 | 3 | 5 | 6 | 3 | 3 | 5 |
| | | | Individuality | 5·9 | 4·1 | 7 | 6 | 4 | 3 | 7 | 4 | 6 | 6 | 6 | 6 | 5 | 6 | 6 | 7 | 5 | 3 | 3 | 5 | 6 | 3 | 3 | 5 |
| | | | Form | 3·2 | 3·5 | 4 | 4 | 1 | 3 | 3 | 2 | 5 | 4 | 1 | 4 | 3 | 4 | 2 | 4 | 3 | 3 | 4 | 4 | 4 | 3 | 3 | 4 |
| | | | Size | 4·5 | 3·6 | 7 | 5 | 1 | 3 | 5 | 1 | 7 | 5 | 5 | 5 | 2 | 5 | 4 | 6 | 4 | 3 | 3 | 5 | 3 | 3 | 3 | 5 |

standard by giving one number (7) for the largest, and one number (1) for the smallest organ in every head. Thus each number in the table not only indicates the relative proportion which a certain organ bears to every other faculty in the same head, but in all the crania of both sexes throughout the tribe. In pursuing this scheme, not only has a fair amount of accuracy been maintained in the observations, but a trustworthy average has been recorded for each organ, and thence—by similar process—of each group in the Toda skull. It will prove an interesting and valuable practical result, if by means of this process, we may be enabled to form a really true estimate of savage type, and learn the precise character and capabilities of any individual wild tribe.

Although amongst these figures the proportions of some of the ablest[1] and most respected members of the tribe are represented, it will be observed how similar the main forms of their skulls are, and that variations are confined entirely to single organs whilst the groups maintain a surpassing uniformity of appearance.

Two portraits—in side and full face—of a man and a woman, photographed to scale, are here given, by which some means are afforded of comparing the descriptions which are given in these pages with examples of 'real life,' and of enabling my readers to supply any other processes of estimating character from forms of crania, or of usefully classifying races that may be known to them.

It is unfortunate that no member of either sex could be induced to submit to having the head shaved. As the practice of cremation is the universal mode of disposing of the dead, the portraiture of a head without hair or of a skull without flesh could by no manner of chance be obtained. The male subject in the picture was selected solely

[1] This reminds one somewhat that the emperor of the Lilliputians was 'taller, by almost the breadth of my nail, than any of his court, which alone is enough to strike an awe into his beholders.'

Nº 3

Nº 4

N°. 5

N°. 6

on account of being one of the baldest men of the tribe, though his head is also above the average. The woman—well, beauty has charms! She was so good-natured or so vain as to put her hair into 'curl-papers' for me; but she was photographed as she now appears because the curls formed artificial 'bumps' interfering with my purposes.

In other parts of this book the portraits of two women will be found who had been chosen on account of unusual development; No. 25, 'The Little Savage,' has the largest Veneration, and No. 16, Avv, the largest Firmness I saw.

Perhaps the most noteworthy information which a close scrutiny of the figures of Table No. 1 affords, is that notwithstanding all the members of this little tribe have—as will be described in future chapters—intermarried most intimately for untold generations, and have lived under precisely similar circumstances, yet *in the midst of the remarkable uniformity of cranial development, which is evidently a result of this incestuous state, individual faculties frequently assume abnormal proportions,* large and small, considerably at variance with the common average. This affords us some slight insight into the working of nature in respect of national growth; enabling us to apprehend with what readiness, varieties may originate in a race whose marriage custom is opposed to incest, or whose families separating from one another, form social unions varying with the differing circumstances in which each may in course of generations be placed. It is the induration of these eccentric organic growths through hereditary descent, which gives us permanent varieties of the human race.

Although this Table bears internal evidence to the fact that the Toda head, simple as it is, is not as simple as it might be, and that in consequence it has no title to be considered as a sample of an absolutely primeval race; yet, amidst many points deserving attention, it possesses one of peculiar interest; through pointing to the nature and amount of difference existing between the sexes, in a tribe

CHAP. III.

# TABLE II.

*Sizes of Heads in both Sexes of the Todas, as obtained by Calliper Measurements.*

| Position of Callipers | | Average size | | Sizes of Individuals, in inches | | | | | | | | | | | | | | | | | |
|---|---|---|---|---|---|---|---|---|---|---|---|---|---|---|---|---|---|---|---|---|---|
| | | | | Males | | | | | | | | | | Females | | | | | | | |
| From | To | M | F | 1 | 2 | 3 | 4 | 5 | 6 | 7 | 8 | 9 | 10 | 1 | 2 | 3 | 4 | 5 | 6 | 7 | 8 |
| Occipital spine . | Individuality . | 7·39 | 7·14 | 7¼ | 7½ | 7½ | 7¼ | 7½ | 7¼ | 7¼ | 7½ | 7½ | 7⅜ | 7¼ | 6⅝ | 7½ | 7 1/1 | 7 | 6¾ | 7¼ | 7½ |
| Occipital spine . | Hole of ear . | 4·67 | 4·70 | 4¾ | 4¾ | 5 | 4½ | 4½ | 4 | 4½ | 4¾ | 5 | 4⅞ | 4¼ | 4¾ | 4½ | 4¾ | 5¼ | 4¼ | 4¾ | 5 |
| Individuality . | Hole of ear . | 4·94 | 4·50 | 5 | 4¾ | 5 | 5 | 4⅞. | 5 | 4¾ | 5¼ | 5 | 4¾ | 4½ | 4⅜ | 4½ | 4½ | 4½ | 4½ | 4½ | 4¾ |
| Firmness . . | Hole of ear . | 5·75 | 5·78 | 5¾ | 6 | 5½ | 5¼ | 5¾ | 5¾ | 6 | 5¾ | 5¾ | 6 | 6 | 5¼ | 6 | 6 | 5¾ | 5½ | 5¾ | 6 |
| Destructiveness . | Destructiveness | 5·41 | 5·17 | 5¼ | 5¼ | 5½ | 5½ | 5⅜ | 5¾ | 5 | 5½ | 5½ | 5½ | 5¼ | 5⅛ | 5¼ | 5¼ | 5 | 5¼ | 5 | 5¼ |
| Cautiousness . | Cautiousness . | 5·44 | 5·17 | 5¼ | 5½ | 5½ | 5½ | 5½ | 5½ | 5½ | 5½ | 5¼ | 5⅜ | 5 1/1 | 5⅛ | 5½ | 5¼ | 5 | 5 | 5 | 5¼ |
| Ideality . . | Ideality . | 4·39 | 4·37 | 4¼ | 4 | 4½ | 4½ | 4⅜ | 4½ | 4¾ | 4¼ | 4¼ | 4½ | 4 1/1 | 4⅜ | 4⅜ | 4½ | 4¼ | 4½ | 4½ | 4¼ |
| Constructiveness | Constructiveness | 4·91 | 4·66 | 4¾ | 4¾ | 5 | 5 | 4⅞ | 5 | 4¾ | 4¾ | 5¼ | 5 | 4½ | 4¾ | 4¾ | 4¾ | 4¾ | 4½ | 4½ | 4¾ |
| Circumference of head through Concentrativeness and Eventuality | | 22·21 | 21·37 | 22 | 22 | — | — | 21½ | — | 22 | 22¼ | 22 | 22¾ | 21¾ | 20¼ | 22 | 21½ | 20¾ | — | 22 | — |

NOTE.—The heads are not in the same succession as those in Table No. 1.

which is not more advanced than the remotely-ancient people living towards the end of the glacial period in Europe, the surviving records of whose dexterous skill and admirable artistic efforts, mark them as having been fully the Todas' equal in point of talent, and who certainly could not have been much their inferior in point of reverential and moral qualities.

The calliper measurements of Table No. 2 distinctly show the mass of the female head of this early type of man to be smaller than that of the male. It appears by the evidence of Table No. 1 to have a small advantage in organs affording the love of children and adhesive feelings, also in Veneration among the moral faculties. But the women are strikingly inferior to the men in respect to the entire range of the perceptive faculties, and even in the reflective powers, small though they are amongst the latter. Amativeness is rather small in both sexes, and it is remarkable and seemingly unaccountable that in the midst of so many large perceptive faculties, the organ of Form should frequently be found undersized. I cannot doubt the correctness in my observation of this organ, for the characteristic I notice, will be found in several places in this book, to be fully borne out by the evidence of facts.

One of three occurrences must have happened; the ancestral Toda must have developed, with the organ of Form alone small: or, supposing all the perceptive faculties to have been originally given to him of small size, Form must have failed to progress from its primeval dimension at the same rate as those other faculties by which we find it immediately surrounded; as for instance, Size, Individuality, Locality, and Weight: or, again, supposing the converse to have happened, that man was originally formed with all the perceptive powers large, this organ must at some subsequent period have become atrophied. The point of interest lies in the speculation; what nature of selection operating on men's characters, what circumstance in which simple races ever find themselves, could have had an impression so great as to have left this permanent stamp on the Toda forehead.

The following description of the physical appearance of the Todas will, I trust, prove of some value.

Eyebrows. Horizontal, straight and of medium length; never short, sometimes long; approach each other. Sometimes fine—willow leaf—generally somewhat bushy, with hairs close and, amongst the women, soft like a beaver's.

Nose. Generally *narrow* and of medium height at the base; nasal bones broad at the lower end; long; superciliary ridge in both sexes often very strongly marked; sometimes aquiline, often nearly so, never *retroussé*. Rather fleshy; nostrils rather dilated, but sometimes long and fine. The nose rarely appears at perfection before mid-age.

Mouth. Somewhat fleshy; rather short upper lip, and rather protruding and pendant lower lip—often strikingly so, becoming more evident with advancing years.

Gums. Generally purple, but often of a bright, highly oxygenated red colour.

Teeth. Sometimes short and broad, in others long; nearly all are even, yellowish, but bright, with rounded edges, set in roomy but not large jaws. With some the teeth are set at intervals, spreading outwards like a fan. In a few cases they were found cramped and crushed together; in one or two instances the eye-teeth were prominent. The teeth last till old age.

Ears. Generally flat to the head, never standing out; long, and with a large fleshy lobe. The orifice is nearly on a line with the eyebrow.

Hair of head. In both sexes black and heavy; in some cases close and tolerably fine, in others as much separate as in a wig, and coarse; wavy rather than curly. Both men and women habitually cut their hair, the former to about the level of the nose, and the latter at the shoulder. There are two or three nearly bald men in the tribe, but no bald women.

Beard and whiskers. As a general rule very thick and coarse, wavy rather than curly, extending to the eyes. A few delicate men are deficient in hair.

Hair on body. At about the age of thirty often covers the entire body, as appears on the full-length photograph, especially over abdomen, chest and shoulders. Boys of fourteen are often covered with down. Women have sometimes fine hair between the shoulder-blades.

Eyes. Of medium size, a few rather large; somewhat long, though some are nearly round; horizontal; in varying shades of brown, from hazel to snaky or beady, never blue or bluish; whites rather yellow. General expression of full average intelligence, some very soft and even sad; doggish; almost all have a great power of lighting up, in some to a wonderful extent, flashing, when under even slight excitement, like brilliants.

Eyelash. Rather straight, and of moderate length and closeness, never short, but sometimes long.

Face. Rather long, oval, of pleasant contour, without anything harsh or unusual in it, but, on the contrary, often refined; a few instances of rather high cheek-bones. The jaw is sometimes, but very rarely, a little prognathous.

Nails of hand. Sometimes short and square, but more generally long and oval; convex, strong.

Nails of feet. Are more flat, probably from walking barefooted on the wet grass.

Fingers. Some square; more often rather taper.

Feet. Of medium breadth. In strong people thick, but among the weakly, thin. The instep is rarely above an average in height, often very low; the heel of ordinary shape, and rather small.

Skin. Of medium texture, brown, much the colour of the Sikhs, often warm and copperish, a few fairer.

Abdomen. Small; a paunch is never to be seen.

Thorax. Moderate; the largest girth does not exceed

CHAP. III.

33 in. Photograph No. 7 is the picture of one of the most sturdy men of the tribe.

Height. Of men, from 5 ft. 4 in. to 6 ft. 1 in.; average about 5 ft. 8 in. Of women, from 4 ft. 10 in. to 5 ft. 4½ in.; average about 5 ft. 1 in. There are no very short people.

Weight. Of men from about 110 to 155 lbs. There are reasons why the weight of women cannot be accurately ascertained; but it is believed to vary between 90 and 130 lbs.

Shoulders. Angular, never sloping, generally with a flat back.

Muscles. Never large; hard rather than full; some decidedly below the average.

The general mass of the tribe are fairly, often well grown; straight and lank, without deformity, but without any really fine people.

The men's carriage is erect, free and unconstrained, without being either bold or athletic. Their manners and tone of voice are self-possessed, suave, quiet, and solemn: the women substituting a pleasing cheerfulness for solemnity. When quiescent, their expression and carriage has much oriental repose in it.

The temperament of such a people as has just been described would in the main be fibrous, with some of the sanguine or the nervous in individuals; especially so in the female sex, many of whom I noticed show a considerable amount of the nervous with advancing years. Such a national temperament is more suited to the display of qualities requiring muscular energy for their support, than of those in which the subtilty of intellect would take part.

We find the cranium, taken as a whole, to be of an average size; comprising certain very strong, and certain equally and lamentably weak, points of form. The singular uniformity in contour of all the heads has already been observed upon.

In order to form a correct, and therefore complete judgment of a man's character, it is not sufficient to take a

No. 7

AUTOTYPE, LONDON.

mere general view of its shape, and imagine it as acting under the influence of an average pressure. But it is necessary to master all its details. Firstly, to study the relative sizes of the groups; which knowledge will give a good general acquaintance with the disposition. Then to fill in this outline by examining all the organs of each group, so that an estimate may be formed of minute peculiarities in the idiocrasy of the person. By these processes we shall ascertain the greatest capacity of the head for acting, when most favourably placed for the display of its highest qualities; and to learn in what direction, and to what extent, it will certainly fail when situated under the influence of adverse circumstances.

By abstracting from Table No. 1, we find the following to be the largest and the smallest groups; the action of which, will, as might be expected, display the real character of the Toda. The medium groups will not exert much active influence one way or the other.

Very large. The Domestic (B) and Concentrative (A) Groups, almost throughout both sexes of the entire tribe, would be considered large in any race; Amativeness, which is of average dimensions, being undoubtedly the smallest organ in them.

The {Perceptive / Statical} Group ($I_2$) is, in the case of the men, nearly equally large as the above; though it varies in size considerably in individuals. Locality, Individuality, and Weight are the largest organs of the group; whilst Form and Colour are often very small, and never attain the highest figure. Amongst the women this group is below average.

Very small. The Invigorating (C), the Reflective (G), the Refining (F), and the orderly-calculating organs of Group $I^1$, are, with little exception, extremely small in both sexes; Comparison and Imitation being exceptionally large; and Alimentativeness, Wit, Wonder, Order, and Number the smallest organs.

CHAP. III.

Medium. Those groups which record events, give self-reliance, and tend to general morality (H, D, E), can neither be termed large nor small; but vary considerably with individuals of both sexes, in the size of their composing organs; Eventuality, Firmness, Veneration, and Benevolence being the largest, and Language, Tune, Caution, and Hope the smallest faculties. Women have a superiority in Veneration and Benevolence over the men; whilst the males are the more observant.

The character of the Toda is written in his acts, described upon the whole face of this book.[2] I see no reason why, if caught young, he should not prove as intelligent and as useful a member of society as the humble Ryot of India. We may at least compare him with the ancient Celt of our own country, of whom it has been written; 'Do not obtain your slaves from Britain, because they are so stupid, and utterly incapable of being taught, that they are not fit to form part of the household of Athens.'[3]

[2] I abstain from giving a diagnosis of the Toda character; such as would be deduced from the sizes of his organs, the nature of his temperament, and the circumstances of his life; fearing to trespass on the patience of my readers.

[3] Cicero's letter to Atticus.

# CHAPTER IV.

## CHARACTERISTICS.

*Talking Voices—Modes of Salutation—Home Life—Frank and obliging Natures—Colour of the Skin—Tattoo Marks—Ornaments—Boys distinguished from Girls—Apparel—Toilette.*



THE Toda talking voice is peculiar; particularly so that of the women. Whilst on the part of the men it is strikingly grave and sedate, spoken almost *sotto voce*: the women's voice, on the contrary, is rather high, appearing to come altogether from the region at the back of the ear—the 'mastoid process.' In both sexes, but particularly with the female, the sound of the voice is somewhat musical and refined, though fatiguing to listen to from its monotonous tone. Indeed, it is somewhat astonishing that some harsh syllables of their language should come so softly from such mouths. The refinement arises doubtless, from the gentleness of their dispositions—void of asperity; its friendliness, accompanied by desire to please. Not from any innate sense of tune, for they have no more ear for music than so many crows.

Their amiability shows itself also in their observance of courteous customs. The salaam of the East, performed amongst the Todas by raising the thumb-edge of the right hand vertically to the nose and forehead, is a respectful form of address; used in addressing superiors, and on approach to sacred places, and other like occasions. When asked by what name they styled that form of salute, they replied: 'Itvâ eshken, swâmi eshken,' or, 'I say, come! I say, Lord!'

That mode of salutation which is most employed amongst

equals, is the short exclamation of 'Tya!' or 'Tcha!' corresponding in its tone and mode of use to our own expression of 'Good morning!' when friends meet or pass one another. The meaning of the word is not known to me. Perhaps it has no actual meaning, though similarity of sound suggests the Hindustani word 'Achḉha,' good, well—as having the same derivation.

The salute called 'Âdabuddiken,'[1] or 'I seize the foot,' is very singular. Performed when people meet who have been apart for some time, it seems to combine an expression of fealty with that of courteous respect, and perhaps of affection. Suppose a case; a group of men and women, conversing in their village, is surprised by an inroad of Toda visitors. The exclamation, 'Here is Beliâni, Beliâni's wife, and her little-sister Penpuv!' The cheerful smile lights up the assembly. Every operation is suspended. Every house discharges its occupants. All rise pleasantly, and with much gentle urbanity, to meet the new arrivals.

What now ensues depends on certain points of etiquette; matters of prudence, quite understood amongst them. In this early stage of society, the dues to sex and to age and relationship, are clearly defined. Early and constant practice has long made every woman acquainted with the position in which she stands with regard to her relatives, and to her husband's parents, elder and younger brothers; and there is little else to remember. Hence, amongst the two groups of both sexes which now meet, a glance of the eye suffices to enable each member to apprehend the position to be taken.

A man never bows down before a woman; not even a son before his mother.

A man does not bow down before another man; but women do so before women.

[1] Âdabuddiken. Aḍi = *foot*, Piḍi or Pattu = *seize, take hold of.* To *seize the foot* is a common Drâvidian expression for *homage, reverence.* [POPE.]

No. 8

AUTOTYPE, LONDON.

A GREETING—ÂDA BUDDIKEN.

A wife never bows down before her *husband*; though she performs the Âdabuddiken before her father-in-law, mother-in-law, her husband's elder brother.

Now each one of the juniors or inferiors—being a female—approaching each of the seniors or superiors—both men and women—in succession, 'falls at his feet;' crouches on the ground before him, or her. On which he, or she, places first the right, then the left foot on her head. Such is the act styled Âdabuddiken.

As every man of the two parties has to perform this ceremony to every female, and each woman to each younger woman, and the men to salute one another and say 'Tcha!' the greeting of parted friends—which has to be carefully gone through, and which no sense of impatience or untimely levity ever occurs to abbreviate—is one that takes time. But the Toda has no wit, and plenty of time to spare and to waste.

Mr. Metz tells me he has seen a son fall at his mother's feet. But the act (a very exceptional one) was committed on the occasion of a funeral, when the family appeared overwhelmed with grief; and the man, actuated by his feelings, performed this token of respect and love.

Nothing but the natural good manners of the people hinders the ceremony of Âdabuddiken from becoming unseemingly slavish. But the cheerfulness of the women, and the men's grave politeness, admits of its being performed with entire good taste.

Toda women indeed, hold a position in the family quite unlike what is ordinarily witnessed amongst Oriental nations. They are treated with respect, and are permitted a remarkable amount of freedom. They perform the legitimate offices of women in Europe; tending children, cooking the family meals, bringing water from the spring, and cleaning the house and premises. Wearing mantles or togas—Putkuli—there is very little stitching to be performed; but they embroider the edges of the mantles which some of the men wear, with blue cotton, in the fashion which some of the photographs in this book will show.

The turbulent cattle are tended solely by men and boys. And the men manage out-door affairs generally.

It is a quiet, undemonstrative, but intensely domestic people; domestic in the wider sense of viewing the entire family, to the last cousin, much as one household, in which everyone is everywhere entirely at home; each one assisting, with the steadiness of a caterpillar, in the easy, progressive task of emptying his neighbour's larder: no one exerting himself by one fraction to raise the family. The great feature in Toda organisation, is the all-absorbing power of his domestic attachments, which, like Pharaoh's lean kine, swallow up all other qualities.

If the Todas lose, in a material point of view, from deficient size in Acquisitiveness, and the propensities generally, yet they certainly are large gainers thereby in the quiet, even tenor of their domestic life, undisturbed by the wrongs of grasping, vindictive, overbearing natures. They no doubt have quarrels, in the course of which they—particularly the women—are known to use very high language indeed and expressive gestures, but they are mere pebbles in a brook as compared with the rocks that break the flow of other waters.

The men maintain their authority in the home circle very sensibly, and without attempt at tyranny; but I saw too a woman who, as was very evident, ruled her husband. She must have acquired this authority by means of some slight superiority in quality of brain, for she had no apparent vantage over him. I was so much interested in this repetition, amongst an unambitious, retiring, and primitive people, of a well-known phase of married life in energetic folk nearer home, that I had hoped to induce the pair to present themselves to be photographed; and the temptation I offered would have succeeded but for their age, which made a long walk over the hills too great an effort.

The general type of the Toda character is most unvarying; singularly frank, affable, and self-possessed, cheerful yet staid: respectful, seemingly from a sense of conscious inferiority rather than from an active principle: fearless, from small cause for fear more than from the stimulus of a latent power of opposiveness: communicative, yet watchful and shy, as if their natures impelled them to divulge what their natures also prompted them to maintain quiet: willing to take money,[1] yet accepting what is proffered with callousness, allowing it to lie on the ground or their children to play with it. In villages without an article *de luxe* beyond a few women's ornaments, one may see naked children decorated liberally with small coin. The investment was no doubt safe round their necks and loins, but the very safety implies an absence of theft and violence, which is fully confirmed by the testimony of the law courts of the district. Their main crimes appear to consist in struggles to avoid payment of their debts for money borrowed on bonds from the Badagas.

According to superior notions, they are not a moral race; yet a knowledge of many little facts that could not well be recorded, leaves the impression on my mind that they have certain limits in decent custom (well understood by them, though rarely primitive to our civilised conceptions of what is respectable) which are probably not often transgressed. I could not hope, without a far greater knowledge of the people than could be obtained except by residing long amongst them, to give anything approaching a just definition of their private ways. I fancy, however, that they are less bounded by acknowledged rule than by the gentleness and simplicity, though rude nature, of their character.

Though their intellect is of a very inferior order, and their force of character extremely small, and no great man of

[1] The Todas living in proximity to the haunts of Englishmen, do not hesitate to importune for money with the greatest and most childlike persistency; yet if unsuccessful are not a bit distressed.

Toda blood may ever arise to influence the tribe, yet what they do know, they know well. They are intelligent within limits. Although they take contracted views of things, yet they work and act within the circumscribed limits of their mental vision with great steadiness, intelligence, and some sense.

I am indebted to the quick-wittedness and patience of both men and women, for the accuracy and definition of the information on the manners and customs of the tribe which I have been able to afford. I cannot present a stronger tribute to their frank and obliging communicativeness, than in stating that we made a habit of very close cross-questioning in tiny villages for three and four hours together. One woman well earned the title of Munshi, by telling us at a sitting the Toda words for the long list of relations given in Chapter VII. Notwithstanding the questions were often repeated, and many of them puzzling, she kept her head quite clear throughout, dexterously speaking with slowness and marked intonation, showing pointedly with tongue and teeth, how the syllables of the difficult words should be pronounced.

Though their brains became fatigued sooner than ours did, I doubt if they tired more quickly than would those of illiterate peasants in other parts of the world.

Travellers have affirmed that the Todas stain their skin by the use of a blue colour; but I have ascertained, both by personal inspection and by direct enquiry, that this statement is incorrect. Dark races are apt to have the skin in some portions of the body naturally of three or even four shades darker tint than in others, indeed often so strikingly dark as to give the impression that those parts had been stained. This peculiarity is nowhere more remarkable than in the nape of the neck. I have often observed it amongst the Sikhs, and it is quite apart from freckling or the effects of exposure. I noticed it so very much the case in one young woman, that I asked her if she had coloured it. The reply convinced me that the practice of staining the skin is quite unknown to them.



They—the women—however, mark or tattoo portions of the body, terming it Gurtu. Dr. Shortt has recorded these marks so carefully, that I cannot do better than quote his own words :—'The women,' he writes, 'are tattooed about the arms, chest, and legs in the following manner: Three semicircles of dots on the outer side of each arm, each semicircle containing nine points ; a double row of dots across the upper part of the chest, about an inch below the clavicle, each row consisting of thirty-six points, about the eighth of an inch apart, the rows themselves being one inch distant from each other. Those on the arms have an intervening space of two inches; two rows, containing eight or nine points each, on the shoulders, commencing in front where the lines on the chest terminate, and extending backwards to a point on a level with the superior semicircle on the arm ; a solitary dot in the centre of the chin ; two circular lines of dots on each leg, the upper circle containing twenty-five and the lower only twenty dots ; and a row across the dorsum of each foot, numbering from nine to eleven points. The terminal point of each row is marked by a ring, the interlinear points being simple dots, frequently taking the form of squares.'[3]

The most characteristic personal ornament amongst them, is that carried by women ; an extremely clumsy metal ring—Tulwaji—weighing sometimes as much as five pounds, which is carried on the upper part of the arm, and worn according to taste ; sometimes one ring on each arm, or sometimes a pair on one arm, kept apart—so that the skin may not be pinched between them—by means of a slip of padding. These rings are often built half of copper, half of brass, so that one day they may be worn presenting the one metal, and another day turned to show the other. In order that the arm may be introduced into this ponderous mass of brass, the ring is cut

[3] Shortt, 'Tribes on the Neilgherries.'

CHAP. IV.

through at one place in the circle, so that by introducing a lever into the crevice it may be opened a little.[4]

The device being so heavy and inartistic, and these rings known to be often ancient heirlooms, I do not doubt we have in this quasi ornament an armlet belonging to very primitive times; one that certainly could not have undergone very great improvement since it was first adopted by the people.

No. 9.

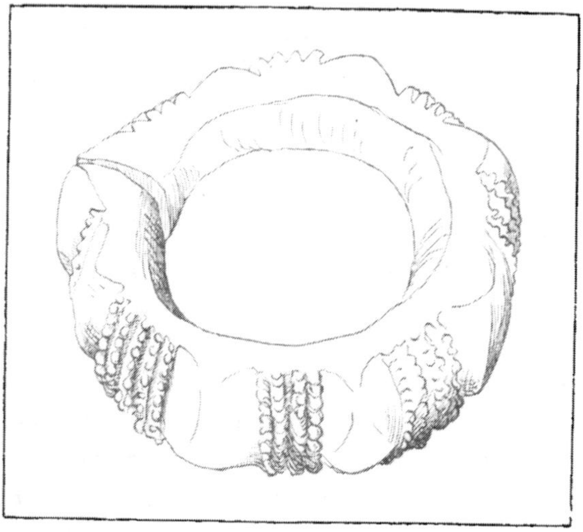

A TODA ARMLET.

Hence it may prove of some value as a means of tracing the Todas to the unknown race from which they sprang and separated.

[4] Curiously enough, on return from the Nilagiris, a friend living at Kheri in Oudh, showed me an armlet which had just been cut out of the stomach of an alligator caught in the neighbourhood. Although the workmanship of this bracelet was far more artistic than that of the clumsy Toda ornament, yet the mode of opening and shutting it was identical, and the general design, suggestive. As it was not in wear amongst any of the civilised natives of the place, and there are known to be primitive tribes living in the neighbouring jungles, it is just possible there may be some real connection between the two armlets, though separated during 3,000 or 4,000 years.

Perhaps the ornaments, likely to be equally primitive with these armlets, are the heavy bunches of coiled iron wire or of little bits of the same metal, worn like charms from both waist and elbow. Very tasteless and heavy.

I do not see, in the form of their finger and ear rings, necklaces and girdles, anything deserving of remark. They do not appear to me to be especially characteristic of the Todas, but rather, just what they can purchase from the tribes surrounding them. The photographs of women, show the nature of necklace worn as marriage tokens.

The nose and lips are never perforated or ornamented ; nor are bangles for the ankles, or bells on the toes, worn.

You may distinguish a boy from a girl by the mode in which the hair is cut. With the latter, the entire back-hair is kept short from infancy till the approach to marriageable age. The former have a band of hair cut short, or shaved, along the head, from the nape of the neck, over the poll to the top of the forehead, and a cross slip carried over the top of the head from ear to ear. The smallest male infants are often so distinguished.

The wearing apparel of the sexes is identical. First comes the loin-cloth—Kûvn—corresponding to the Hindustani Lungoti, over which the toga—Putkuli—measuring about six feet long by four feet broad, made of coarse unbleached cotton, and worn double ; ornamented at the two ends with red and blue stripes, and sometimes with a little embroidery in blue cotton. This mantle is sufficiently large to envelope a woman most completely. A decent though cumbersome garment to wear, better suited for sitting and sleeping in than for any purposes of labour. Pockets are made in the corners of the mantle, by sewing the double cloth together at those places. This dress is more properly Drâvidian than mere Toda, and is purchased in the bazaars.

They are a dirty people ; yet very much of their dirt arises from circumstances somewhat beyond their control; such as crowded establishments and poverty. They bathe their bodies in the running brook, and even sometimes use hot-water for the same purpose. Yet I do not remember to have seen a Putkuli fresh from a wash.

A pretty sight, that rewarded one of my expeditions, was a group of women and girls just returned from the stream, sitting, clean and bright, curling one another's hair. The locks were separated neatly, and the partings made accurately with the finger-nail. Each lock having been dressed straight, either with the fingers or a forked stick, is twisted and twisted until it has formed a tight coil, when the end is tucked in among the roots. The *well developed* female back-head looks remarkably pleasing under this treatment—unadorned, adorned the most. The curls are opened out in the morning.

The eyebrows are sometimes touched up with a charred stick from the fire-place; the fancy being to join them over the bridge of the nose.

If they would only not grease the hair with butter, I could close this description of the toilette without unpleasant reminiscences of some phrenologising experiences.

The mouth and teeth are often kept in wonderful order up to a late age. But they take care of them; using daily a little wood ash—not charcoal—and the forefinger, for dental purposes. I have seen people of all ages with teeth as bright, and mouths as fresh-looking as an infant's—or a dog's.

AUTOTYPE, LONDON.

REDUCED FROM A PHOTOGRAPH BY MESSRS BOURNE & SHEPHERD. SIMLA.

THE LAND HE LIVES IN.

THE NILAGIRI PLATEAU.

## CHAPTER V.

### THE LAND HE LIVES IN.

*The Todas a very ordinary people: the Interest they attract greatly due to Association—Habits and Manners free from Eccentricity—The Scenery of the Country: its Silence and Grace—A cool Morning grows to a Summer Day—Tasteless Toda.*



A MOST interesting people is this to contemplate. The well-marked Assyrian stamp of face, amidst more clumsy types, would, if for no other reason, make them attractive to us.

But when one has actually witnessed and realised what I am about to describe; the patriarchal mode of life in all its wonderful artlessness: the antique religious usages—effete, the forms remaining, their motives lost: the quiet deam-like lives;· the even tenour of which reposes on custom, whose rare simplicity and immemorial practice indicates a strange proximity to primeval man;—then the interest in them redoubles, and one appreciates the fact, that he actually views a state of society more primitive than, though somewhat similar to that of our own Celtic ancestors, who *tilled* British soil. And the traces in his language, of what is cognate to the Celtic, increases the points of curious resemblance.

But it must be acknowledged that the interest we take in the Todas, is chiefly due to these associations: for of themselves, and apart from considerations connected with the evidences of the vast antiquity of their habits, or with their relationship to other races of which we may have especial knowledge, there can, I think, be no doubt they must be held a very ordinary people; whose peculiarities result mainly from combinations of negative qualities, and the contrast they present to all the activities we have been accustomed to.

It is humanising, however, to recognise in them—ignorant, dirty, and unkempt—the likeness to ourselves, inheritors of many centuries of civilisation. Their children laugh and play as ours do. Their tricks are the tricks of our own boyhood. Their women display, with direct simplicity, many of the exact same characteristics of ours; even the most refined, even the debased. And they are repositories of family lore—staunch conservatives. The men rule their households on principles of worldly policy as we do, and without any striking point of dissimilarity; and, as I have already noted, are treated somewhat arbitrarily by their wives too, as we are apt to be also. Their natural language is precisely the same as ours; not a sign, not a demonstration of the feelings, not a movement, but may be understood at a glance as well as if we had all been brought up from infancy together.

The customs of the people strangely seem to suggest the germs of many that even now exist among us. Indeed, nothing in their ways surprised me more than to see them act so much as we do; to an extent, even, that deprived them of much interest in my eyes.

The country in which we find the Todas, though not by many moves perhaps the seat of his origin, is worthy of notice; for thus we shall better realise how man lived in days when he had advanced scarce more than one step from the period of his rude simplicity; in what style of place he gradually acquired forms and social habits, that he never forsook entirely; and how he multiplied unobserved, until his country could no longer contain his progeny—then migrated and founded nations.

Picture an abrupt-edged table-land, on the apex of a solitary mountain—a very Laputa in its complete isolation of some 7,000 ft. in altitude—whose evergreen surface is one continued intermixture of rounded hills, with tracts of rolling prairie. The hills as accessible as those of Malvern; the prairie land as ceaseless, in its long undulations, as the billows of an ocean. Short coarse grass, clothes the whole, save where the deep forest holds possession of the damp secluded valleys, or the cool little woods moss the banks of the prolonged gulleys, through which the trickling streams or dashing bourns course down the silent hill-sides: then collect, and, through successive vigorous rapids and tumultuous cataracts—where from behind the clouds of spray and mist, noise roars its prolonged approval—precipitate themselves into the plains below. Wherever, in fact, rich soil and a perennial supply of moisture may be found, there are the ever silent woods; for the periods of annual drought are long: the monsoon rain flows quickly off the hard surface of the exposed hills, and the scorched grass containing the young saplings is yearly fired.

These woods and forests, and lovely glades, whose perfect quiet is broken only by the calls of wild animals and birds, or by the rustic sounds of Toda cattle—almost equally wild—herding in the open, form pre-eminently the characteristic features of the scenery; adding emphasis to the singularly peaceful beauty of the view.

The grass, in spots where the buffalo has not grazed it short, and where moisture favours growth, is crowded with wild flowers. Climbers, in great variety of grace and form, swing in festoons from the limbs of the gnarled old forest trees, bearded with hoary lichen, or ornamented with varieties of flowering orchids, which cling to the branches of the moss-covered timber. In the dank secluded shades a great variety of ferns; from the tree-fern to those of the smallest size, grace the gloom:—

> 'O, might I here
> In solitude live savage, in some glade
> Obscured, where highest woods, impenetrable
> To star or sunlight, spread their umbrage broad.'

All round the circle of this high-perched green plateau, one

CHAP. V.

unbroken sweep of low flat country, dotted with hills. Picture it an island in a tropical archipelago; storm, cloud, and driving mist intervening between periods of brilliant sunshine. Try to realise the equatorial sun acting through this ever-changing sky and rarified atmosphere, both on the sweet inland prospect, and as you turn to take an eagle's view outwards, over the grand panorama of the long horizon. Both are unique and lovely.

There is one view, on the precipitous western ridge of the plateau, below Makurti Peak—

'The last hill that parleys with the setting sun,'

which seems to unite all the *possible* beauties of such a land. Such a mixture of the lovely properties which a landscape may derive from the presence of stupendous depths, brilliantly transparent and buoyant atmosphere, delicate distances, changing tints, and wonderful shadows, I have not seen combined, even in the Himalayas; and, I believe, few spots in the world can exhibit.[1]

Had the Toda made this spot the entrance to his heaven—Amnôr (of which, more in its proper place), he would at one step have placed himself on a pinnacle of good taste, from which it would not have been easy to dislodge him. But to have omitted all notice of these extraordinary beauties, marks him as the tasteless man he is.[2]

Let me here describe an *inland* scene; which, though casually witnessed by myself, must often be surveyed by the

[1] The artist in search of a study of aërial effects, could nowhere find them so complete and satisfying as in this view. Owing to monsoon rains, clear days in which to watch it cannot often be got before the month of October. To be seen to perfection, both sunrise and sunset should be witnessed.

[2] In Chapter I. I have quoted a Toda legend, that the souls of men and cattle leap from Makurti on their journey to Amnôr; but in the expression of this belief there appears to be no appreciation of the beauty in the scene;—merely that Makurti is the highest and westernmost hill, nearest the setting sun (See Chapter XII.), and therefore the *most suitable locality* for the purpose.

people living their lifetime in the midst of such sights. A brilliant and powerful sun is no such rare object to those who have dwelt in tropical climates, as, under ordinary circumstances of heat and dazzle, to merit a description of its effects. They are but too well known by actual familiarity to many Englishmen. But few have experienced the pleasure of spending an hour or two under this equatorial sun, when it strikes through the attenuated atmosphere of high elevations, filtered by means of the deposit of moisture through *frost*, as realised in the cold season of this favoured land. And I can hope but approximately to depict the rare sight, which has made a lasting impression on my memory.

After a perfectly still, clear, cold night, the dawn had broke on the green country, suffused with moisture ; close hoar-frost in the damp valleys, dense dew on all the high lands—a frosted emerald.

The slanting beams of the yellow rising sun, as they glance over the hills, illuminate with cold shades of prismatic colours all the drops of dew hanging in rich completeness suspended from the delicate seed-stalks of the summer grass with which the foreground is clothed. It is cold. The breeze that accompanies the dawn, waves the water-laden herbage, and in the pulsation of the full drops and the fresh sparkling of their lights, an interest is attracted. 'Tis the passage of Aurora! She sweeps lightly along over the drooping grass stalks, scattering their burdens as she goes ; reminding one of all that is fresh and cool—fountains, crystal, the happy tinkle of silver bells!

Soon we find that cheerful draught has awoke all living nature. The birds are shaking out their feathers, and calling from tree to tree. The Toda buffalo in his pen looks over the fence at his pastures, and moves towards the gate. His master opens the little door of his hut, and, putting his towzled head into the air, mutters 'Êrigitâshk!'—dawn, rising time. All creation is alert ; the day has begun!

CHAP. V.

As the luminary continues to ascend, his rays, now grown brilliant, penetrate more and more the frosted valleys: and nature shows herself in a new phase. The little patches of water glare like daring mirrors; the hoar frost melts at once, and its vapour ascends in volumes on every side, filling the atmosphere as it rises. The zealous sun now reigns supreme —its floods of light illuminate the steaming mass; its dark beams, through which the view behind is seen, radiates from the skies into the bright mist carrying the elongated shadows of trees and hill-sides balanced and undefined upon it. The close cattle herd tracks the hill-sides through the dewy grass.

A near view of the sedgy swamp below, presents at this time a rich picture of quiet nature in a dynamical fit. The dark mass of green reeds seems, though the only quiet thing, to be on the eve of movement; its outlines all brilliant with the melted frost, and undefined through the sun's halo: the shadows hazy and drowsy green. The while the glaring water is giving forth clouds of vapour. Insects and creatures, forgetful of their cold night, revel in the present heat, and animate the air with their busy progress. The water-rat, returning from a nocturnal excursion, pushing through the swamp with emergent speed, partakes of the glory of the water, his little body idealised as to appear a magnified spot in the sun.

As the mist continues its rise and fills the air, that which in the early morn was cold and steel-coloured, then steaming and busy, now becomes quiet, genial and radiant up to the zenith. The trees on the distant hills stand out distinctly, each in its dark blue patch of shadow. The cattle lie ruminating in the swamps. And all nature smiles. The clear morning sky is flecked with fleecy clouds, till the midday summer heat dispels the whole, and

> 'O'er heaven and earth, far as the ranging eye
> Can sweep, a dazzling deluge reigns.'

This wonderful country, ever beautiful and expressive,

silent yet speaking, quiet and secluded, forms the *bèau idéal* of a breeding-place and nursery for infant races.

The Toda buffalo has roamed over this land for centuries, and his master, calling his orders to the cattle he leisurely tends, has witnessed the many beauties of nature which I have merely suggested. But I do not find, by his language, religion, or tastes, that they have had any effect on him. He sees the grass. Ha! He sees the dew. Ha! He sees the forest. Ha! But apparently it is only so much cattle's food with water on it, and fuel in the distance. Ha! The sun is shining on it, and the water will soon dry; then the cattle will grow thirsty!

The prevalent idea is that primitive man, uneducated man, working man, is so engrossed in cares and in the occupation of providing himself with food, that he has no leisure for contemplating nature's beauties. The phrenologist knows better; and you, reader, will shortly agree that the Toda has unlimited leisure, as I now show that he has endless opportunity of noting the beautiful.

These hills are covered with good soil—indeed in the moist hollows it is pre-eminently rich and productive, and the land is very accessible to the plough. There is excellent clay for pottery. A laborious, acquisitive race, conserving the glorious water supply, would render this land a paradise. But the Toda scheme is simpler far. He has cattle who afford him all he wants; why should he work? Why should he plough? And from the lazy man's point of view, perhaps he is right.

# CHAPTER VI.

## THE MAND.

*Todas a pastoral Race—Definition of a Nomad—Todas migrate, but are not nomadic—The Mand or Village—Construction of Houses—Interior Arrangement of Houses—The surrounding Wall—The Cattle-pen—The Dairy or Pâlthchi—Typical Plan of a Mand—Selection of Village Sites—Names of Villages.*

CHAP. VI.

THE TODAS are a purely pastoral race; occupying themselves almost entirely in the bucolic pursuit of herding buffalos, of which they are in possession of a very fine species. They keep no other description of animals, save cats—Kotti.

As they do not attempt cultivation of the soil, they have rather hastily been styled nomads. Taking that term to imply a tribe which, *without fixed place of residence*, wanders in quest of food—whether that be game or pasture for its cattle—the word is a misnomer as applied to the Todas.

Indeed, from the many primitive races found in various parts of the world, which with striking deficiency of development in the organs of Acquisitiveness, Constructiveness, Order, and Number, are also distinguished by the peculiarity, common to them all, of not tilling the soil, we may select links of a complete gradation in idle mode of life; from the lowest, or ever-wandering predatory class which lives by begging and theft: through several varieties of the nomadic shepherd and hunter: up to the *settled* pastoral races, amongst which we class the Todas; who, with a very strong bias in favour of a permanent home, *yet migrate* once a year, compelled to do so, simply in order by change of pasture, to obtain a sufficiency of food for the cattle, on whose milk they almost entirely subsist.

I make free to assert that no tribe of people, having the organ of Concentrativeness so largely and so uniformly developed as it is with the Todas, will ever be found to be habitual wanderers. Whether it be, that in the early days of the human race, circumstances having forced a family of man to become nomadic, the form of its skull gradually changed in the course of many generations, so as to adapt the man's disposition to his necessities; or if, on the contrary, the wandering habit be largely the result of defective size of that faculty; certain it is, that practice and corresponding cranial form are now in harmony, and that a small development of Concentrativeness will be found ever accompanied by a centrifugal tendency; attachment to a settled home being strong in proportion to the organ's volume, strong even to the extent of producing nostalgia when thwarted, if associated with remembrances of home and landscape.

Toda families reside in permanent villages—Mand or Madd—having each a certain tract of grazing ground surrounding it. Each minor division of the family has a house —Ârsh—in the Mand, and a share of the village land.

Nearly every Mand, however, has its duplicate, sometimes its triplicate, to which the entire body of the inhabitants migrate at certain seasons of the year, both for the sake of fresh pasturage and with the view of escaping the inclemency of situations which become exposed to the west-monsoon rain and wind.

These storms drive at times with such intense severity over the wilds, that although at the time, the actual thermal state may be far from low, yet the evaporation induced by the extreme violence of the rain is known to lower the temperature of the body so as frequently to cause death to man and beast. Wild animals cower during these storms under

CHAP. VI.

the protection of secluded woods, or migrate like the Todas for the period of the monsoon season.

It is also a Toda custom to vacate a house, or even the entire village, for a certain limited period, if one of their number should have died, or sickness be rife amongst the community or attack their cattle.

In these matters they follow the dictates of sorrow, of prudence, or of necessity, much as we do under very similar circumstances. We too, who can afford the luxury, have a town as well as a country house; take trips to the sea-side, or at times vacate the tenement which some dear one has just left for ever. These people do no more. *No* Toda is so persistently migratory as thousands of our own countrymen are.

From what is here written it will be understood why the Nilagiris may have upwards of one hundred Mands on its surface, yet not more than forty of the number be actually occupied.

I have ascertained, in the course of a careful census of eleven Toda Mands—the detailed results of which will be found tabulated in Chapter X.—that they contain from two to three dwelling-houses or huts, whose general appearance is depicted on the frontispiece. Most of these houses consist of only one room or cabin, but many are formed by the juncture of two, and sometimes even of three rooms in a line; each with its own door leading direct into the external air and unconnected with one another. The Toda name for a room and for a house is the same.

The rooms, though all of the exact same shape, vary somewhat in size; from five to six cubits square in area, and from five to six cubits high. Thus, a house of two rooms would be about 8 ft. by 16 ft.; and a house of three rooms would measure some 8 ft. by 24 ft.

Each room holds one entire subdivision of a family.

The roofs of all houses are thatched with grass and

bamboo, fastened with split rattan, and are either constructed in curved outline like the tilt of a waggon, or brought to an angle at the top, with a wooden ridge-pole, similar to the form of construction met with in more civilised life. The first method of roofing—which is peculiar, not being found amongst any of the surrounding tribes—is that universally employed amongst the well-to-do. The latter, which is probably cheaper, and certainly more simple to make, but endures less the violence of storms, is ordinarily adopted by poor people, and for houses of a temporary nature requiring to be erected in a hurry.

The two end walls, which are invariably gabled, are made of very stout planking: and where the house consists of more than one room, the partition wall is of the exact same construction as the outer walls. The side walls, in the tilt-waggon houses, are formed by carrying the roof down to the ground, in which the ends of the curved bamboo rafters are all imbedded. At the line of junction with the earth, flat stones are used in order to throw the water off from the domicile. All the interstices and holes in the planking are carefully filled in with clay, mixed with cow-dung.

The doorway, presenting the appearance of a ship's port-hole, and about two cubits high by one and a half cubits broad, is to be found in the middle of the gable wall, when there is only one room to the house: if there are two or three rooms, the second and third doors will be found in the sides, so arranged that all the doors may be to leeward; usually the south or south-east. These doorways, which are closed at night with a flat stone or solid slab of wood, kept in place by a stick thrust vertically into the floor at either side of the opening, form the only passage for the household, and for light, smoke, and air.

The roof projects two cubits beyond the gable walls; thus forming a pleasant open verandah facing the morning sun, and sheltered from the wind. Here the primitive family sit,

CHAP. VI.

air themselves, and perform various offices of a domestic and social (entomological) nature.

The people have been at much pains to exclude every particle of external air from their dwellings: and were it not for cracks, caused by the contraction of the material of which they are constructed, their rooms might have been rendered quite uninhabitable. As primitive folk, living in an elevated climate, have far more to fear from cold than from heat, these 'beehives' are, on the whole, well adapted for comfort and for the preservation of infant life.

I think that when these houses were originally built, they were designed with one room only. I judge so, partly from the Toda name for a house and for a room being identical, and in part from the symmetrical arrangement of the door and verandah; also, from noticing that the second and third doors at the side, appear like an after-thought, out of keeping with the original design, and holding awkward positions in a house whose roof is continuous to the ground. I deduce from these appearances that their numbers have increased since they first established themselves where we now find them.

It may be interesting to my readers to be able to form an idea of the mode in which the very small area of a savage's house is utilised for cooking, eating, and sleeping purposes.

Be it remembered that the room is 8 ft. long, 8 ft. broad, and 8 ft. high; and that, as Chapter X. shows us, as many as eight people board and lodge in this diminutive space. The plan (No. 11) which, without any deviation, is that of every Toda dwelling, shows the mode in which room is economised. Against the walls, at a convenient height over both store and fire-place, slips of split cane are fastened vertically, so as to form slings; into which firewood is neatly inserted, and in which it rapidly dries. The women are careful to keep a supply of dry wood in this manner: hence they are able to cook without making much smoke, using as they do, with a skill that seems to be the common property of all the natives of India, only one or two little sticks at a time. The correctness of this observation is corroborated by the striking freedom of adults and children from eye-complaints. CHAP. VI.

A. The pestle and mortar—Kudi.

B. The fire-place—Vorsh, or Vorshkall.

C. The store or space, measuring $4\frac{1}{2}$ ft. by $2\frac{1}{2}$ ft., in which brass cups and plates, bamboo milk-pails—Honnu—are placed.

No. II.

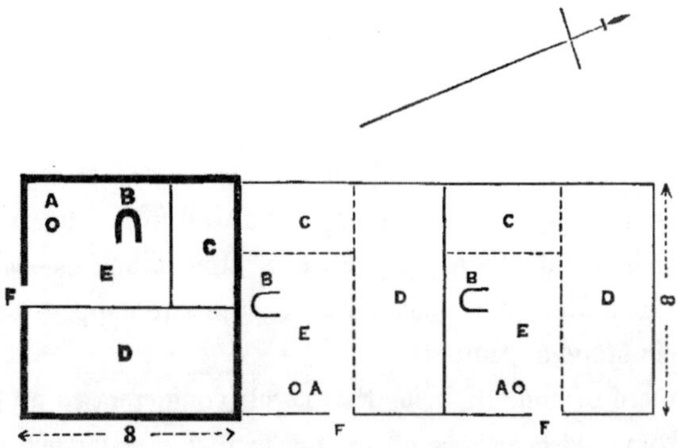


THREE TODA HOUSES.

D. Raised bed of clay, measuring 8 ft. by $3\frac{1}{2}$ ft., for the elders.

E. Vacant space on the floor, 5 ft. by 3 ft., where the family eats, and where the juniors sleep.

F. The door.

Nearly every Mand, and in some instances each house, is surrounded, at the distance of three or four paces. by a low enclosure wall—Tûar[1]—built neatly but without cement. This wall, which in all cases bears the appearance of age, is so low (about 3 ft. high) as to preclude the possibility of its having

[1] Tûar, Tûel. Tamil, Suvar. In all the Drâvidian dialects *s* and *t* are interchangeable. Thus Shrî becomes Tiri. Ar and El are affixes which are used in the formation of nouns. [POPE.]

CHAP. VI.

originated in any defensive project, whether as protection from the attacks of man or the inroads of wild animals. Taken with the extreme narrowness of the gap left in it for egress, there seems no doubt of its having been designed merely to keep the half-wild cattle off the premises, lest they should trample on the children in their stampedes, or should rub their bodies against the low houses in their hours of ease. Neither the wall nor the enclosed area is in any degree sacred.

In close proximity to the Mand will invariably be found the pound or pen—Tûel[2]—into which the buffalos[3]—Êsm [illegible] c, Er a female—of the village are driven every evening on return from the grazing grounds. This pen, which varies in dimensions according to the wealth of the community in cattle, is fenced in strongly ; in some places by a wall from four to five feet in height : at others by a fence of stout branches—when it is termed Mên Tûel—according as the site happens to be prolific in stone or timber.

The herd of buffalos, being thoroughly competent to protect itself from wild beasts, is left in this pen without further protection, and, indeed, without any shelter, though the calves —Koan a male, Karr a female—whilst quite young are shut up at night in little huts situate close and often contiguous to the people's dwellings.

Deserted cattle pens have at times been mistaken for Druidical circles. When the enclosure wall has been made of large blocks of stone, and where from paucity of material it had been constructed of double rows of stone filled in with soil, and the earth had in due course been washed away, then the stones left standing would remain in very religious form ;

[2] Tûar, Tûel. Tamil, Suvar. In all the Drâvidian dialects *s* and *t* are interchangeable. Thus Shrî becomes Tiri. Ar and El are affixes which are used in the formation of nouns. [POPE.]

[3] When Todas talk of their cattle generally, the word Êr is invariably used.

most attractive to the wandering archæologist who did not know of the primitive habits of this pastoral race. CHAP. VI.

In addition to the dwelling houses just described, every Mand, without exception, contains a house devoted solely to the purposes of a dairy—pâlthchi—consisting of two rooms;

No. 12.

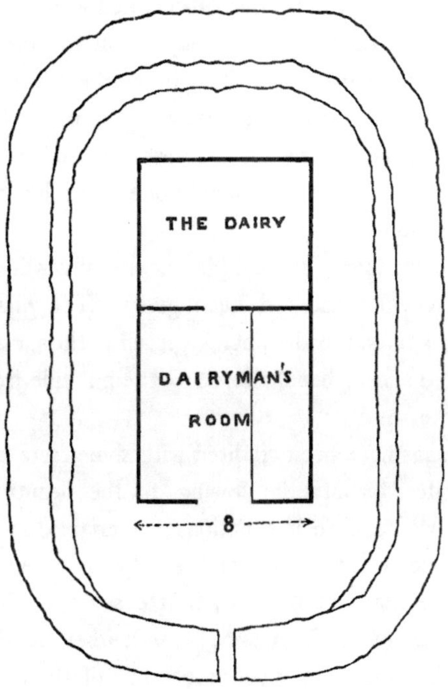


THE DAIRY—PÂLTHCHI.

the outer—porram-âl-g-ârsh—for the residence of the dairyman—pâlkarpâl[4]—and the inner room—ulg-ârsh—for the storage

[4] Pâlkarpâl. This is one of the most remarkable examples of the identity of Toda and Tamil.

This is pâl—karr—p—âl; (1) (2) (3) (4) where (1) is the Drâvidian word for *milk*; (2) is the root of the verb = *to milk*; (3) is the suffix forming the verbal noun, *milking*; (4) = *person*. [POPE.]

CHAP. VI.

of milk—pâl—and for its conversion into clarified-butter.[5] This building varies in size according to that of the village herd; from the dimensions of an ordinary house of two rooms, to one perhaps half as large again. It is situated somewhat apart from the Mand, and—presumably for the sake of coolness—is generally found on a site which has been partially dug out from the side of the hill, on the slope of which the Mand is situated. The dairy is always enclosed within its separate wall, which is built very close up to it, and the outside of the wall often earthed in. The outer door is much of the size of those in ordinary dwellings, but that in the partition wall, forming the only means of access to the dairy room within, is of minute dimensions; probably one cubit high and about half a cubit broad.

The accompanying typical plan of a Mand will explain the description which has just been given. The village itself is invariably situated in the open, exposed to the sun almost from daybreak to sunset, but sheltered by the hill side from the full force of the wind.

The Todas have been credited with some taste in the selection of sites for Mands; owing to the beauty and often romantic nature of their situations; invariably on some open grassy slope, where wood and spring or rivulet combine. But I more than doubt if any innate sense of the beautiful influences them in the choice; for neither do their heads, nor do their other acts, give probability of the possession by them of any taste. I am disposed to attribute the success of these happy selections to the fact that, acting with a very strong practical sense of the advantage of localities, they have, whilst seeking shelter for themselves and cattle from the monsoon storms, with a dry bit of soil in proximity to water and fuel—the whole centrical with regard to pasture—obtained, by means of the natural advantages of a lovely land-

[5] Known in India as ghi; in Toda termed nei.

No. 13

AUTOTYPE, LONDON.

A TYPICAL MAND.

A = RESIDENCES. B = DAIRY. C = CATTLE PEN.

scape, an harmonious whole, very striking to visitors of cultivated tastes. CHAP. VI.

A knowledge of Drâvidian dialects would probably show the names of their villages, of which the following are a few samples, to be mainly descriptive of localities.

| | |
|---|---|
| Diljavênu. | Bângâdu.[7] |
| Kakhodi. | Karshk.[8] |
| Beresthro. | Mênmadd.[9] |
| Koana-koar.[6] | Keshkir.[10] |
| Ebgodu. | Kirzho. |

Melkarshk.[11]

[6] Koan = *male calf*; karr = *female calf.*

[7] Bân = *sky.*

Gâdu, or godu, or gudu, affixes to names of villages; from kudu = *come together*; the same as Mand, which is Tamil for *collection.* [POPE.]

[8] Karshk = *stone.*

[9] Mên = *wood, forest*; Madd = Mand. See above.

[10] Ir, or iri, or ari, affixes to names of villages; from the Drâvidian root, which is variously written ir, ur = *be, exist.* Ûr, *a village* in Tamil, is from the same root. [POPE.]

[11] Mel = *upper*; karshk = *stone.*

# CHAPTER VII.

## THE FAMILY.

*Parturition—Midwives—Confinements—Infanticidal Mother taken red-handed—Name this Child—Men's Names—Nicknames—Women's Names—How married people call to one another—List of Relationships.*

CHAP. VII. THE act of bringing forth children seems very generally to be considered an easy one. In the course of my enquiries into the causes of death amongst adult women, I was told of two who had died in labour. If I were to judge solely by the opinions of the male sex, I should have no hesitation whatever in recording that the process of child-birth was a mere trifle: yet even after seeking more correct information from the women themselves, I could arrive at no other conclusion than that parturition, though a delicate matter, was an act which almost invariably passed off without great difficulty.

Men are never present during these family events, but apparently have to await the result outside. Three or four women—the house-full in fact—remain in attendance; one of whom is said to sit behind the patient supporting her frame: the others performing various offices tending to alleviate pain, and for the reception of the infant.

May not the ill-understood expression, 'She shall bear upon my knees,' Gen. xxx. 3, have reference to the position in which we find the person, who with a knee on each side of the expectant mother, squats behind to support her body?

'We call a midwife merely old woman—kelachi'[1]—said my informant—an elderly gentleman with a large family—'why give a name for midwife when every woman can act?' This, though from the male point of view, is nevertheless a statement whose truth is borne out by facts.

'The umbilical cord—pokku—is severed by laying it on a piece of wood, and cutting with a knife.'

'What! tie it with string first!' raising his eyes roguishly to the roof, as if looking for a piece of string projecting from the thatch. 'I have plenty of children, but have never heard of such a thing! ha! ha! ha! Tie it with string! ha! ha! ha!' Here the old man turned the laugh against us, protesting that such a thing was never done. Whether the cord is tied, but that he had for so many years remained in ignorance of the fact: or if it is really never bound, in savage life, I had no further opportunity of enquiring: but leave the narration as it was given to me by a great authority.

On the morning after the child has been born, the mother is removed to a shed—purzârsh[2]—which has been erected for her in some sequestered spot of the village wood, in anticipation of the approaching event. There she remains till the next new moon—muttu[3]—whether that phase occur in the course of 3 or of 30 days. These people cannot explain the reason for this removal: but possibly they may suppose the monthly aspect or reappearance of the moon to have some periodic effect on women. I did not succeed in eluci-

[1] Kelachi = *old woman*; Kelâl = *old man*. Tamil: kirra = *old*. Kirra van = *old man*; Kirra tti—*old woman*—tti pronounced chi—Âl = *man*. Keladi, in ancient Kanarese = *a female friend*. [POPE.]

[2] Purzârsh. In Tamil we have purra = *outer*. Sansk. âlayam = *dwelling*. Any termination may be converted in a Toda mouth to a guttural sound made up of l, r, and sh. [POPE.]

Mr. Metz is of opinion that purzh = *mud*; and that purzârsh means a *mud hut* or *temporary house*.

[3] Muttu, new moon = *jewel, pearl*, in Sansk. and Drâvid. [POPE.]

Tiggalu, full moon, the moon. Ti is a part of dina = *day*. Glau = *the moon*, Sansk. In Tamil, tingal. [POPE.]

dating any expression of such belief from them: but the profound ignorance in which they are steeped is amply sufficient to account for all want of knowledge of reasons. The custom is probably an extremely ancient one. Some notion, of the nature I have described, may have founded the practice, though all trace of its origin or cause, may have been forgotten long ages ago.

For a month after her return home, she appears to have the house to herself: her husband remaining indebted to friends for shelter meanwhile.

I had the pleasure of being introduced to a woman just after her return from the purzârsh. In the course of my inquisitorial visits, which will be more fully described in Chapter X., I had ascertained in a certain village, that there was a young female infant which had not been shown to me: and this might be an infanticide! Almost hoping such might be the case, and that I had discovered a mother red-handed, I enquired after its health. 'Oh,' said the women, airily, and with the true maternal interest in young babies, 'they are both in the house round the corner.' Thither accordingly I went, and found the young mother awaiting a visit, hoping to receive for her small one—kin-minthki[4]—one of the little silver-bits she heard were circulating so freely amongst the children of the Mand, from whose society she was still debarred.

Studying the Frontispiece and the pictures of Toda women in this book, anyone of artistic taste can fancy the little picture; which in its way was pretty and interesting. Scene; an old-looking and water-stained log hut, belonging to a primæval tribe of the glacial period: summer time: brilliant sun: green herbage: forest background. The imagination is now sufficiently developed to appreciate the tableau! A

[4] Kin-minthki = *female infant.* Kin = çin = *little*: a Drâvidian root. Minthki is probably a corruption of manujâ or manushî = *woman*—Sansk. [POPE.]

Popen = *male infant.* This is a mere term of endearment. Drâvidian pomma is a *puppet*; with which it may be compared. [POPE.]

young mother—infanticidal, polyandrous—is sitting on the earthen floor, just within the doorway, enveloped in a mantle of unbleached cotton. On her left arm, snuggling next her bare body, inside the garment, lies something like a comic doll, with long black hair, cream-coloured skin and pink points. The palm of the woman's right hand, uppermost, is directed towards the child. Her body, foreshortened by reason of the lowness of the door. The nut brown gipsy face, all eyes and teeth, just a bit delicate, is upturned towards the visitor: and speaking volumes by look and by attitude of hand, appeals for a present for the one-month-old. The inside of the room—such as remains visible—pitch-dark. There she was, smiling away, little knowing of my groundless suspicions.

A boy is named—peru or pesru or hesru=a name—and his ears are bored some time within about three months of his birth.

The child appears to be kept out of sight until the naming day; when the father, unaccompanied by the mother, takes it, hidden in the folds of his mantle, up to one of the sacred buildings of his Clan: and standing in front of the door, but outside of the surrounding wall, salutes the sanctuary with hand to forehead. Then kneeling on the ground, he for the first time opens out the infant's head to vision, and pressing its little forehead down till it touches the soil, names the child, reciting the following prayer; 'dânenma, mokh ultama, âl ultama, êr ultama, karr ultama, ellam ultama;' the meaning of which is: 'Be beneficent: may it be well with the children, the people, the cattle, the calves, and everyone.'[5]

I see now before me, a woman who had accompanied her husband till *within sight* of the building, standing on an eminence, witnessing from a distance, with hand shading

[5] Strictly speaking, the prayer means, 'May it be well with the *male* children, the *men*, the *cows*, the *female* calves'—in fact, all that is useful —'and everyone;' in which latter category are probably included the women and girls.

CHAP. VII.

intent and loving eye, and with wide-open mouth, the naming of her son. YE-A-AH! YEN POPEN! she said, tenderly.

The father also names the girls. But they are not taken to a temple for the purpose. 'It grows up with the name by which its father calls it in the village' say the Todas.

'No children may enter the outer wall—tûar—of sacred places, until they have cut their teeth.' Such is the unchanging law of these Medes and Persians. The reason why, is not known: it is sufficient that 'our forefathers always did so.' Perhaps as a matter of cleanliness: but probably to obviate the necessity for their mothers running after them within the precincts. As *women are not held unclean*, it is likely this rule may result from prudential grounds.

A feast—a little more sugar and a little more nei—is given about the time a child is named; apparently so soon as both mother and infant are strong; and perhaps seasons favouring.

The following are the names of men:

| | |
|---|---|
| Netarâdi. | Kirnâl. |
| Beliâni. | Tinkuttan. |
| Narikutti. | Nidiabên. |
| Azavom. | Kêdâlbên. |
| Pernâl. | Kêvi. |

Nearly every man has one or even more nicknames—porra[6] hesru—which have been given to him by his associates, mainly on account of some incident in life; sometimes from gait or physical peculiarities, though more rarely so, for the similarity between Todas is great, and their freedom from eccentricity so remarkable, that salient points in figure and manner do not often present themselves. No Toda, however rich he may be, having landed property, and no trade being followed by anyone, or other occupation than those of a priestly nature, names cannot be obtained from

[6] Porra = *outside*.

those ordinary sources. Nor, as I notice, are they ever called 'of such a village,' 'of the brae,' 'of the hill;' presumably because every Mand has its duplicate, with a different appellation and varying nature of locality.

An informant acknowledged with much laughter and shamefacedness, that his own nickname was Gurugudugan or Gurugurgan—so far as could be understood through his modesty. It appears that when driving an *old* buffalo—let this be remembered when we describe funeral obsequies—purchased from a Badaga village for funeral purposes, it died on the road. And this word, whatever its meaning may be, seems to have been given him in ridicule for having purchased an animal that at once died.

His father, he said, was termed Bülta, from Bült, a bird; being noted for swiftness of foot in his occupation of driving cattle.

Here are a few nicknames:

| | |
|---|---|
| Kalkutti. | Mûrukâlu. |
| Kûndagalla. | Kûndemati. |
| Bira. | |

Some *sobriquets* have, as might be expected, indecent meanings.

'Are you called by your name or by your nickname?' I asked of a young man. 'Generally by my porra hesru; but when they want anything of me they are more civil, and use my proper name.'

I do not know if women have any such *sobriquets*. Indeed some delicacy is shown in mentioning women's names at all. And I experienced difficulty in obtaining the following: each man being willing to tell those of every man's wife and daughter but his own. I observe in a book on the Todas by a late author, that the designations he has given are literally 'wife or daughter of so and so'—being a man—but not the actual name of a woman:

CHAP. VII.

| | |
|---|---|
| Quêldirth. | Jinvani. |
| Tushquilth. | Nastufi. |
| Muneth. | Ânchaguti. |
| Penpuv. | Chizarêm. |
| Dirthavilli. | Pentirêm. |

A woman retains her maiden name on marriage; being known, for instance, as Nastufi, the wife of Beliâni.

It is etiquette in speaking of another man's wife to term her either kottê or pannê;[7] the first, if her husband is of the Pyki clan, the second if of the Pekkan, Tôdi, Kenna, or Kuttan clans.

A man calling to his wife, or a wife to her husband, would not say 'come here Nastufi or Beliâni,' but 'kukh itva, come here woman,' or 'âl itva, come here man.'

But the more proper term by which a man speaks of his wife is yen kâtvoti.[8]

According to these rules, people talking of the woman Nastufi, would describe her as Beliani pannê, or kottê. *He* would mention her as kâtvoti. He would *call out* to her as kukh.

*List of Relationships.*

| | |
|---|---|
| Man, person, husband . . . | Âl. |
| Man—young . . . . . | Varsh.[9] |

[7] Kottê. Pannê. Such terms are difficult. They are frequently of a depreciatory character.

Kôṭṭa = *a fort* or *large dwelling*. Kôṭṭi = *a person of a fort, a superior inhabitant*. Paṇi = *jewel*. Paṉi = *work*. [POPE.]

[8] Yen Kâtvoti. Yen or en = *my*, constantly prefixed in Drâvidian to words indicative of relationship.

Kaṭṭu = *bind, join*. V is an insertion of tense, used in forming verbal nouns with a future or indefinite temporal signification.

Ati is a feminine termination.

The word means, '*she who is bound to me*.' [POPE.]

[9] This is, I think, Sansk.: purusha. But there is vîras, *a hero*.

In old high Tamil we have virral, and the termination al becomes in Toda sh as a general rule. [POPE.]

| | |
|---|---|
| Boy, son . . . . . | Mokh. |
| Woman, girl, daughter, wife | Kukh.[10] |
| Father . . . . . | App'n, êyan, ên, or ênin. |
| Mother . . . . . | Avv. |
| Wife . . . . . . | Kâtvoti. |
| Youth, bachelor . . . | Mokh varsh. |
| Child—son . . . . | Kin mokh. |
| Child—daughter . . . | Tüj mokh.[11] |
| Infant—son . . . . | Popen.[12] |
| Infant—daughter . . . | Kin minthki.[13] |
| Twins . . . . . | Mor mokh. |
| Fatherless, Motherless, Orphan . . . . | Tobbâri.[14] |
| Widower . . . . . | Baruda.[15] |
| Widow, barren woman . . | Mudegitti,[16] barudi. |
| Great-grandfather . . . | Pêvian. |
| Great-grandmother . . . | Pêviavv. |
| Grandfather . . . . | Pîyan. |
| Grandmother . . . . | Pîavv. |
| Brother—elder . . . | Ennon. |
| Brother—younger . . . | Ennorvet, enta. |

[10] The etymology is doubtful. One is reminded of Greek, gunaik.
In Tamil kokku = *copulatio*. [POPE.]
Kuk = *a receptacle*, also *pudendum muliebre*.

[11] Tüj mokh. Here mokh = *child*. High Tamil, maga.
Tüj is a difficulty. In Kanarese, tush = *inferior*. I imagine this is the idea. [POPE.]

[12] [13] The derivations of these words have already been given in this Chapter.

[14] Tobbâri. Tagappan = tam + appan = *their father*, or simply *father*; Tamil. This is pronounced commonly tôppan.
Âri = '*one deprived of*.' Drâvidian root aru. [POPE.]

[15] Baruda. In old Kanarese, barru = *decay*, *die*, *fail in strength*.
In Tamil this root is varru.
Sansk.: vridda = *old*.
Tamil: maladi = *barren women*. [POPE.]

[16] Mudegitti, moṭṭai = *baldness*; muṇḍai = *bald*, *a widow—whose head is shaved*. [POPE.]

CHAP. VII.

| | |
|---|---|
| Sister—elder . . . . | Enakkan. |
| Sister—younger . . . . | En norvet kukh, enta. |
| Father's brother—elder . . | Ennin perud. |
| Father's brother—younger . . | Ênnin kirud. |
| Father's sister—elder and younger | Mâmi. |
| Mother's brother—elder and younger | Mâman. |
| Mother's sister—elder . . | Perud avv. |
| Mother's sister—younger . . | Kirud avv. |
| Son's wife . . . . . | Mortwirth. |
| Daughter's husband . . . | Enman mokh. |
| Husband's mother, Wife's mother . . . | Mâmi. |
| Husband's father, Wife's father . . . | Mâman. |
| Husband's brother—elder . . | Yen âl ennon. |
| Husband's brother—younger . | Yen âl norvet. |
| Wife's sister—elder . . . | Yen kâtvoti akkan. |
| Wife's sister—younger . . | Yen kâtvoti norvet kukh. |
| Wife's brother . . . . | Pâyâl or Bēiâl. |
| Grandson—son's son . . . | Yen mokh ver et mokh. |
| Granddaughter—sôn's daughter | Yen mokh ver et kukh. |
| Old man . . . . . . | Kelâl. |
| Old woman . . . . . | Kelachi. |
| Family, relation . . . | Anatama, pâltiâl, pâyâl,[17] kutasaram.[18] |
| Ancestor . . . . . | Mûpu, doddavan. |
| Clan . . . . . . . | Kôleh—in Badaga language. |

[17] Pâltiâl, pâyâl. In old high Tamil we have pâttil = *house*.

Âl is the constant abbreviation for avargal = *they*. Thus the word pâttiâl = *those belonging to the house*.

The Sanskrit root pâ = *protect, cherish*.

The two words are probably different forms of the same. [POPE.]

[18] Kutasaram. Tamil, kûda = *together*; çaram = *a going*.

In Sanskrit kuṭumba is *family*. [POPE.]

The word Anatama,[19] which means elder and younger brother, is the generic title given to all very near relations. CHAP. VII.

Regarding the appellation for cousins, the people say they have no names for them—'The son of my little-father, ênnin kirud, is the same as my brother.' Yen perudên kirudên mokh yen aṇan taman ershchi.

[19] Anatama. In Kanarese, aṉṉa|tamm|andaru.
elder younger they (who are)

So in Telugu, anna|damu|lu. Here we have soft n, d for t and pluralising particle lu.

In Tamil, aṉṉan = *elder brother*; tambi = *younger brother*.

The Drâvidian root aṉa = *upper*, and may be compared with Greek ἀνά. Tam = *one's own*; so in terms of relationship = *my own*, *my*, a familiar kindly expression. [POPE.]

# CHAPTER VIII.

## FOOD.

*Diet—Kûtu—Badaga and Kota Neighbours prey on the Todas—Todas give away valuable Property—Not flesh eaters—Ceremony of eating Buffalo flesh—Don't drink Spirits—Children's Food—Family Meals—Grace before Meat—No Weapons of the Chase—No variety of Live Stock.*

CHAP. VIII.

THE Todas have no sports or games, except the innocent tip-cat, corresponding in its play very much with our boys' game of rounders. No violent exercise. No means of settling disputes by scientific personal conflict, as in wrestling, fencing, or boxing. Nothing in fact pointing to natural turbulence of character and surplus energy. They wear no weapons of offence or defence. They do not even hunt, either, for the sake of providing themselves with food, or for the pleasure of the chase.

They do not attempt to till the ground.

The products of the buffalo form the main staple of Toda diet. No doubt, at some time or another, they depended upon that animal more than they do now; in a period when they were isolated from contact with agricultural races. Now they are well supplied with the ordinary cereals of the country, as rice, wheat, barley, varieties of the pea, millet and other small grain, also sugar, salt, and tobacco; all of which items are, and for many generations have been, either purchased from the surrounding tribes by the barter or sale of their own surplus nei, or obtained by the levy from their neighbours, the Badaga[1] tribe, of kûtu,[2] or tribute due to them as lords of the soil. This kûtu, which implies a permission to the Badagas to cultivate the land, is said[3] to be a certain portion of the produce, varying from $\frac{1}{10}$ to $\frac{1}{8}$, and shows that the Todas are the earliest *existing* race occupying the plateau of the Nilagiri Mountains.

Each Toda Mand has a claim on certain Badaga villages for their kûtu. Members of each family of the Mand go out in turn on a begging expedition to the village from which it is entitled to draw for support. And as no very accurate accounts are kept, either of the amount of kûtu due in any individual year, or of the quantity of grain which has already been supplied, this foraging stands with the Toda in lieu of sport, in so far as the uncertainty of the results is concerned; it being to the interest of the Badagas to postpone and shirk payment of grain as long as possible: whilst on the other hand, the state of the Toda stores, and his natural persistency combined, are urging him on to repeat the visits for the renewal of his granary. The result being that the Toda gets exactly as much grain as will just satisfy his actual necessities: the Badaga acquires land on cheap terms of rental.

Thus we find that these people have, for several centuries, been in the enjoyment of a considerable variety of nourishing and digestible articles of diet: probably as much in quantity, and nearly as great in variety, as most other races have access to: acquired too with the very smallest amount of personal labour; the mere tending of cattle.

From the fact of the strong similarity which is known to exist between the Toda and Kanarese dialects; and of the Badagas having followed the Todas from the hot plains of

[1] Badagas, a Kanarese people of the Hindu faith.

[2] Kûtu. See Chapter VI., note 7.

[3] This statement was made in a Report, dated 1835, from Mr. J. Sullivan, collector of Koimbatore—in which district the Nilagiris lay—to the Government of Madras, in the Revenue department.

the low country, into a district so cold, wild, and inaccessible as this must, by contrast, have appeared to them, we have strong presumptive evidence of the two tribes having, previous to their migration, long lived side by side, mutually dependent one on the other; the Todas, for the supply of grain they had not the energy to raise for themselves: the shrewd Badagas, for the nei which they obtained so easily from this most unmercantile people.

Similarly, another native tribe—the Kota—not so advanced as the Badaga, but more laborious, and thus skilled, than the Toda, followed the fortunes of this simple people on retirement to the Nilagiris; possibly influenced, amongst other motives, by knowledge of the fact that the live male buffalos, the carcasses of the females, and the skins and horns of both, were to be had almost gratis, so long as they maintained adherence to their old friends. Thus we see—no matter how primitive the stage of society, how microscopic the tribe—the universal mundane process at work; of the strong preying on the weak, and the clever on the stupid: races, like individuals, supporting themselves by utilising and depressing their simpler brethren.

> Big fleas have little fleas upon their backs to bite them;
> Little fleas have lesser fleas; and so on *ad infinitum.*

To what other cause but grievous national improvidence can we attribute their having acquiesced in promptings to part with an amount of meat sustenance, that would, if utilised, nearly double their food supply? And to permit skins and horns of vast herds—whose sale would have brought a very welcome addition to their revenue—to be removed as return payment for a little trumpery Kota music, and primitive iron-mongery?

What the buffalo is to the Toda, so is the Toda to these slightly superior tribes; the milch-cow.

There is good reason for believing the Todas' assertion;

that they have never at any time eaten the flesh of the *female* buffalo; for they set an immense value and importance on the milk-giver. And there are very strong grounds also for crediting their statement; that they *never made a practice of eating the males*, even though they may have died from accidental causes. In fact they are not, and never were, flesh eaters. Not that they dislike the flavour of meat; for a meal of venison is one of those events so rare and pleasurable as to form a datum in a man's life from which to time all incidents.

CHAP. VIII.

Yet there is a yearly exceptional occasion on which all the adult males in the village join in the ceremony of killing and eating a very young male calf—seemingly under a month old. They take the animal into the dark recesses of the village wood; where the Vorshâl[4] kills it by blows of a club made of their holy tree,[5] reciting the ejaculatory prayer beginning dânenma, which has been given in full length in the last chapter. Although fire may readily be procured from the Mand, a *sacred* fire is created by the rubbing of sticks: and the flesh, which is then roasted on the embers of certain trees, is eaten only by the men—the presence of women not being permitted.

No information can be had as to the origin or object of this curious and apparently sacrificial ceremony. 'It seems,' writes Mr. Tylor, 'scarcely too much to assert once for all, that meaningless customs must be survivals, that they had a practical or at least ceremonial intention when and where they first arose, but are now fallen into absurdity from having been carried on into a new state of society, where their original sense has been discarded.'[6]

[4] Vorshâl. This is a sacred character, of whom we shall read more in Chapter XVII.

Ve, vê, are Drâvidian roots indicative of *heat*.
Varhis is Sanskrit for *sacrificial fire*.
Virragu is Tamil for *firewood*.
Vrishmi is Sanskrit for Agni, *god of fire*.
Vrishâkapi is the same. [POPE.]

[5] For further information regarding the tûde tree, see Chapter XIV.

[6] Tylor, 'Primitive Culture,' vol. i. p. 85.

CHAP. VIII.

The Todas state it, as a matter of tradition amongst them, that the time was when they subsisted largely upon roots. They are even now partial, amongst others, to that which is known in India by the name of Salup Misri—orchis mascula—a terrestrial orchid which grows in great abundance on these hills. The woods also abound in edible varieties of wild-fruit—pôm—and herbs of sorts.

Intoxicating liquor or drug had never been utilised by these people prior to the arrival of the English. And tobacco is still a luxury.

Infants are nursed by their mothers, as a matter of general habit, for about three years: and it is not uncommon, for them to be still suckling when in the sixth year. Boiled millet or rice warmed in milk is a common article of diet for young children.

As a general rule, food is either eaten uncooked or boiled: but is sometimes baked or parched.

The Todas have no 'caste' prejudices; those Âryan fears of contamination which haunt the population of the plains, requiring that persons not of the precise same grade of life or family, should cook and eat apart: and which place obstacles to the intermarriage of those of different castes, as insuperable as if they were of foreign religions or nationalities.

Their two meals—which the women almost invariably cook—are eaten between the hours of 9 and 10 in the morning, and of 7 and 8 in the evening, in their little houses, but never in the dairy.

Men and women do not eat together at home, but the adult males of the family dine first, then the females. This as a matter of etiquette; which is not however so stringent as to preclude the women from eating before the men if there should be just occasion for them to do so. Children of both sexes have their meals either with the men or with the women. When one comes to consider the smallness of their houses and the primitive nature of their practices, one cannot but see that both convenience and good habits have been consulted in following these rules. CHAP. VIII.

Before eating, each member of the family takes a little of the food in his fingers, and raising it to the forehead says Swâmi! Swâmi![7] then places it on the ground as a present to bhumi tai[8] or mother earth. After meals these offerings are swept out of doors.

Before the Englishman came to the Nilagiris, and colonised the Todas' land, the country was full of game; hares, pea-fowl, partridge, jungle fowl, and numerous small birds, filled the secluded woods: deer of sorts, bison, and jungle-sheep roamed their open pastures: the tiger and leopard were common: and packs of the wild dog—chen nai[9]—running mute, hunted the largest deer with the unerring certainty of fate. The Toda buffalos, half-wild, had learnt to defend themselves and their young by tactics, the offspring of their bravery and skill; forming a rough triangular phalanx, with the courageous and strong bulls at apex and flanks, and the females and young in the hollow of the base, they would face the common enemy, and charging him in a body, gore and trample him under foot. The Todas, confident in the prowess of these animals, leave them to be herded by mere striplings armed with light wands; knowing that the amimals, and the children under their protection, would be perfectly safe.

Yet in the face of these attractions of sport: in the presence of considerable danger: and with the example of the brute creation before them, they have not adopted a weapon, even one so simple as a spear. They neither make nets, nor do they construct traps or pitfalls. They do not employ any of

[7] Swâmi = *lord.*

[8] Bhumi tai = *earth mother.* It appears likely that both the words and the practice have been copied from the Badagas.

[9] Chen = *red,* nai = *dog.* May not the French *chien* be derived from chen = *the red* (*one*)?

CHAP. VIII.

the processes for driving game known throughout India. No idea of defence appears to have been entertained, or of obstruction, brighter than that of making the doors of their houses so small, that to enter them they must crouch, and crawl through the openings on all fours. No mode of catching game, more skilful than is implied in the beating the wild-dogs off the prey they have hunted down and are worrying, is known to them.

Had the Todas felt any disposition to add to the varieties of their food, or to increase the amount of their animal stock, or to indulge in meat diet, the surrounding country at once afforded them precedents and examples of people who had domesticated cows, sheep, goats, pigs, and poultry. Some exception might have been taken by them to the introduction of cows and sheep on pasture land which the august buffalo alone, should be permitted to enjoy : yet, as they narrate, they have brought home young bison, hoping to tame them, though failing in their attempt to do so. But fowls, pigs, and goats would have kept entirely to the woods adjoining the villages.

## CHAPTER IX.

### SAVAGE ANTITYPE.

*Cause of idleness of primitive Races—Their attributes—Toda qualities, and form of Cranium—The most primitive form of Skull—How to judge of Cannibal heads—Tylor, on the Development of the Human Race—Dolichocephali the natural Inhabitants of warm Zones: Brachiocephali the result of harsher circumstances—Endogamy and Dolichocephaly—Why pure Brachiocephali are not met with—Caste inimical to advance—Brachiocephaly the counterpoise to Dolichocephaly—Correlation between Brachiocephaly and Broad Shoulders.*



IT will no doubt appear phenomenal to many of my readers, much in the same way as surprise has been excited in myself; that notwithstanding the example of certain tribes living contiguous to the Todas, and cognate to them in blood as in the stage of their barbarism, who earn a living by various modes of occupation, pursuit, and industry, the Toda should persist in maintaining an isolation of idleness so complete, that not one of the many means which these other tribes have adopted for improving their circumstances, and none of the impulses to action by which they have been moved, should in the least have commended themselves to this remarkable people living in their very midst.

The North-American Indian is well known to be receding before the advance of the white-man; from an inability to adapt his wild habits to the too-rapidly changing times, so absolute as to give the appearance of his having deliberately and proudly elected to accept extinction, rather than compromise with civilisation by altering the pristine customs of his race. And we greatly—and with much apparent justice—

CHAP. IX.

attribute this failure in self-adaptation, in general terms, to the immensity and abrupt nature of the change he is called on to make, if he would pass from his free and thriftless hunting and warring life, to the quiet of a frugal cultivator of the soil or trader.

But this aversion to all forms of *profitable* labour, and incapacity for commercial pursuit, is not more conspicuous in the untamed Red-Indian than in the self-restrained domestic Toda, surrounded as he is by industrious tribes not far elevated from his own primitive status; from whom—had he felt desire to change—he could at once have adopted simple expedients, as sufficient for his own purpose as they have been for theirs. I will endeavour to account for this persistency in idleness, of primitive and unprogressive races.

In the first place, and as regards the Todas, I assume as if a fact established, what indeed has every appearance of truth; that their present mode of life precisely suits the constitution of their minds—any important change appearing to them to be for the worse—that however much they must certainly, at some early periods of their career, have suffered from the failure of supplies, owing to the increase of their own numbers, and to their having depended on one source of food—which must have failed—yet as we find them, their natures and surrounding circumstances are practically in a condition of equilibrium. That is to say, they have perfected a dairy system enabling them to live entirely at ease and without labour: and which, owing to there being a ready market for surplus produce, now places them in a considerable degree of homely comfort—a happy state, which is likely to last so long as the land affords room for the people to expand.

Although in the estimation of many, this perfect contentment with a very little may be considered a proof of good sense, and be held a great virtue, yet it must be acknowledged that the phase is not one the best races of the world would acquiesce in. If they will not trade, and to work are ashamed, yet why none of the ordinary short cuts to wealth and honour, by means well known in all ages, and to most nations? No exciting and glorious war, with plunder! the feathers of the chief, the titles of the hero! No women to be attached, or prisoners to be enslaved or tortured! No food but a milk diet and grain, whilst the woods are full of game, and flocks and herds to be had for the taking! What is the meaning of all this? Have we come on the tracks of an aboriginal reign of conscience? And was man originally created virtuous as well as very simple?

It appears to my mind, that in this *absence of vigorous qualities: in the disregard of gain and of thrift:*[1] *as well as in their ultra domesticity, we have the attributes of a primeval race*, which at an era, when other families of man were undergoing the vivifying effects of such processes of natural selection as tend to eliminate the weak-minded and the weakly, and produce brachycephalic-headed and broad-shouldered men, had remained almost unchanged, through avoiding conflict with nature and man, in the seclusion of the sequestered jungles of warm climates; migrating—where it had to emigrate from its cradle land—either in vast numbers, for mutual protection, or in company with and patronised by more advanced and warlike tribes, glad perhaps to utilise its herds of cattle as their commissariat.

People of such torpid and inefficient natures would maintain—as the Todas have done till lately—the aboriginal habit of man; in living on wild fruit and roots, and the milk of cattle it had tamed: whilst other races, made more spirited,

[1] The causal organs excepted, no faculties are more uniformly defective in primitive races than Acquisitiveness, Constructiveness, Number and Order. When collectively small, they form the invariable sign of a recent 'primitive' origin; implying the unthriftiness, innocence of the value of property, contentedness with the simplest dwellings, and dislike to orderly rule, which are also the cause of their backward state. Tune is equally small: and such people have but little sense of music.

clever, and persevering through ages of strife with fellow-man, and conflict with difficulties presented by nature, had either risen in civilisation by means of a preliminary course of cultivation of the soil, and become great nations, or, on the contrary, had—like the North-American Indians under other and less favourable circumstances—developed qualities which, whilst retaining the primitive dislike to profitable labour, and the innocence of commercial skill displayed by the Todas, superadded other traits so ferocious as to render their immediate civilisation almost as hopeless as the taming of wild animals. The Toda is merely a simple, thriftless, and idle man, who will never, so long as his blood remains unmixed with that of superior tribes, or, by selection, is improved almost beyond recognition, work one iota more than circumstances compel him to do: but without taint of the ferocity of savagery.

I proceed now to compare the known qualities of the Toda with the form of his cranium: for if my supposition be correct; that in his general inefficiency, and callousness to wealth, combined with intense gregariousness and domesticity of character, we have prominent physiologic evidence of extreme primitiveness in condition of race, then it will prove most interesting and valuable, if, in addition to the objects of our immediate study, I may be successful in demonstrating even one practical means, by which, in judging of ancient skulls, we may be competent to decide between two chief candidates; of late years styled the brachycephalic and dolichocephalic—terms which, owing to want of definition, are unsatisfactory to the phrenologist, but which I use as being well understood by ethnologists—which is the oldest, most primitive form.

I feel the conviction that aboriginal man must, like the Todas, have been eminently gregarious, fond of children, and practical; for the simple reason, that without such combination of valuable qualities, he must, in the days of his ignorance and inexperience, have been killed off in detail, and his infant progeny have perished by neglect. That the Toda skull is remarkably well developed in all the domestic organs, and in the necessary perceptive—practical—faculties, a glance at the photographs in this book will show to everyone.

Next. In the dark prehistoric age, whose duration appears unlimited, but through which all families of man have passed, *that race which possessed the greatest capacity for overcoming obstacles*—taken in the very widest sense—must, *cæteris paribus,* inevitably have remained the survivor in struggles with the weaker, and therefore, by laws of progression, more primitive race. Now *these active qualities are invariably accompanied by large size in the groups of organs, which, situated at the sides of the cranium, form, when well developed, the brachycephalic head.*

The Toda tribe is entirely, and without individual exception, narrow-long-headed—dolichocephalic—every person in it, of both sexes, being deficient in every organ at the sides of the skull; and, as I have before stated, having the perceptive organs over the eyebrow (group $I^2$), and the Domestic group at the back of the head, large. If we add to these indications, the deficiency in moral and in superior mental organisation which appears to be an universal attribute of almost entirely undeveloped peoples, we can, I think, make up our minds without hesitation, as to what form of skull is the most primitive of those of which we have yet discovered remains.

In races which, though still dolichocephalic, are seemingly *growing*—advancing towards brachycephaly—we find the *sides of the skull in stages of development,* varying in directions and degrees of growth, with each different race. This phenomenon is capable of explanation:—We might anticipate that so long as the marriage practice of a tribe is what Mr. M'Lennan has termed[2] endogamous, the form in skull of that tribe—as the Todas—from every individual being affected by

[2] M'Lennan, 'Primitive Marriage.'

the self-same causes, would be identical, or nearly so. It would either grow with considerable uniformity, or remain unaltered throughout the tribe. But when marriage custom changed to exogamy, in alliances with neighbouring races, or through the capture of female prisoners in war, then we might expect to see the tribal skull exhibiting great variety in shape.

We find the dolichocephalic Toda, careless of a meat diet, and without an intoxicating beverage. Setting moral considerations apart—and savages are not much troubled with morals—the practical *necessity* for flesh and stimulants arises from the craving of the organs of destructiveness and alimentativeness; properties of the brachycephalic head. The same organs acting under deep emotions, and perhaps under exceptional geographical restrictions, would produce cannibalism.

From what has just been written, it may be gathered that from the shape of a skull we may judge of the possibility of the race to which it belongs, having been cannibals. We shall see, in the course of future chapters, that we may also estimate, by the same process, the probabilities of its having been infanticidal, polyandrous, or much imbued with polygamy.

Mr. Tylor, in sustaining the thesis of the progression of civilisation, as contrasted with its rival, the degeneration theory, expresses his views in words which give great support to the ideas I have ventured to advance, on the improvement in form of the human skull: 'The savage state,' he writes, 'in some measure represents an early condition of mankind, out of which the higher culture has gradually been developed or evolved by processes still in regular operation as of old, the result showing that, on the whole, progress has far prevailed over relapse. On this proposition, the main tendency of human society during its long term of existence has been to pass from a savage to a civilised state. Now all must admit a great part of this assertion to be not only truth, but truism. Referred to direct history, a great section of it proves to belong, not to the domain of speculation, but to that of positive knowledge. It is mere matter of chronicle that modern civilisation is a development of mediæval civilisation, which again is a development from civilisation of the order represented in Greece, Assyria, or Egypt. Thus the higher culture being clearly traced back to what may be called the middle culture, the question which remains is, whether this middle culture may be traced back to the lower culture; that is, to savagery? To affirm this is merely to assert that the same kind of development in culture which has gone on inside our range of knowledge, has also gone outside it, its course of proceeding being unaffected by our having, or not having, reporters present. If anyone holds that human thought and action were worked out in primæval times according to laws essentially other than those of the modern world, it is for him to prove, by valid evidence, this anomalous state of things, otherwise the doctrine of permanent principle will hold good, as in astronomy or geology.'[3]

If the arguments which I have adduced in these last few pages, be reasonable, probability has been shown that the earliest races of man—of whom it is believed the Todas form a somewhat advanced sample—were the mild dolichocephalic natives of a terrestrial zone where nature is most gentle and favourable to human growth. We may suppose that in the course of ages, population increased, until having occupied all regions where man could live without the exercise of much labour or skill, it then began to encounter the difficulties destined ultimately to form its character; of which the chief would be experienced by those branches of the human family which spread into the most severe and inhospitable tracts. These wanderers would grow, by means of the process of natural selection, and in the course of long ages, brachycephalic, savage, and strong-bodied.

Rather than continue their national growth in intractable

[3] Tylor, 'Primitive Culture,' vol. i. p. 28.

climes, these races, now hardy and warlike, would turn back their hordes in anticipation of the easy conquest of the rich lands occupied by the more effeminate and now wealthy populations from which they had originally sprung. All eventful history of which we have written record, teems with experiences of the oft-repeated inroads of northern barbarians on their luxurious or weak southern neighbours. I have, therefore, substantial grounds for entertaining the conviction that conquests of the more mild, dolichocephalic races, by the brachycephali, must have been in constant operation, in greater or less scale, and in varying quarters and directions of the globe, from the earliest point of prehistoric age at which population began to crowd, and races to find a difficulty in providing food for the ever-increasing number of mouths.

It is suggested that thus we may, amongst other causes, account for the fragmentary remains of some races, and the living existence of others, which advance of anthropological discovery proves to have been, at one time, near neighbours, and possibly of the same stock, though now dispersed and separated at the extreme limits of the inhabitable world. In those instances where these scattered races had intermarried amongst themselves alone—*practising endogamy* in social alliance—and where the progress of their passage, migration, or flight from the tropics had been so rapid and free from conflict, that natural selection had not had time or opportunity to make modifications, ere the tribes died out in the country of their refuge; there we should expect their exhumed skulls would show them to have been *entirely dolichocephalic.* But where the tribes had, in the *observance of exogamy*—whether resulting from choice or through incorporation with their conquerors—intermixed with brachycephalic peoples: or if they had, in their turn also, been long exposed to the action of natural selection; there we should meet *either modified-dolichocephalic crania, or find the narrow and the broad skulls intermingled.*

It is a matter of actual experience, that endogamous and exogamous tribes may coexist as neighbours in the same limited territory.

Although dolichocephalic races are not uncommon: if we *do not find a purely brachycephalic tribe*—one in which every individual member is broad-headed—we may remember, primarily; that this form of skull—according to this theory—was in the first instance shaped by natural selection; in which action every person would not be equally affected, nor both sexes exposed to all the same influences. Secondly; such a race being by its nature warlike, and strong in its animal propensities, would be little disposed to accede to restrictions limiting its members to marriage within their own tribe; hence, in their domestic alliances with people of other families of man, the probability of connectionships being formed with dolichocephali, and the consequent introduction of narrow-headed individuals into their midst, would be increased. Thirdly; there would appear to run throughout composite nature, animate and inanimate, a tendency to deterioration; to be resolved into original simple elements; for instance, of the most enduring metals to corrosion, and the hardest granite to disintegration. Similarly a process is at work; term it atavism, degeneration, or what you will, by force of which man—amongst other animals—tends to lapse, or revert to a more dolichocephalic strain. Though nature provides antidotes to this process, in different forms of selection, instances of degenerate form must always exist.

This deteriorating action is particularly observable in the breeding of domestic amimals. The difficulty in maintaining breadth in dogs' heads is well known. And the very same tendency may readily be observed in the human family. Doubtless there must be some limit to which the healthy subject can thus degenerate. And probably we shall not be very far in the wrong if we consider the Toda cranium to afford us a sample of what man—as a race—uninfluenced by selection, and living an open-air life, tends to revert to. I have seen many individuals of the Âryan family far more dolichocephalic than any Toda: but never an entire race or tribe.

The caste system of India; which I believe to be merely the religious bias, or impulse, which a designing priesthood gave to a dolichocephalic and naturally endogamous people, is eminently opposed to brachycephalic improvement, through interfering with natural selection. Even in peaceful pursuits; as in war, and contentions with climate, we are always struggling against the difficulties presented by competition; over which the most energetic—the brachycephalic—has most chance of success; of outliving the other.

*Brachycephaly produced by selection, forms the natural counterpoise to dolichocephaly obtained through degeneration or inherited from primitive ancestors.*

In the assertion of the belief I expressed; in the correlation existing between brachycephaly, and broad shoulders; it is not wished to imply, in the face of ample and frequent evidence to the contrary, that the rule has not many exceptions. Indeed narrow-headed men have often strong frames. But dolichocephalic *races* may well be noted as having light figures compared with their converse. I incline, however, as the result of my personal experience, to attribute variations from the principle I have laid down; to the marriage amongst exogamous races, of the two different descriptions of head to two different styles of body; by which the individual offspring we may notice as a departure from the rule, probably derived his cranium from one parent and his bodily frame from the other.

# CHAPTER X.

## CENSUS.

*Mode of taking Census—Census Table—Todas hide nothing but Number of Cattle—Review of the Table—Crowding—Number of Todas—Vital Statistics—Does the Tribe increase, or is it dying out?*

CHAP. X.

'AMONG the various objects of Political Economy, one of the most important and interesting,' wrote Dugald Stewart, 'has been always understood to be the augmentation of the numbers of the people.'[1]

I am about to lay before my readers the *boná fide* results of a detailed census (Table No. 3), taken by me in the year 1870, of a considerable portion of the Toda tribe. It will be found to well repay close scrutiny; for more precise information as regards actual domestic custom and the social condition of very primitive races can be deduced from what at first sight will appear to be a mere collection of dry facts and figures, than from a far larger amount of written description of events.

A second sheet, termed 'Statistics of Toda Families,' recorded at the time of taking the census, will be found in Table No. 4.

Both of these tables were compiled with as much scrupulous care and accuracy as could probably have well been bestowed on them. The process of collecting information was as follows;—Arriving at each village, every soul, male and female, old and young, would be summoned before us. The

[1] Dugald Stewart, 'Lectures on Political Economy.'

## TABLE No. III. *Census.*

| Mands: Toda Names | Mands: Badaga Names | Houses: Dwelling Rooms | Houses: Dwelling Houses | Houses: Sacred Houses | Houses: Deserted Houses | Houses: Total of Houses | Inhabitants, Male: Widowed Adults | Male: Married Adults | Male: Single Adults | Male: Children | Male: Total | Female: Widowed Adults | Female: Married Adults | Female: Single Adults | Female: Children | Female: Total | Grand Total | Particulars regarding Inhabitants | Remarks (M = Mands, I = Inhabitants) |
|---|---|---|---|---|---|---|---|---|---|---|---|---|---|---|---|---|---|---|---|
| Diljâvenu | Karikall | 3 | 3 | 2 | 1 | 6 | — | 3 | 3[1] | 4 | 10 | 1[2] | 2 | — | 6[3] | 9 | 19 | 1. Two younger brothers of the married men. One dairyman aged 18 years. 2. Mother of one of the married men and of the dairyman. 3. Two of 12 years of age. | M. Well sheltered and drained. Doors face east. I. Healthy and fairly vigorous. Comfortable. |
| Kakhodi | Kakhodi | 2 | 2 | 1 | 1 | 4 | — | 3[1] | — | 2 | 5 | — | 2[2] | — | — | 2 | 7 | 1, 2. One man and one woman, lately married: hence the small number of children. | M. Well sheltered, but imperfectly drained. Doors face north. I. Tolerably hale, but not vigorous. Very poor. |
| Beresthro | Karrsthro | 2 | 1 | 1 | — | 2 | — | 4[1] | — | 3 | 7 | — | 4[2] | — | 1 | 5 | 12 | 1, 2. One father, one mother, two sons, two wives of sons, one daughter, and one husband of daughter. Two of these pairs having lately married, the number of children is small. | M. Not well sheltered or drained. Doors face west. I. Hale, and fairly vigorous. Very poor. |
| Koana-koar | Koana-korrâi | 3 | 2 | 1 | — | 3 | — | 4 | 3[3] | 3 | 10 | — | 4[2] | 1[3] | 1[4] | 6 | 16 | 1. Two dairymen. 2. One aunt and two nieces. 3. A cripple from birth, aged 20 years. 4. Aged 14 years. | M. Exposed, but well drained. Doors face south. I. Healthy, and fairly vigorous. One cripple from birth. |
| Ebgodu | Ebgodu | 4 | 3 | 1 | 1 | 5 | 1[1] | 4[2] | 4[3] | 3 | 12 | 1[4] | 4[5] | — | 6[6] | 11 | 23 | 1. About 85 years. Admitted to this Mand through kindness, having lost his own children and quarrelled with his grandchildren. 2. Aged 16 years. 3. Two are dairymen. 4. About 75 years of age. 5. One in | M. Well sheltered and well drained. Doors face south-east. I. Hale and vigorous. Very comfortable. An old man nearly deaf. An infant |

CHAP. X.

| | | | | | | | | | | | | | | | | | | | |
|---|---|---|---|---|---|---|---|---|---|---|---|---|---|---|---|---|---|---|---|
| | | | | | | | | | | | | | | | | | | childbed. 6. One of 14 years, one of 12 years. One infant with a disease of the skin.—The four married men, and four single adults, are six brothers and two nephews. | with disease of the skin. A woman in childbed. |
| Bângâdu . | Bângâdu . | 4 | 2 | 1 | — | 3 | 2[1] | 4 | 2[2] | 6 | 14 | 2[3] | 4 | — | 4[4] | 10 | 24 | 1. Both brothers of one of the married men. 2. One aged 22, engaged to be married. One aged 16, a dairyman. 3. One mother of one of the married men. One mother of two of the married women. 4. Two about 12 years of age. One sister to one of the married men. | M. Much exposed, but well drained. Doors face east. I. Healthy, but not vigorous. Very poor. |
| Karshk . | Kandal . | 5 | 3 | 2 | — | 5 | — | 10 | 6 | 4 | 20 | — | 10 | — | 2 | 12 | 32 | One father, one mother, one married son, one son a dairyman. One father, one mother, one married daughter. Three married sisters. Three women lately married. One woman barren. Three with small families. | M. Fairly sheltered and well drained. Doors face south-east. I. Healthy and fairly vigorous. Comfortable. |
| Mêâmadd . | Mardini . | 3 | 3 | 1 | 1 | 5 | 1[1] | 6[2] | 1[3] | 3 | 11 | 2[4] | 6 | — | 4 | 12 | 23 | 1. Son of one widow. 2. Four sons of same widow, and two grandsons. 3. Son of same widow, a dairyman. 4. The second widow is mother-in-law of widower; also mother-in-law of one of the grandsons. One a child-marriage. | M. Well sheltered and well drained. Doors face east and south-west. I. Healthy and fairly vigorous. Comfortable. |
| Keshkir . | Kakkeri . | 3 | 2 | 1 | — | 3 | — | 6[1] | 1[2] | 5 | 12 | — | 6[3] | — | 3 | 9 | 21 | 2. Two are sons of one married woman. One is a son of another married woman. Two are boys, aged 12 and 15. 2. A dairyman, 24 years of age. 3. Two are daughters of one married woman. One is a daughter of another married woman. Two child-marriages. | M. Fairly sheltered and well drained. Doors face south-east. I. Healthy and fairly vigorous. Poor. A girl squints. A woman blind of one eye from an accident. |
| Kirzho . | Kundetro . | 2 | 1 | 1 | — | 2 | — | 2 | 1[1] | 2 | 5 | 1[2] | 2 | — | 1[3] | 4 | 9 | 1. A dairyman, 15 years of age. 2. Mother of one married woman and of one married man. 3. One aged 12 years. | M. Fairly sheltered and well drained. Doors face south and east. I. Healthy and vigorous, except one man. Comfortable. |
| Meikarsk . | Manchakâll . | 4 | 3 | 1 | — | 4 | 1[1] | 3 | 1[2] | 1 | 6 | — | 3[3] | — | 1[4] | 4 | 10 | 1. Father of girl of 14. 2. Dairyman aged 15. 3. One is mother of one of the other married women. 4. Aged nearly 14 years. | M. Exposed, but well drained. Doors face south-east. I. Healthy and vigorous. Comfortable. |
| | | 35 | 25 | 13 | 4 | 42 | 5 | 49 | 22 | 36 | 112 | 7 | 47 | 1 | 29 | 84 | 196 | | |

women would invariably be placed in front; as it would be from them we should obtain information of the nature we required for census purposes; experience telling us that on points of mere family lore, they, without fail, are more reliable and intelligent than the men. It is they especially who know of the births, deaths, and marriages, and who can compare the dates of those interesting family events, by the heights, or comparative ages of individuals in the group standing before them.

At first we found the people in front of us, an apprehensive little assembly. The women, squatting on the ground, would close up together, looking shyly at us from the corners of the eye. The men, seated about on the surrounding-wall, were surly and suspicious. Breathless boys, who, hearing of the gentlemen's arrival at their Mand, had run in from buffalo-tending, stood open-mouthed, leaning on their sticks. The girls would stroll about, nursing the babies, now and then crouching in to the houses, to look after the fire which their mothers had been invited to leave. After a general explanation of our object in paying their retired home this very unexpected visit—most carefully avoiding all allusion to the subject of infanticide—and following on a judicious distribution of small coin, made amongst the infants, in order to open the mothers' hearts, we would commence our examination.

One woman at a time. She points out her husbands, her boys, her girls: accounts for the absent; one tending cattle, one the dairyman, two gone to collect kutu: and describes her relationship to the other males and females in the Mand.

What chance had such a simple people of eluding us, when enquiry took the form of a series of most unimportant questions? Not the most suspicious would object to tell if their parents were alive or dead: and what relation the members of the group were to one another. When was your daughter married, my good woman, and how many boys and how many girls have you? So sorry to hear you lost two daughters and a son. How old were they? And so on, and so on we went, examining one woman after another, and village after village. Had they shown, at any time, a desire to deceive—which, as regards human population, they never did—we could have readily detected the attempt, and outwitted them. A striking characteristic of the Todas is their inability to avoid giving an answer; but as the reply will, however, not always be true, leading questions should be avoided as much as possible. If you wish to ascertain a fact; undermine it, stalk it down, follow up enquiries with others that test it. Their only recipe to avoid answering a disagreeable query, is to tell a lie; a lie as palpable as that of a child.

My belief is, that, with the exception of the number of their cattle, they have nothing to hide. Now as there is no way of stalking down such a subject, and they will not, or cannot, tell you truly how many head there are in the village herd: and the Mands are situated wide apart over the hills: and the cattle are not driven home till evening; I was unable to count the buffalos myself, or to form any test of the numbers which they told me. I have therefore left that subject an open question. The food supply is one that I have not been able to determine, even approximately.

To some minds this may appear to be an imperfect census; both because the inhabitants of all villages were not taken on the same day, and because every soul was not actually present. Practically speaking, it is as accurate as could be obtained, and nearly as perfect as could be desired; for the people are very primitive and the Mands are very small—containing from two to five houses or rooms—the inhabitants have few pursuits to lead them away from home, and on cloudy cold days they rarely go abroad. Above all, ignorance of the fact that they were being numbered, robbed them of object in deceit.

CHAP. X.

Before proceeding further, I will review this Census Table, especially selecting those facts which may be useful to us hereafter.

α. We find that Toda males of *all ages*, bear the proportion to females of all ages, of 112 : 84, or of 100 : 75. In a census of the North-west Provinces of India, taken during the year 1866, the proportions between the sexes were found to be as 100 : 86·6. And in the Punjab as 100 : 81·8.[2] In Oudh, the census of 1868-69 taken in ten districts suspected of infanticide, gave 100 : 75·6 of all ages.[3]

β. The male *adults* are to the female adults, as 76 : 55, or as 100 : 72·4.

γ. The male *children* under fourteen years of age, bear to the female children of the same period—ages estimated from their personal appearance—the ratio of 36 : 29, or of 100 : 80·6.

Although, as we find, there is a somewhat larger proportion of females to males among children than amongst adults, I am disposed to attribute the discrepancy either to the score of the limited number of instances which the census contains: or to my having recorded as children, some who should have been accounted adult women.

δ. There is 1 unmarried girl—a cripple from birth—out of 55 adult females, or 1·8 in 100.

ε. There are 22 young men who are said to be unmarried. If we deduct from these 22 adults, the 10 recorded as dairymen; who, during the term of office, are compelled, through religious usage, to live *en garçon*: we have yet 12 men of marriageable age who are stated in the Table to be leading a single life. From actual knowledge of the people, I form the opinion that these 12 are Benedicts, *de facto*.

[2] Selections from the Records of the Government of India. Foreign Department. Dated 1867.

[3] Statistics deduced from a census of Oudh in 1868–69, relating to female infanticide among Rajput families.

ζ. We find there to be 49 undoubtedly married men, and 47 married women.

If this ratio was strictly true, I should be in a position to announce that the practice of polyandry had become extinct. But if to these 49 men, we add the 12 who are married *de facto*, we get 61 husbands for the 47 wives, or the proportion of 100 : 77. Such, in my belief, is the existing state of polyandry in the tribe—formerly, the discrepancy was perhaps as much as 100 : 40.

η. The total of the Table gives a return of 196 people; from whom, if we deduct the 10 dairymen who live apart, we find that 186 people, of both sexes and all ages, live in 35 rooms, the dimensions of which we know to be 8ft. by 8ft. each; or 5·3 persons, on an average, in each of such rooms. Such is the average domiciliary condition of the tribe. But in village Mênmadd, 23 are shown to be living in 3 rooms, or 8 in some rooms.

If such be the custom of the people when in a state of health, we can scarcely form a conception of their miserable plight when epidemics arise: but we can at once comprehend how fatal any form of contagious disease is too sure to become, if it obtains a footing in the homesteads of any primitive race. Let this essential condition of savage life make a deep impression on our minds, if we would realise any one of the numerous forms of suffering, hardship, or disaster, to which our forefathers must all, from time to time, have been exposed. Rapidly as intelligence spreads amongst civilised nations in these modern days, through the quick interchange of ideas; we may feel very confident, that in the retirement of mountains, swamps, and jungles, at an era when all mankind was young and inexperienced; isolated tribes each gaining their separate knowledge through means of the repeated hard knocks to which their own ignorance of the working of natural laws had rendered them liable, must have undergone the severest trials.

A perusal of the column in Table No. 3, which affords

CHAP. X.

particulars regarding the inhabitants, will give a curious insight of the social economy of the Mand. It may be viewed as a house occupied by one family; in each room of which a subdivision of the family lives. If we look closely into the details of—for instance—villages Diljâvenu and Koana-koar, we find in the former, 3 rooms in which live 5 adult men, 3 adult women, 2 girls twelve years of age, besides 8 other children of both sexes. In the latter village are 3 rooms containing 6 adult men, 5 adult women, one of whom is unmarried, 1 girl of fourteen years, with 3 small boys.

The people do not set apart a room as bachelor-hall, as some equally rude tribes do; the Kôls for instance.

I find in a statistical Report of the Nilagiris,[4] submitted in the year 1847 to the Government of that day, that the Todas were then estimated at only 337 people. Owing, perhaps, to the low figure at which the number is fixed; partly also to the existence of certain mistakes, which have of late been discovered in the names and positions assigned to certain villages, an impression exists that the data are not to be entirely relied upon. But the record, given as found in the carefully compiled Report, is, I believe, not very incorrect. No census having been published since 1847, I am indebted to the kindness of the late Commissioner of the Nilagiris,[5] for the most reliable statement of the number of the Todas, extant. Mr. Breeks believes that in the year 1867 they amounted to 455 males and 249 females, of all ages; giving a total of 704 souls.

*6.* Referring to the Census Table of 11 villages of various sizes; it appears that there are 112 males + 84 females = 196 souls in those Mands, or 17·82 as the average number in each. Of these 112 males, 49 + 22 = 71 are in the prime of life.

[4] Captain J. Ouchterlony, Madras Engineers, 'Statistical Report of the Nilgherry Hills. 1847.'

[5] Mr. J. Breeks.

The precise number of Mands occupied at any one time, has not been ascertained, but the best authorities consider them to be not less than 40. Hence, by a short calculation, we find that the tribe consisted, in 1870, of not less than 407 males + 306 females, or 713 souls; of whom 258 were men in the prime of life.

Now, if the Report from which I have just quoted, should be correct, it would appear that the tribe has more than doubled in about 23 years; and the opportunity, has been lost to me; of witnessing the process, and of ascertaining the causes, by means of which a race may die out. With every desire for the happiness of existing Todas, I still grieve to have been deprived of the interesting study.

It is very much to be lamented that no vital statistics exist of the people: and that such as I have been able to collect, cannot be depended upon, absolutely; being merely approximate.

1. Of the 196 people found noted in the Census Table, I ascertained by personal inspection that there were only 2 cases of natural malformation; viz., in the village of Koanakoar, a young woman who was a cripple from birth: in Keshkir, a girl squinting with one eye.

2. Only 3 people possessed defects that would either tend to shorten life or to evidence the probability of its soon drawing to a close; viz., in Ebgodu, a man nearly deaf and blind from old age: in the same village an infant with a skin disease: and in Kirzho, a middle-aged man in bad general health.

Many were scored on the shoulder as a remedy for rheumatism. One woman was in quarantine after child-birth. And one woman was blind of an eye from a spark of fire having flown into it. It is said that contagious disease is not uncommon, but I am greatly disposed to doubt the statement, as applied to the present day. None came before me marked by smallpox. A case of leprosy was met with; but as the man afflicted with that dreadful malady, was not amongst the 196 people of the census, the case cannot be used in these calculations.

As regards the general appearance of the people; a large proportion of both sexes and of all ages are doubtless in excellent health. Up to the age of fourteen, the children are certainly, and almost universally, hale and hearty. The young women look well, too: but the young men are often bottle-nosed, with a general appearance of deficient circulation, insufficient food, and of athletic exercise. Nature seems to make competent arrangements, by means of which the female sex is able to bear children during the extra period that young men require for the purpose of completing their growth. It is probably a consequence or a portion of this design, that renders girls as a general rule more easy to rear than boys. Be that as it may, these rather weedy youths fill out in course of time, and complete their features with mature age—the large nose is rarely, or perhaps never, apparent in the young; and seems not to attain its climax till near the age of thirty—the women in advanced years are often draggled in appearance, from poverty and child-bearing. The full-grown men look strong and well.

Now for our examination into the augmentation of the numbers of the people.

If we allow, that out of the 3 people recorded in paragraph (x) to be in a state of health unfavourable to prolonged existence, 2 die in the course of the year. And suppose that another 2 die in the same period from other causes—a high rate for those who, living a pastoral and quiet life in a healthy climate, are exposed to few vicissitudes—we have then 4 deaths amongst 196 people, in the course of twelve months; or 2 per cent. per annum, as the extreme death-rate for *all ages*.

In the years between 1838 and 1861, the average ratio of mortality in Great Britain—a country in which high civilisation and competition, expose its people to vicissitudes from which the Toda is entirely exempt—was 1 in 45, or 2·23 per cent. per annum.[6]

λ. We shall find in a succeeding chapter on Infanticide, Table No. 7, that of 26 M + 20 F, or 46 children, who—judging from the ages of the mothers—were of different ages, varying from 1 to 20 years, 5 died. In other words, 10·87 per cent. of children born, die of *youthful* maladies.

μ. If, from the same Table, we calculate the number of children, whose mothers being less than 27 years must themselves be under 10 years of age, we see that of 23 born, 3 died; or that 13 per cent. died of *infantile* disorders.

An average taken of the mortality of several countries in Europe, gives 38·3 per cent. of children who died in the year 1825, 'from birth to the age of 10.'[7]

Not to fatigue my readers with further preliminaries, I will now submit the brief calculation which is to show whether the Todas are dying out or increasing in numbers; and at what rate of progress. Mathematical accuracy cannot, with justice, be expected; for, even with the most perfect census possible, there are obvious reasons why exactness is unattainable. I will premise, in the words of Dugald Stewart, that 'the rate at which the multiplication of different races would go, seems to depend on the following particulars; (1) the age at which the parent becomes prolific; (2) the time that elapses in pregnancy; (3) the frequency of breeding; (4) the numbers of each brood; (5) the period during which the parent continues prolific.'[8]

Suppose then we begin our reckoning with 177 married Todas of both sexes. Paragraph (ζ) of this chapter informs us that of this 177, there will be 100 men and 77 women.

Tables Nos. 6 and 7 show that the average of women—

[6] Adam Smith, 'The Wealth of Nations.'

[7] Malthus, 'Essay on the Principle of Population.'

[8] Dugald Stewart, 'Lectures on Political Economy.'

CHAP. X.

including a proportion of the sterile—bear children for 20 years, at the rate of 6 children for each woman.

We know from paragraph (λ), that of 100 children born, 10·87 die before they attain to the age of 20.

The natural death-rate of *all ages* is allowed in paragraph (κ) to stand at 2 per cent. per annum; which rate is here taken for the proportion of *adults* only, who die—a very high figure. Hence 18·29 per cent. will give the number of deaths during the ten years which forms the *mean* period of child-bearing.

*Calculation.*

| | |
|---|---|
| 77 | Number of women who commence to bear children. |
| 77−18·29= 58·71 | Average number of women who bear children for 20 years. |
| Then | |
| 58·71×6=352·26 | Number of children born to those women at the expiration of 20 years. |
| Deduct | |
| 52·26÷10·87= 32·41 | The number of children who die before attaining 20 years. |
| 319·85 | The number of children who survive at the expiration of 20 years. |
| | During these 20 years, the original 177 people have decreased by 2 per cent. per annum; or 33·21 per cent.=58·78. |
| Thus | |
| 177−58·78=118·22 | |
| 438·07 | |

We see therefore that in the course of 20 years, the 177 Todas have theoretically expanded to 438. Thus doubling in 16·2 years. 'In the back settlements of America, where the inhabitants applied themselves solely to agriculture, and luxury was not known, the people were found to double themselves in 15 years.'[9] And it has been shown by Adam Smith, that 'when the means of subsistence are supplied in sufficient abundance, the principle of increase is powerful enough to cause population to advance in geometrical proportion, or in the ratio of the numbers 1. 2. 4. 8. 16.'[10]

It follows therefore, taking the present number of the Toda tribe at 713, and the term of doubling at 16·2 years, that

| | | | |
|---|---|---|---|
| in the year | 1886 | they will have become | 1426 |
| „ | 1902 | „ „ | 2852 |
| „ | 1918 | „ „ | 5604 |

and so on; of which numbers, nearly one-third will be men in the prime of life.

[9] Malthus, 'Essay on the Principle of Population.'

[10] Adam Smith, 'The Wealth of Nations.'

# CHAPTER XI.

## FAMILY STATISTICS.

*The day approaches when the Nilagiris will not afford support for the Todas—Occupations which the Todas might take to—A little education would give them a good start in life—Toda Males bear to Females the ratio of* 100 : 75*—The cause of this disparity between the Sexes—A male-producing variety of man, formed by Infanticide—Useful Family Statistics.*

CHAP. XI.

SUPPOSING that the Toda cattle should multiply at the same rate of progress as their masters are shown to be doing, still the time must sooner or later arrive, when the available grazing land on these mountains will be insufficient to feed them all. I may repeat, that the food, on the due supply of which the Toda depends, is derived from two sources only; viz., that which is obtained as a cess from the Badagas in lieu of rent for the Toda land they cultivate: and that which is acquired by the consumption and sale of the products of their own buffalos. The first is a fixed quantity; the second will become a fixed quantity also, so soon as the cattle have attained their largest practicable number.

If then the Todas persist in adhering without deviation, to their present habits and customs, it is clear that the time must be approaching when the tribe will drift into a condition of great distress. 'Food,' wrote Adam Smith, 'is indispensable for the support of human life; and it may be said that this condition of our existence has a natural tendency to make every man perish of hunger! In point of fact, however, very few perish of want; and the tendency in question is, in the great majority of cases, far more than counterbalanced by the opposing principles to which it gives rise—by the industry and foresight which it enforces on the attention of every man.'[1]

Two sources of food, entirely apart from those to which I have alluded, are available; the adoption of either of which would not only rescue the Todas from immediate danger, but might stamp an era whence their rise in the world would date, viz., the physical labour of the men: and the sale of male cattle, of horns and hides, of which they are at the present time cheated by the Kotas. Both cooly-labour and cattle-breeding, should be occupations suitable to an able-bodied pastoral people.

With a race that labours, everything is possible. Civilisation owes to labour her first impulses. It gives to nature the opportunity of selection, which the Todas have avoided; that process, by means of which, the fittest survive, and the inefficient gravitate first, into the lowest ranks of a population: then die out through the want and maladies which are the results of their own ignorance and want of vigour.

A modicum of worldly education; a little writing and ciphering, would give them a start in life: some local geography and knowledge of the world, inculcated by the enforced travelling of some of the more intelligent of their number, would enlarge their ideas. For the rest they must act for themselves. Thus when the time arrives—as come it enevitably must do—that, in spite of labour and cattle-breeding, the small Nilagiri plateau can no longer contain their ever-increasing numbers; the little colonies they would throw off, would not retire into the depths of the surrounding country, as ignorant and barbarous as these their ancestors; to be preyed upon by offshoots from their present wily neighbours: but would have a good chance of becoming independent and improving peoples.

In paragraph (α) of the last chapter, I showed that the

[1] Adam Smith, 'The Wealth of Nations.'

CHAP. XI.

Toda males of all ages bear to the females, the proportion of 100 : 75; and the correctness of this statement is somewhat confirmed by the ratio in adults and in children, given in paragraphs (β) and (γ) bearing a similar discrepancy. This excess of males is a very striking fact, and its truth may be accepted without doubt or mental reserve. I think we cannot quite account for the universal paucity of females without acknowledging, either that infanticide is, or has recently been practised to a very sensible extent: or that more boys are *born* than girls.

To what cause may we attribute this wide departure in nature, from those of her well-established laws; by the operations of which, equality between the sexes, is, within certain limits of divergence, known to be preserved, in all countries of whose population we have accurate knowledge? If we are disposed to describe the cause, in some general expression, as 'race peculiarity,' we still cannot be satisfied with less than the discovery of the physiologic reason for such eccentricity. We note the food and clothing, the mode of life, the climate; and fail to see sufficient reason for ascribing what we seek to any such origin. In fact, as regards the Todas, we can with certainty pronounce, that in only two respects can their surroundings be considered to differ widely in an important manner, from that of vast masses of mankind to whom great variation between the sexes has never been traced; viz., in their marriage system, and in the practice of infanticide.

We have learnt that relationship is, with the Todas, intimate far beyond that witnessed in any country approaching civilisation. Intimate to such a degree, that the whole tribe, where not parents and children, brothers and sisters, are all first-cousins, descended from lines of first-cousins prolonged for centuries. Let me show emphatically and distinctly that such is in truth the case. The tribe consists of about 713 persons, divided between 5 clans; of which two are almost extinct. The remaining three clans, being nearly of equal number, must contain about 200 members of all ages each. But one of them—the Peiki clan—marries solely within itself. Hence, this small body of 200 people have intermarried from time immemorial. And the intercourse must have become very promiscuous. I do not attribute disparity between the sexes to this close intercourse; but it is interesting to review the primitive practice, as a custom connected with the paucity of numbers arising from infanticide, and with the polyandrous habit which is found in junction with it.

In future chapters we shall see that the practice of infanticide as observed by the Todas, was the habitual destruction of all daughters in every family, except one or sometimes two. And we know that the average size of Toda families is 6 children born to each woman.

Now let us for the purpose of illustration take three families as representing an average of the entire tribe; say that one mother gives birth to 6 daughters and no sons: a second mother has 6 sons only, whilst the third mother has 3 sons and 3 daughters. The first mother—following the triba custom—destroys 4 daughters and preserves 2. The second retains her 6 sons. The third kills 2 daughters and keeps 1, as also her 3 sons. We have then, from the three families, 9 sons and 3 daughters with which to continue the breed. But whilst the males belong to families in which the tendency to produce sons is great, the females are of those of a converse inclination. Thus the bias strengthens with each generation, until, as we find, families grow to have habitually more sons than daughters. This habitude *outlasting the depraved practice which caused it*, indurates more or less, into a fixed characteristic of the people: and *a male-producing variety of man is formed.*

In presenting Table No. 4, containing what I have termed 'Statistics of Toda Families,' to the indulgence of my readers,

## TABLE No. IV. *Statistics of Toda Families.*

| No. on the List | Name of Mands | Wives | | | Husbands | | | | | Children | | | | | | Remarks |
|---|---|---|---|---|---|---|---|---|---|---|---|---|---|---|---|---|
| | | Clan | Apparent present ages | Probable number of years since married | Clan | Apparent ages of those alive | Probable ages of those dead, and number of years since dead | | Degree of relationship to one another | Apparent ages of those alive | | Probable ages of those dead, and the number of years since dead. | | | | Notes.—No. 5 column has been determined either by reference to age of eldest child or where the period was manifestly short, from the woman's own statement. The remaining columns are the result of *vivâ voce* examination of parents, or of personal inspection. |
| | | | | | | | | | | Males | Females | Males | | Females | | |
| 1 | 2 | 3 | 4 | 5 | 6 | 7 | 8 | 9 | 10 | 11 | 12 | 13 | 14 | 15 | 16 | |
| 1 | Diljavenu | Tôdi | 27 | 13 | Tôdi | 28 | | | Brothers | 4, 2 | 12, 10 | — | — | — | — | Child-marriage. |
| 2 | | ,, | 25 | 12 | ,, ,, | 26, 25 | — | — | | 11 | 8, 1½ | 1 | 3 | — | — | There is a fourth brother to these three husbands, aged 18; the village dairyman. Child-marriage. |
| 3 | | ,, | 40 | 16 | ,, | D | 67 | 6 | Brothers | 25, 18, 11 | 12, 10 | — | — | — | — | This woman was put away by her first husband, in order that he might marry his brother's widow. She was not living with her deceased husband's brothers, but with her own sons. |
| 4 | Different Mands | ,, | 65 | 46 | ,, | 70 | — | — | Brothers. | 38, 35 | 28, 24 | 6, 3 | 39, 29 | 6, 2 | 14, 10 | |
| 5 | | ,, | 60 | 43 | | 65 | — | — | | 42, 35, 30 | 24, 20 | | | | | |
| 6 | | ,, | D | — | ,, | D | 66 | 12 | | 4 No. | — | — | — | 8, 6 | 10, 10 | |
| 7 | | ,, | D | — | ,, | D | 45 | 8 | | — | — | — | — | — | — | Mother died in first travail. Sex of child—which died—not known. |

| | | | | | | | | | | | | | | | | |
|---|---|---|---|---|---|---|---|---|---|---|---|---|---|---|---|---|
| 8 | Kakhodi | Peiki | D | — | Peiki<br>,,<br>,, | D<br>68<br>65 | 57 | 20 | Brothers | 20<br>12<br>8 | 22<br>18 | 12<br>5 | 3<br>7 | 20<br>10 | 4<br>7 | Twins. This woman died five years ago. On her death the two widowers married a woman (9) *known* to have been barren all her life: and therefore set aside. Having already a family, they married for the sake of having some one to cook. |
| 9 | | ,, | 50 | 5 | ,,<br>,, | 68<br>65 | | | Brothers | — | — | — | — | — | — | Barren. |
| 10 | Beresthro | ,, | 38 | 25 | ,,<br>,, | D<br>42 | 42 | 8 | Brothers | 22<br>19<br>17<br>10<br>6 | 24 | 6 | 7 | — | — | |
| 11 | | ,, | 24 | 4 | ,, | 25 | — | — | | — | 2 | — | — | — | — | Not pregnant. |
| 12 | | ,, | 18 | 2 | ,, | 22 | — | — | Brothers | — | — | — | — | — | — | Pregnant. |
| 13 | | ,, | 18 | 1 | ,, | 19 | — | — | | — | — | — | — | — | — | Not pregnant. |
| 14 | Koana Koar | ,, | 18 | 2 | ,, | 28 | — | — | | — | — | — | — | 1 | 1 | Pregnant. The husband has a brother aged 18; the village dairyman. |
| 15 | | ,, | 40 | 26 | ,, | 58 | — | — | | — | 23<br>20<br>17<br>14 | 15<br>2 | 10<br>6 | — | — | One female child is a cripple from birth. The husband has no brother. |
| 16 | | ,, | 22 | 3 | ,, | 30 | — | — | | 2 | — | — | — | — | — | The husband has a brother, aged 24; the village dairyman. |
| 17 | Ebgodu | ,, | 75 | 61 | ,, | D | 75 | 4 | | 60<br>58<br>56<br>48<br>42 | 54 | 32 | 6 | 32<br>34<br>12 | 18<br>12<br>23 | This widow says she never had more than one husband. |

| No. on the List | Name of Mands | Wives | | | Husbands | | | | | Children | | | | | | Remarks |
|---|---|---|---|---|---|---|---|---|---|---|---|---|---|---|---|---|
| | | Clan | Apparent present ages | Probable number of years since married | Clan | Apparent ages of those alive | Probable ages of those dead, and number of years since dead | | Degree of relation-ship to one another | Apparent ages of those alive | | Probable ages of those dead, and the number of years since dead | | | | Notes.—No. 5 column has been determined either by reference to age of oldest child, or where the period was manifestly short, from the woman's own statement.<br>The remaining columns are the result of vivâ voce examination of parents, or of personal inspection. |
| | | | | | | | | | | Males | Females | Males | | Females | | |
| 1 | 2 | 3 | 4 | 5 | 6 | 7 | 8 | 9 | 10 | 11 | 12 | 13 | 14 | 15 | 16 | |
| 18 | Ebgodu | Peiki | 35 | 17 | Peiki | 40 | — | — | Brothers | 16<br>10 | 14<br>12 | — | — | 4 | 12 | |
| 19 | | ,, | 30 | 11 | ,, | 35 | — | — | | — | 10<br>3<br>1½ | — | — | — | — | These two husbands have a younger brother, aged 38 ; the village dairyman. |
| 20 | | ,, | 19 | 2 | ,, | 16 | — | — | | — | — | — | — | — | — | Not pregnant. Child-marriage. Wife older than husband. |
| 21 | Bangadu | ,, | 50 | 34 | ,, | D | ? | 3 | | 28<br>26 | 30 | 3 | 15 | 18 | 15 | This man had three younger brothers, married and living in different mands. |
| 22 | | ,, | 45 | 21 | ,, | D | ? | 2 | | 16<br>14<br>13 | 20<br>18 | 1 | 7 | 2<br>2 | 8<br>9 | This man had four brothers, who died ; one as a child, three married separately. |
| 23 | | ,, | 42 | 23 | ,, | 50 | — | — | | 22<br>14 | 12<br>3 | 1<br>1 | 7<br>5 | — | — | This man has two brothers, widowers, living in the same mand. |
| 24 | | ,, | 20 | 7 | ,, | 28 | — | — | | 1½ | 3 | — | — | — | — | Not pregnant. Child-marriage. |
| 25 | | ,, | 18 | 1 | ,, | 25 | — | — | | — | — | — | — | — | — | Not pregnant. |
| 26 | | ,, | 28 | 10 | ,, | 25 | — | — | | 8½ | — | — | — | — | — | This man has a brother, aged 23, married in another mand. |

| | | | | | | | | | | | | | | | | |
|---|---|---|---|---|---|---|---|---|---|---|---|---|---|---|---|---|
| 27 | Karshk | Kuttan | 55 | 41 | Kenna<br>,, | D<br>65 | 60 | 10 | | 30 | 40<br>32 | 20<br>8<br>6 | 15<br>10<br>8 | — | — | |
| 28 | | Tôdi | 60 | 35 | ,,<br>,, | D<br>63 | 65 | 1 | Brothers | 30<br>25<br>20 | 28 | 20<br>14 | 14<br>18 | 8<br>6<br>4 | 18<br>18<br>18 | These men have a third brother. The three brothers had two wives in common. |
| 29 | | Kenna | 24 | 8 | Peiki | 28 | — | — | | — | 6 | — | — | — | — | Pregnant. |
| 30 | | ,, | 22 | 1 | Kuttan | 25 | — | — | | — | — | — | — | — | — | Not pregnant. |
| 31 | | ,, | 18 | 1 | Peiki | 24 | — | — | | — | — | — | — | — | — | Not pregnant. This man has three married brothers, living in different mands. |
| 32 | | Kuttan | 30 | 8 | Kenna<br>,, | 35<br>30 | — | — | Brothers | — | — | — | — | — | — | The woman is looked on by the people as barren. These husbands have a brother aged 20; the village dairyman. |
| 33 | | ,, | 19 | 3 | ,, | 30 | — | — | | — | — | — | — | — | — | Not pregnant. |
| 34 | | ,, | 19 | 2 | ,, | 30 | — | — | | — | — | — | — | — | — | Not pregnant. |
| 35 | | Kenna | 28 | 5 | Kuttan | 40 | — | — | | — | — | — | — | — | — | Not pregnant. |
| 36 | Mênmadd | Peiki | 45 | 31 | Peiki | 50 | — | — | Brothers | 30<br>14<br>4 | 18<br>16<br>2 | 6 | 4 | 2 | 10 | |
| 37 | | ,, | 45 | 29 | ,, | 45 | — | — | | 28<br>26<br>22 | 27<br>24<br>18 | 6<br>9 | 8<br>4 | 1 | 8 | These husbands have a fifth brother, aged 20; the village dairyman. |
| 38 | | ,, | 25 | 13 | ,, | 28 | — | — | | 12 | 2 | — | — | — | — | Child-marriage. |
| 39 | | ,, | 14 | 4 | ,, | 23 | — | — | | — | — | — | — | — | — | Not pregnant. Child-marriage. |

CHAP. XI.

| No. on the List | Name of Mands | Wives | | | Husbands | | | | | Children | | | | | | Remarks |
|---|---|---|---|---|---|---|---|---|---|---|---|---|---|---|---|---|
| | | Clan | Apparent present ages | Probable number of years since married | Clan | Apparent ages of those alive | Probable ages of those dead, and number of years since dead | | Degree of relationship to one another | Apparent ages of those alive | | Probable ages of those dead, and the number of years since dead | | | | Notes.—No. 5 column has been determined either by reference to age of oldest child, or where the period was manifestly short, from the woman's own statement. The remaining columns are the result of vivâ voce examination of parents or of personal inspection. |
| | | | | | | | | | | Males | Females | Males | | Females | | |
| 1 | 2 | 3 | 4 | 5 | 6 | 7 | 8 | 9 | 10 | 11 | 12 | 13 | 14 | 15 | 16 | |
| 40 | Mênmadd | Peiki | 25 | 11 | Peiki | 30 | — | — | Brothers | 4 | 1 | — | — | 6 | 4 | |
| 41 | | ,, | 14 | 2 | ,, | 14 | — | — | | — | — | — | — | — | — | Child-marriage. |
| 42 | | ,, | 50 | 31 | ,, | D | ? | — | | 28<br>26<br>25<br>23 | 30<br>14 | — | — | — | — | |
| 43 | | ,, | 55 | 31 | ,, | D | ? | — | | 30<br>20<br>18<br>14 | 16 | 23<br>4 | 5<br>3 | 16<br>14 | 10<br>2 | |

| | | | | | | | | | | | | | | | | |
|---|---|---|---|---|---|---|---|---|---|---|---|---|---|---|---|---|
| 44 | Keshkir | Tôdi | 40 | 29 | Kenna | 60 | — | — | | 28<br>15<br>8 | 25<br>12 | 4<br>2 | 12<br>3 | 18 | 1 | The daughter died in her first travail. Sex of child, which died, not known. The husband has a brother married in another mand. Child-marriage. |
| 45 | | Kuttan | 45 | 30 | ,, | 55 | — | — | | 12 | — | 20<br>12 | 9<br>6 | — | — | This husband had three younger brothers who died in childhood. |
| 46 | | ,, | 30 | 13 | ,, | 50 | — | — | | 12<br>9<br>6<br>1 | 11 | — | — | — | — | This husband has a brother married in another mand. |
| 47 | | Kenna | 11 | 1 | ,, | 12 | — | — | | — | — | — | — | — | — | Child-marriage. |
| 48 | | ,, | 12 | 3 | ,, | 15 | — | — | | — | — | — | — | — | — | Child-marriage. |
| 49 | Kirzho | Tôdi | 55 | 36 | ,, | D | 55 | 6 | | 35<br>24<br>15 | 26 | 24 | 2 | — | — | This man had a brother, who died young. |
| 50 | | Kenna | 24 | 10 | ,, | 28 | — | — | | — | — | — | — | — | — | Not pregnant. Looked on by the people as barren. |
| 51 | | ,, | 26 | 12 | ,, | 26 | — | — | | 8<br>4 | 10 | — | — | — | — | Pregnant. Child-marriage. |
| 52 | | Tôdi | 20 | 6 | ,, | 35 | — | — | | — | — | — | — | — | — | Not pregnant. |
| 53 | Melkarshk | ,, | 65 | 43 | Peiki | 70 | — | — | | 40<br>25 | 42<br>35 | 18<br>12<br>10<br>12<br>18 | 20<br>18<br>18<br>14<br>6 | 22 | 10 | This husband had three brothers, who died young. |
| 54 | | Peiki | 42 | 26 | ,, | 56 | — | — | | — | 25 | — | — | — | — | Not pregnant. This husband has a brother married in another mand. |
| 55 | | Kenna | 20 | 10 | ,, | 26 | — | — | | 1 | — | — | — | — | — | Child-marriage. This husband has a brother married in another mand. |

CHAP. XI.

## TABLE No. V.

*Information deduced from 'Statistics of Toda Families,' Table No.* IV.

| No. on the List | Present ages of: Wives | Present ages of: Husbands—oldest | Present ages of: Child—oldest | Present ages of: Child—youngest | Calculated ages when: Wives married | Calculated ages when: Oldest Husbands married | Calculated ages when: Wives commenced child-bearing | Calculated ages when: Wives left off child-bearing | Children: Number alive | Children: Number dead | Children: Number born | Remarks |
|---|---|---|---|---|---|---|---|---|---|---|---|---|
| 1 | 2 | 3 | 4 | 5 | 6 | 7 | 8 | 9 | 10 | 11 | 12 | 13 |
| 1 | 27 | 28 | 12 | 2 | 14 | 15 | 15 | — | 4 | 0 | 4 | Child-marriage. |
| 2 | 25 | 28 | 11 | 2 | 13 | 16 | 14 | — | 3 | 1 | 4 | Child-marriage. |
| 3 | 40 | 73 | 25 | 10 | 14 | 47 | 15 | 30 | 5 | 0 | 5 | |
| 4 | 65 | 70 | 45 | 12 | 19 | 24 | 20 | 53 | 4 | 4 | 5 | |
| 5 | 60 | 65 | 42 | 20 | 17 | 22 | 18 | 40 | 5 | 0 | 8 | |
| 6 | D | 78 | — | — | — | — | — | — | 4 | 2 | 6 | |
| 7 | D | 53 | 0 | 0 | — | — | — | — | 0 | 0 | 0 | |
| 8 | D | 77 | 24 | 8 | — | — | — | — | 5 | 4 | 9 | |
| 9 | 50 | 68 | 0 | 0 | 45 | 63 | — | — | 0 | 0 | 0 | Barren. |
| 10 | 38 | 50 | 24 | 6 | 13 | 25 | 14 | — | 6 | 1 | 7 | |
| 11 | 24 | 25 | 2 | 2 | 20 | 21 | 22 | — | 1 | 0 | 1 | |
| 12 | 18 | 22 | 1 | 1 | 16 | 20 | 17 | — | 1 | 0 | 1 | |
| 13 | 18 | 19 | 0 | 0 | 17 | 18 | — | — | 0 | 0 | 0 | |
| 14 | 18 | 28 | 2 | 2 | 16 | 26 | 16 | — | 0 | 1 | 1 | |
| 15 | 40 | 58 | 25 | 8 | 14 | 32 | 15 | 32 | 4 | 2 | 6 | |
| 16 | 22 | 30 | 2 | 2 | 19 | 27 | 20 | — | 1 | 0 | 1 | |
| 17 | 75 | 79 | 60 | 35 | 14 | 18 | 15 | 40 | 6 | 4 | 10 | |
| 18 | 35 | 40 | 16 | 10 | 18 | 23 | 19 | — | 4 | 1 | 5 | |
| 19 | 30 | 35 | 10 | 2 | 19 | 24 | 20 | — | 3 | 0 | 3 | |
| 20 | 19 | 16 | 0 | 0 | 17 | 14 | — | — | 0 | 0 | 0 | Child-marriage. |
| 21 | 50 | — | 33 | 18 | 16 | — | 17 | 32 | 3 | 2 | 5 | |
| 22 | 45 | — | 20 | 8 | 24 | — | 25 | 37 | 5 | 3 | 8 | |
| 23 | 42 | 50 | 22 | 3 | 19 | 27 | 20 | — | 4 | 2 | 6 | |
| 24 | 20 | 28 | 3 | 2 | 13 | 21 | 17 | — | 2 | 0 | 2 | Child-marriage. |
| 25 | 18 | 25 | 0 | 0 | 17 | 24 | — | — | 0 | 0 | 0 | |
| 26 | 28 | 25 | 8 | 1 | 18 | 15 | 20 | — | 2 | 0 | 2 | |
| 27 | 55 | 70 | 40 | 14 | 14 | 29 | 15 | 41 | 3 | 3 | 6 | |
| 28 | 60 | 66 | 34 | 20 | 25 | 31 | 26 | 40 | 4 | 5 | 9 | |
| 29 | 24 | 28 | 6 | 6 | 16 | 20 | 18 | — | 1 | 0 | 1 | |
| 30 | 22 | 25 | 0 | 0 | 21 | 24 | — | — | 0 | 0 | 0 | |
| 31 | 18 | 24 | 0 | 0 | 17 | 23 | — | — | 0 | 0 | 0 | |
| 32 | 30 | 35 | 0 | 0 | 22 | 27 | — | — | 0 | 0 | 0 | Barren. |
| 33 | 19 | 30 | 0 | 0 | 16 | 27 | — | — | 0 | 0 | 0 | |
| 34 | 19 | 30 | 0 | 0 | 17 | 28 | — | — | 0 | 0 | 0 | |
| 35 | 28 | 40 | 3 | 3 | 23 | 35 | 25 | — | 1 | 0 | 1 | |
| 36 | 45 | 50 | 30 | 2 | 14 | 19 | 15 | 43 | 6 | 2 | 8 | |
| 37 | 45 | 45 | 28 | 9 | 16 | 16 | 17 | 36 | 6 | 3 | 9 | |
| 38 | 25 | 28 | 12 | 1 | 12 | 15 | 13 | — | 2 | 0 | 2 | Child-marriage. |
| 39 | 14 | 23 | 0 | 0 | 10 | 19 | — | — | 0 | 0 | 0 | Child-marriage. |
| 40 | 25 | 30 | 10 | 1 | 14 | 19 | 15 | — | 2 | 1 | 3 | |
| 41 | 14 | 14 | 0 | 0 | 12 | 12 | — | — | 0 | 0 | 0 | Child-marriage. |
| 42 | 50 | — | 30 | 14 | 19 | — | 20 | 36 | 6 | 0 | 6 | |
| 43 | 55 | — | 30 | 7 | 24 | — | 25 | 48 | 5 | 4 | 9 | |
| 44 | 40 | 60 | 28 | 5 | 11 | 31 | 12 | 35 | 5 | 3 | 8 | Child-marriage. |
| 45 | 45 | 55 | 29 | 12 | 15 | 25 | 16 | 33 | 2 | 2 | 4 | |
| 46 | 30 | 50 | 12 | 1 | 17 | 37 | 18 | — | 5 | 0 | 5 | |
| 47 | 11 | 12 | 0 | 0 | 10 | 11 | — | — | 0 | 0 | 0 | Child-marriage. |
| 48 | 12 | 15 | 0 | 0 | 9 | 12 | — | — | 0 | 0 | 0 | Child-marriage. |
| 49 | 55 | 61 | 35 | 15 | 19 | 25 | 20 | 40 | 4 | 1 | 5 | |
| 50 | 24 | 28 | 0 | 0 | 14 | 18 | — | — | 0 | 0 | 0 | Barren. |
| 51 | 26 | 26 | 10 | 4 | 14 | 14 | 16 | — | 3 | 0 | 3 | Child-marriage. |
| 52 | 20 | 35 | 0 | 0 | 14 | 19 | — | — | 0 | 0 | 0 | |
| 53 | 65 | 70 | 42 | 24 | 22 | 27 | 23 | 41 | 4 | 6 | 10 | |
| 54 | 42 | 56 | 25 | 25 | 16 | 30 | 17 | 17 | 1 | 0 | 1 | |
| 55 | 20 | 26 | 1 | 1 | 10 | 16 | 19 | — | 1 | 0 | 1 | Child-marriage. |

## Table No. VI.

*To ascertain the 'ages at which Toda women commence and leave off Child-bearing.'*

*Compiled from Tables No.* IV. *or* V.

| Commenced Child-bearing | | | | |
|---|---|---|---|---|
| No. on the List | Present age of Wife | Age of her oldest Child | Calculated age when she commenced Child-bearing | Remarks |
| 1 | 27 | 12 | 15 | In the compilation of this abstract, the younger women have, as a rule, been taken, as conducive to accurate results. |
| 2 | 25 | 11 | 14 | |
| 3 | 40 | 25 | 15 | |
| 10 | 38 | 24 | 14 | |
| 11 | 24 | 2 | 22 | |
| 12 | 18 | 0 | 18 | P |
| 14 | 18 | 2 | 16 | |
| 15 | 40 | 25 | 15 | |
| 16 | 22 | 2 | 20 | |
| 19 | 30 | 10 | 20 | |
| 22 | 45 | 20 | 25 | |
| 23 | 42 | 22 | 20 | |
| 24 | 20 | 3 | 17 | |
| 26 | 28 | 8 | 20 | |
| 29 | 24 | 6 | 18 | |
| 35 | 28 | 3 | 25 | |
| 36 | 45 | 30 | 15 | |
| 37 | 45 | 28 | 17 | |
| 38 | 25 | 12 | 13 | |
| 40 | 25 | 10 | 15 | |
| 44 | 40 | 28 | 12 | |
| 45 | 45 | 29 | 16 | |
| 46 | 30 | 12 | 18 | |
| 51 | 26 | 10 | 16 | |
| 54 | 42 | 25 | 17 | |
| 55 | 20 | 1 | 19 | |
| 26 | | | 452/26 | = 17·4 { Average age at which the women commence child-bearing. |

| Left off Child-bearing | | | | |
|---|---|---|---|---|
| No. on the List | Present age of Wife | Age of her youngest Child | Calculated age when she left off Child-bearing | Remarks |
| 3 | 40 | 10 | 30 | In this abstract, only those women have been entered, who from their own age or from that of the youngest child, appear to have left off child-bearing. |
| 4 | 65 | 12 | 53 | |
| 5 | 60 | 20 | 40 | |
| 15 | 40 | 8 | 32 | |
| 17 | 75 | 35 | 40 | |
| 21 | 50 | 18 | 32 | |
| 22 | 45 | 8 | 37 | |
| 27 | 55 | 14 | 41 | |
| 28 | 60 | 20 | 40 | |
| 36 | 45 | 2 | 43 | |
| 37 | 45 | 9 | 36 | |
| 42 | 50 | 14 | 36 | |
| 43 | 55 | 7 | 48 | |
| 44 | 40 | 5 | 35 | |
| 45 | 45 | 12 | 33 | |
| 49 | 55 | 15 | 40 | |
| 53 | 65 | 24 | 41 | |
| 54 | 42 | 25 | 17 | |
| 18 | | | 674/18 | = 37·4 { Average age at which the women leave off child-bearing. |

CHAP. XI.

## Table No. VII.

*To ascertain the 'size of Toda Families:' the 'period during which the women bear children;' and the 'number of years intervening between the birth of children.'*

*Compiled from Tables No.* IV. *or* V.

**Wives who have left off Child-bearing**

| No. on the List | Calculated age when commenced Child-bearing | Calculated age when left off Child-bearing | Total number of years in Child-bearing | Number of Children born |
|---|---|---|---|---|
| 3 | 15 | 30 | 15 | 5 |
| 5 | 18 | 40 | 22 | 5 |
| 15 | 15 | 32 | 17 | 6 |
| 17 | 15 | 40 | 25 | 10 |
| 21 | 17 | 32 | 15 | 5 |
| 22 | 25 | 37 | 12 | 8 |
| 27 | 15 | 41 | 26 | 6 |
| 28 | 26 | 38 | 12 | 9 |
| 36 | 15 | 43 | 28 | 8 |
| 37 | 17 | 36 | 19 | 9 |
| 42 | 20 | 36 | 16 | 6 |
| 43 | 25 | 48 | 23 | 9 |
| 44 | 12 | 35 | 23 | 8 |
| 45 | 16 | 33 | 17 | 4 |
| 49 | 20 | 40 | 20 | 5 |
| 53 | 23 | 41 | 18 | 10 |
| 54 | 17 | 42 | 25 | 1 |
| 17 | | | 333 | 114 |
| 9 | | | 0 | 0 |
| 32 | | | 0 | 0 |
| 50 | | | 0 | 0 |
| 20 | | | 333 | 114 |

Remarks: The total 'number of children born' divided by the 'total No. of wives on the list' gives the average 'size of Toda families'; or $\frac{114}{23} = 5·7$. But if the barren women be excluded from the calculation, then $\frac{114}{17} = 6·7$ is the average. The total 'number of years in child-bearing' divided by the 'No. of wives on the list,' gives the average 'period during which the women bear children'; or $\frac{333}{17} = 19·6$.

**Wives continuing in Child-bearing**

| No. on the List | Calculated age when commenced Child-bearing | Apparent present age | Total number of years in Child-bearing | Number of Children born |
|---|---|---|---|---|
| | | | 333 | 114 |
| 1 | 15 | 27 | 12 | 4 |
| 2 | 14 | 25 | 11 | 4 |
| 10 | 14 | 38 | 25 | 7 |
| 11 | 22 | 24 | 2 | 1 |
| 12 | 18 | 18 | 1 | 1 |
| 14 | 16 | 18 | 2 | 1 |
| 16 | 20 | 22 | 2 | 1 |
| 18 | 19 | 35 | 16 | 5 |
| 19 | 20 | 30 | 10 | 3 |
| 23 | 20 | 42 | 22 | 6 |
| 24 | 17 | 20 | 3 | 2 |
| 26 | 20 | 28 | 8 | 2 |
| 29 | 18 | 24 | 6 | 1 |
| 35 | 25 | 28 | 3 | 1 |
| 38 | 13 | 25 | 12 | 2 |
| 40 | 15 | 25 | 10 | 3 |
| 46 | 18 | 30 | 12 | 5 |
| 51 | 16 | 26 | 10 | 3 |
| 55 | 19 | 20 | 1 | 1 |
| | | | 500 | 167 |

Remarks: The total 'number of years in child-bearing' divided by the total 'number of children born' gives the average 'number of years intervening between the birth of each child'; or $\frac{500}{167} = 3$.

Note.—The wives in child-marriages, and those who, having lately married, have not yet given birth to children, have been excluded from this Table.

it is advisable to mention, that although as much patient care was taken to collect the evidence it contains, with the same accuracy as that bestowed on the Census, yet there are reasons why it could not be attained. For the latter purpose the people were nearly all present; whereas in the process of collecting statistics, dependence had, in the main, to be placed on the statement of uneducated people describing births and deaths, many of which took place long years before. Supposing even they remembered in all cases the number of each sex that died, they would still have to represent their own notions of the ages at which they did so, and the period that had elapsed since those events happened. All, therefore, that can with confidence be asserted, is, that the best was done in the face of these inevitable difficulties to eliminate error.

For instance—and one will suffice—if it was required to ascertain the particulars of a child who had died. The mother was present; the husband also sat close by. Some relation, also present, had a wife, or husband, or child, as the case might be, who had been a playfellow of the departed. Or the child was said by its mother to have been either so much older or so much younger than one standing before us.

For the sake of those who wish to utilise the statistics, Table No. 5 has been compiled from Table No. 4, which will render it easy to extract the most valuable points of information.

In order to obtain reliable data on which to base deductions as to Toda nature and Toda progress, it seems a matter sufficiently important, to record with all the exactness that available information admits of, certain averages relative to the size of families, and the ages at which their women commence and also leave off child-bearing. The details of these points of information, collated from Tables No. 4 or 5, will, therefore, be found tabulated in Nos. 6 and 7 Tables. A point has been made, not to omit any of the instances of Table 4 or 5, that might prove of value; only the women in child-marriages, or those who having lately married, have not yet given birth to progeny, have been left out.

We see from these tables that,

| | | |
|---|---|---|
| I. | The *earliest* age at which women commence child-bearing is about . . | 14 years. |
| II. | The *average* age at which women commence child-bearing is . . . . | 17·4 years. |
| III. | The average age at which women leave off child-bearing is . . . . . | 37·4 years. |
| IV. | Women bear children during a period of | 19·6 years. |
| V. | The average interval between the birth of children is . . . . . . | 3 years. |
| VI. | Including barren women, the average size of families is . . . . . | 5·7 children. |
| VII. | Exclusive of barren women, the average size of families is . . . . . | 6·7 children. |

## CHAPTER XII.

### RELIGION.

*Prayers to Sun and Moon—The Mysterious confused with Godhead—No clear conception of a Supreme Being—The use of a God—Toda Belief—Amnôr—Where situated—Sin, Punishment, little Gods, Spirits, Witchcraft—Toda Religious Belief, whence derived.*



IF by the word religion, we mean to imply devotion, piety, duty, as applied to the worship of God, Creator and Ruler; then the Todas are most certainly an irreligious people, judging of them, as we can alone judge, by their actions; whether we compare them by our own standard or through the rites and performances of simple races more in keeping with themselves.

They salaam to the rising and setting sun—bîrsh—and the moon—tiggalu [1]—at night, reciting the one formula of prayer which they use on all devout occasions; danenma, mokh ultama, âl ultama, êr ultama, karr ultama, ellam ultama, the meaning of which has already been translated in note 5 of Chapter VII. To see a man amongst his family, stand out on a moonlight night with hand to forehead, asking most gravely this blessing on his house, from one of the givers of light, is an impressive spectacle, though the address may have been made only to the moon.

We see from this formula what they acknowledge to be the fact; that they look on these luminaries as Gods, Lords—Dêr, Swâmi—not that they are, in the least degree, clear on the subject of their power, or the mode or limits of their

[1] See note No. 3 of Chapter VII.

CHAP. XII.

action. They rest satisfied that they *are* Gods. But with them, there is a tendency for everything mysterious or unseen to ripen into Dêr; cattle, relics, priests, are, as we shall see, confused in the same category, until it would seem that Dêr, like Swâmi, is truly an adjective-noun of eminence.

They fence in those who perform what they consider holy offices, with rigid rules of conduct. But such offices, although from their point of view, holy, can barely be held to be religious: more perhaps on the confines, affording us samples of the germs of religious belief and action and the growth of religion, from punctilious form.

They do not address supplications, or confessions of sin, to any personal God, of whose attributes or power they entertain an even approximately clear conception. They have no idols or images, either of loved and respected objects to be courted, or of dreaded beings to be appeased: whether ever-present, as in house or village, or to be casually met with in groves, at springs, or on hill sides. They make no oblations, beyond the act of eating periodically a little buffalo flesh,[2] displaying in its ceremonial, the rudimentary stage of sacrificial or festive observance. In fact they can scarcely be said to trouble themselves on the subject of religion proper.

I am not prepared to say that these people have actually no God: for they acknowledge the existence of Ûsuru[3] Swâmi, the Lord above, the High God; but it will be perfectly evident to all who read through this book, that their conception of a Supreme Being is entirely without definition. Indeed almost at a stroke of the pen, I can show this to be the case; for, the reason having been given why the Pekkan clan had no 'holy place,' that it had no property: it was explained to

[2] See Chapter VIII.

[3] Ûsuru. In Tamil y and s are constantly interchangeable. Thus uyir or uçir is *life*; uyaru and uçaru are *to be exalted, lifted up*. In Kanarese, uçar = *life, power*. There may be a connection with Sanskrit uccha = *high*. [POPE.]

me, that the Pekkans are poor and have few herds, therefore *they have no occasion for a God* to protect them. I see the man now before me shaking his grave head, 'Aha, they don't want a God.'

'First divest your mind of cant,' said Dr. Johnson. The Toda anticipated that sage advice long years ago. What is the *use* of a God if not to protect life and property? And no property, no God! I dwell on this phase of the primitive mind, for it will liberate us much from the necessity for searching for evidences of religious worship in the customs, whose description I am entering upon.

The sum of real Toda belief is, that they were born, they and their cattle, somehow—rose out of the earth. When they die they go to amnôr,[4] which is a world exactly like this; whither their buffalos join them, to supply milk as in this state—*voilà tout.* They look on this migration from the nomad point of view: but do not appear to be quite clear whether they and their cattle go to amnôr in the body or the spirit. Some practical difficulties appear to present themselves, to whichever belief they bend. The abstruseness of the question is acknowledged. They are satisfied that they *do* get there, and don't care to speculate and reopen a matter which has so long and so satisfactorily been settled!

A good opportunity presenting itself, in a visit with which I was favoured by an important religious character, I asked him where amnôr was situate. He did not appear surprised at the question, or in a moment's doubt as to the locality. Looking about him in the sky as if to ascertain the cardinal points of the compass; as all Orientals do; who living without clocks or barometers, read the signs in the heavens for guidance

[4] Amnôr, amnâr, ômunâr = *the next world.*

Nâr or nâḍu = *district, country.* This is Tamil.

Ôma is a difficulty. Yaman is the '*God of death.*'

It seems to be = avaṉ, which in Tamil = *there,* and is sometimes used for *the other world.* In Tamil, ammai = *the next state* or *stage in transmigration.* [POPE.]

CHAP. XII.

and information, he pointed direct to the west. 'Where the sun goes down'[5] he said. The quiet certainty with which he spoke, then ceased to speak, was impressive, leaving a feeling of sadness as from the vibrations of an air just played, or of 'a tale that is told;' to think that the place of their future residence—where Toda shall, without fail, meet Toda—was known to them; that this man in his simple belief should be so clear on a subject which has engaged the religious mind of refined nations for ages in vain.

The Toda makes use of the word pâpum for sin, but I more than doubt if he has any word for hell. In reality neither one nor the other subject engages his attention. What has already been described, is his deep-grounded belief: any little matters, as sin and punishment, may be looked on as after-growths. He has also Gods—a little g should be sufficient for them—presiding over certain hills and villages, but he seems to know nothing about them. Spirits and ghosts—bhût—devilry and witchcraft—pilli—also occupy a position in his beliefs. But the Todas are not communicative on these or indeed on any subject connected with religion or the unseen. Most probably they have but little to tell; and superstitious dread of the invisible or half-known, prompts them to keep that little, dark.

A reference to the vocabulary, will show that most words connected with what is commonly termed religion, are almost pure Sanskrit: whilst those relating to the extraordinarily simple practices in course of narration, are either much corrupted Sanskrit, or are free of Âryan influence. From these facts I deduce the possibility that prior to their migration into India, the Âryas of that era, when probably of a somewhat similar stage of culture to the Todas, may have influenced their rudimental religious proclivities. But that any ideas they now possess on religious subjects have come to them quite in modern times from Brahmanical sources; through

[5] See note 2 of Chapter V.

the Hindu Badagas, with whom they have for several generations been on intimate terms: whose mode of worship they have had opportunities of noticing: and with whom they have often conversed on elementary religious topics. Thus, as I have noted, they have seized on a few words, and the names of a score of small Gods connected with maladies and diseases, of whom they know nothing but their names; but without having adopted a religion.

# CHAPTER XIII.

## THE BELL-GODS.

*A religion based on the care of the Cow—Milk a Divine fluid—The Cattle-bell, a God—The Bell-cow—Her ancestral line—The Bell-god—Installation of the Bell-cow—The Tirièri—The sacred Herd—Bulls of the Herd—Sanctification of Bulls—Agnate law amongst the Todas; Female succession for their Cattle—Antiquity of Bell-gods.*

CHAP. XIII.

NOTHING amongst the peculiarities of this very peculiar people is more striking than the absorbing importance they attach to all duties connected with the management of the buffalo and her chief product. The animal is the focus of all village life; the nucleus or centre upon which their entire religio-social system is based. One cannot imagine the Toda apart from a consideration of his buffalo; and when we reflect how entirely dependent the man is upon the animal—how, with only a light and pleasant expenditure of patience and perseverance, he finds the coarse grass of his hills turned into good nutriment; the care of the buffalo, so far from appearing anything extraordinary, only fits into its natural place as a necessary sequence. We are reminded, too, that the milk-giver and the bull have been, and still are, objects of especial care and of worship amongst other races that own Western Asia as their cradle-land. It also carries us back to the time when man depended upon his flocks and herds for existence. We actually see him in process of forming a religion, based upon the care of the cow.

'Few,' writes Mr. Tylor, 'who will give their minds to master the general principles of savage religion, will ever again

No. 14

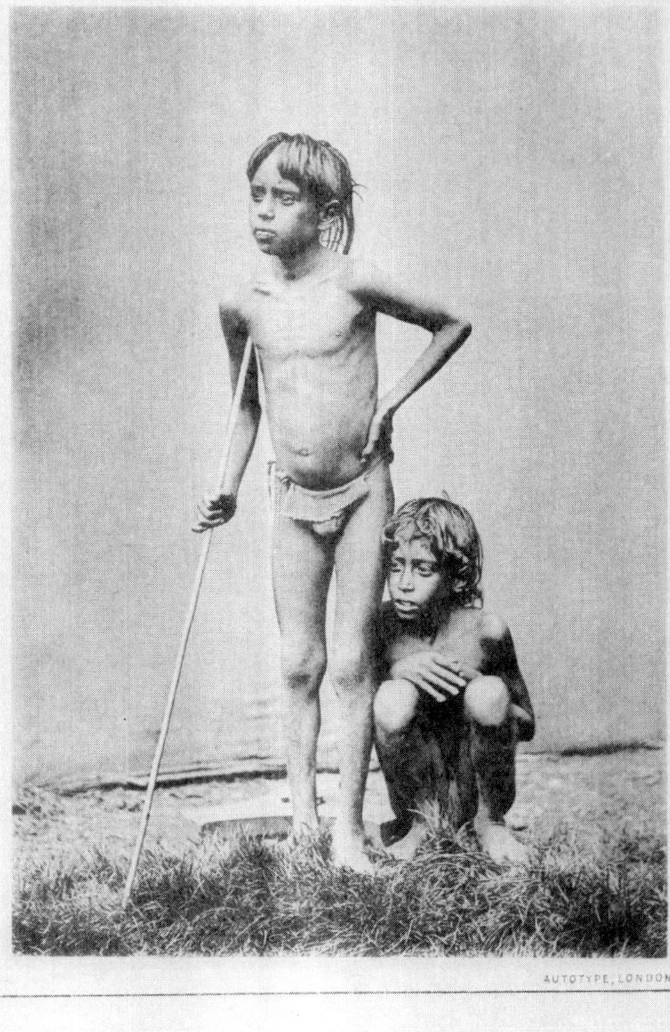

AUTOTYPE, LONDON

CHILDREN TENDING CATTLE.

think it ridiculous, or the knowledge of it superfluous to the rest of mankind. Far from its beliefs and practices being a rubbish-heap of miscellaneous folly, they are consistent and logical in so high a degree as to begin, as soon as even roughly classified, to display the principles of their formation and development; and these principles prove to be essentially rational, though working in a mental condition of intense and inveterate ignorance.'[1]

Our friends appear to *dream* buffalo. Sitting, apparently 'thinking of nothing at all,' a man will pick up a bit of cane or forked twig from the ground, and like the typical Yankee is supposed to whittle a stick while he speculates, so the Toda will employ himself for an hour at a time, splitting his bit of cane or rounding the little branches of his twig into the likeness of buffalo horns, as he muses. Children may be seen coming in from cattle-driving, with strings of these small horns. And these treasures are found lying about their houses and haunts. Two of them are shown in Photograph No. 15.

In the history of most, if not of all nations, savage and civilised alike, we may trace the alliance, more or less intimate, of religion, in its various rites and performances, with food; in its nature, source, or care, or in the occasions or symbols of its use. This correlation is certainly a marked feature in Toda customs. Though the Todas have no actual religion or system of faith leading to the performance of duties to a God, yet they hold to certain practices and certain habits in daily life, which are to them in the place of a religion; being performed with all the strictness and certainty that should be bestowed on sacred observances.

These performances or habits are intimately allied with the care and distribution of the *divine fluid*—milk. The buffalo is to a certain degree held sacred, as being the

[1] Tylor, 'Primitive Culture,' vol. i. p. 21.

CHAP. XIII. chief gift of the Gods: and the fountain of all milk. Hence they hold the care and milking of these animals and the charge of the dairy, to be amongst the highest and most respected offices. The buffalo is treated with great kindness, even with a degree of adoration, by the people; scarcely touched with the light wands they carry, but guided and called by a sort of buffalo-language which they understand, and obey with some intelligence.

But they give away the young bulls to the Kotas. It has been a question whether or not they ever eat the flesh themselves, and I experienced much difficulty in ascertaining what I now believe to be the truth; that they part with the bulls, because, whilst they will not eat the flesh, they cannot permit them to crowd on land required for the grazing of the cows. That they do not sell them, may no doubt be in part attributable to the uncommercial nature of their dispositions. But I think it also possible that the Badagas and Kotas work on the sense of respect for the animal, which the Todas are known to entertain, to make it a custom not to dispose of the buffalo for money. Although it is certain that no Toda will eat buffalo flesh unless in part of the ceremonial described in Chapter VIII., yet, curiously enough, they do not hesitate to mortgage even the cows to the Badagas, though knowing that in such an act, the chance must always exist of the animal's being seized for the non-fulfilment of the terms of the bond; when of course it would be impossible to say what would become of them.

There exists a marked connection between the buffalo and the chief material objects to which any form of religious service is paid; viz., certain ancient cattle-bells, which originally came from amnôr, and though only cattle-bells—konku—yet by virtue of a great antiquity are now venerated as Gods, and styled konku Dêr or maṇi Dêr.[2] This is the Toda faith.

Every village drove does not own a bell, but certain bell-

[2] Konku dêr = *bell-god*, maṇi dêr = *relic-god*. See Chapter XVII., note 6.

cows of the sacred herds only, which are attached to the holy Mands, termed tiriêri.[3] The size of the droves varies, from accidental circumstances, between the numbers 10 and 60: and somewhat in proportion to the dimensions of the herds, from one to three bell-gods belong to a tiriêri. CHAP. XIII.

The bell-cows, for whom, by the way, the Todas have no specific name, are not selected on account of their good milking qualities, their size or beauty, but are the descendants in direct female line from certain originals whose early history has been lost. I have the following information on the subject from the highest authority; viz., a priest of the tiriêri, styled pâlâl, retired from the active business of his calling. He told me that no matter how old and worthless the bell-cow might become, the bell belonged to her till she died: when, without fail, it was transferred to her daughter. Moreover, that if the mother should have left no such female issue, a bell-cow would be procured from one of the other tiriêris: or the holy Mand would itself be broken up, and the entire herd amalgamated with that of some tiriêri still possessing a bell-cow.

The bell-god is never worn by the bell-buffalo, but is always kept in the priest's house; no one but a man of that office being permitted to touch or even to see it.

The same holy man who gave me the above information, also described the installation of a new bell-cow. Twice a day, morning and evening, for three successive days, the priest waves the bell with his right hand, round and round the head of the bovine heiress, talking to it the while, much as follows:

What a fine cow your predecessor was!
How well she supported us with her milk!
Won't you supply us in like manner?
You are a God amongst us!

[3] Tiriêri = *holy place.* Tira or tiri is the recognised Drâvidian corruption of the Sanskrit shrî = *holy*, *sacred.*

Ari or iri, from the Drâvidian root, which is variously written ir, ur = *be*, *exist.* Ur = *a village*, is from the same root. [POPE.]

CHAP. XIII.

Don't let the tirièri go to ruin!
Let one become a thousand!
Let all be well!
Let us have plenty of calves!
Let us have plenty of milk!

During three days and nights the bell is kept fastened round the cow's neck. On the morning of the third day it is removed from her neck, and lodged in the priest's house. It is never worn again during that cow's lifetime.

The entire tirièri herd is far more sacred than any of the ordinary village droves of buffalos, and the bell-cows are infinitely more sacred than any other cows of the sacred drove. So far as I could ascertain: whilst the bell-cow is the direct lineal descendant, from mother to daughter, from some remote but sacred ancestor, the remainder of the tirièri herd are the offspring of some original drove, whose members are probably related to the bell-cows.

A certain number of bulls are retained in the sacred herd; those male calves which are not wanted being given away to the Kotas. The finer animals are retained. When a young bull has arrived at mature age, and has proved his vigour, he undergoes a process of sanctification before he is permanently installed; by being isolated for a day and night in a small pen in the sacred woods of the tirièri, during which time he is deprived of food, though allowed access to water. He is not a very sacred character. In fact it is permissible to introduce a bull from an ordinary drove, after due sanctification.

It appears to me as somewhat remarkable that a people so fond of simple regulation and undeviating rule, should permit the principle of female succession amongst their cattle, whilst maintaining agnate law amongst themselves. I cannot admit the contrast between the two systems to be merely the result of accident. Knowing the direct simplicity and good sense of the savage mind, I see the probability that once on a time, the scheme of inheritance and of kinship, both among themselves and for their buffalos, was identical; viz., through the female line. And the more remotely ancient the mode of Toda life, and the nearer it approached to man's primæval condition, the greater the probability that the habits of animal and man approached one another in general similitude.

Before proposing for consideration the conclusion which I draw from the facts of early identity and present difference in such customs, I will give an extract from a well-known work on primitive marriage. Mr. M'Lennan in striving to show 'that the most ancient system in which the idea of blood-relationship was embodied, was a system of kinship through females only,' writes: 'considering that the history of all the races of men, so far as we know it, is the history of a progress from the savage state; considering the social condition of rude tribes still upon the earth—remembering that the races which can be traced in history had all a previous history, which remains unwritten—it cannot seem a very strange proposition that there has been a stage in the development of human races when there was no such appropriation of women to particular men—when, in short, marriage as it exists among civilized nations was not practised. We believe that we shall show, to a sufficient degree of probability, that there have been times when marriage in this sense was yet undreamt of. Wherever this has been the case, the paternity of children must have been uncertain; the conditions essential to a system of kinship through males being formed, would therefore be wanting; no such system would be formed; there would be—there could be—kinship through females only.'[4]

In Chapter XXVII. reasons for my belief are given, that with polyandry came the change from promiscuous unions and kinship through the female line, to inheritance through males

[4] M'Lennan, 'Primitive Marriage.'

CHAP. XIII.

only—the system which now obtains amongst these people—in which argument I am glad to find Mr. M'Lennan almost entirely with me.

Now therefore, I would advance the suggestion, that the system of kinship in cattle, through their *cows*, is perhaps contemporaneous with the age when the Todas also, prior to the introduction of polyandry, held to the practice of kinship through the female line. In which belief are grounds for confidence in the very high antiquity of the Toda bell-gods.

The worship of the *bull*, may possibly be a further development of cattle worship.

## CHAPTER XIV.

### TIRIÊRI PRIESTS.

*The Pâlâl—The Kâvilâl—The Pâlâl is a God—The Peiki Clan termed 'Sons of God'—Duties of the Pâlâl—No mysteries—Sacred nature of Priests—The Pâlâl becomes man again—Purification for holy orders—The Tûde tree; its botanical name and distribution—The use of the Tûde, an ancient practice—The Pâlâl enters on his duties.*

CHAP. XIV.

EACH tiriêri, with its drove of cattle, is in the charge of an ascetic milkman or priest, styled pâlâl,[1] and an equally ascetic, though not equally holy, herdsman or kâvilâl.[2] And according as the herd may be small or large, there are found from one to two of the former, and from one to three of the latter, attached to the tiriêris.

The pâlâl, whose personal acquaintance I had made in the course of taking information on the interesting subject of the bell-god, was a man of about thirty-five years of age, who had spent some fifteen of them in holy orders, vacating his post in favour of a brother. The effect of that lengthy period of ascetic and solitary life on his personal appearance, was somewhat striking. It was perhaps *de rigueur* for one who had so long been in sacred office to wear his hair dishevelled, and to neglect the cleanliness of his person: but the more than usually motionless eyebrow, the gloomy solemnity of his look and his

[1] Pâlâl, pâl, is the Drâvidian word for *milk*; âl = *person*.

[2] Kâvilâl, kâval = *guard*; âl = *person*.

The former is a Turkish word. Yet kâ is the Drâvidian root for *protect*, *guard*. In Tamil we have a kind of reduplication of it; thus, pâtu kâ. The Sanskrit corresponding root is pâ. [POPE.]

fixed wooden face, were not the results of fashion, but the action of a second nature that had been moulding him for years.

But bread and sugar hath its charms. Under its influence, he softened out and became affable. Waiting till he had finished the meal I had given him, the first of a series of questions suitable to an *ex*-pâlâl, was put. 'Is it true that Todas salute the sun?' I asked: 'tschâkh!' he replied, 'those poor fellows do so, but me,' tapping his chest, 'I, a God! why should I salute the sun?' At the time, I thought this a mere ebullition of vanity and pride, but I have since had opportunity of testing the truth of his speech. The pâlâl for the time being is not merely the casket containing divine attributes, but *is himself a God.*

Let me here describe the duties of the pâlâls and the mode of their ordination. These holy men, who must invariably be selected from the Peiki clan—the members of which style themselves Dêr mokh, or children or sons of God or of the Gods—are not in any way educated to their office; nor by mature age, superior talent, wealth, or other form of influence, are they of themselves worthy of unusual respect. They are just ordinary ignorant villagers, with sufficient shrewdness or impecuniosity, to note in the lonely post, certain very material advantages, combined with those of a more ethical nature, sufficient to compensate for the monotonous duties and isolation of the life.

No Toda being able either to read or write, and each pâlâl being as absolutely ignorant as the last, and as his own successor will be, it is quite clear there can be no dogmas of an abstruse nature, and none but the most simple rites to transmit at time of relief.

The universally defective size in the organs of Caution and Secretiveness observable in the tribe, produces an open nature of disposition, such as renders it almost impossible to conceive the existence of any very mystic rites among them. Whatever is done in these tiriêris, is known to every intelligent

No. 16

AUTOTYPE, LONDON

ADAM AND EVE
ÂL=ÂD=ÂD'M=MAN. AVV=MOTHER.
OF THE PEIKI CLAN – DÊR MOKH OR SONS OF GOD.
GENESIS VI. 2.

member of the male community, and I have little doubt, to every inquisitive woman also. That these performances have hitherto remained unknown to the English public, arises from the simple cause, that they have not been carefully enquired into. I have before stated that the people do not talk freely on subjects they hold to be sacred; from some feeling of awe or reverence. But, if spoken to quietly, they will be found to be like sieves, and to reveal everything they know.

The simplicity of their faith and the crudeness of their rites is such, that the circumstance of their traditions being handed down by memory, is deprived of any element of the wonderful, more especially so when it is remembered that the entire detail of each tradition is known throughout the tribe. Notwithstanding, nothing is more possible than that names, rites, and traditions, transmitted in such fashion, may undergo a certain degree of change in the course of generations. How can there be mysteries without a permanent priesthood?

Not only pâlâls but kâvilâls also, though mostly married men, yet live celibate lives, separating themselves from family and relations during the period of their holy vocations. The pâlâl, as being by far the more sacred, may be touched by no one on earth but a pâlâl, not even by his fellow-labourer and servant, the kâvilâl. The breath even of a human being is defilement—not so that of a buffalo—men must therefore keep at a respectful distance; which appears to be about five yards. Women are not permitted to *approach* either tiriêri or holy men. Even the pâlâl's father must bow down before him. *He is a God*, and for the time loses his personal name, being known only as the pâlâl of such a tiriêri.

These sacred characters may however resign their posts when they tire of their solitude, so soon as a substitute can be found willing to devote himself to the life of celibacy and privation. And the pâlâl may become man again, by the simple process of setting aside his black mantle: though he retains

CHAP. XIV.

through life, amongst his fellow-men, a large amount of respect, as having once been a God.

The following description of the process, which *all* men undergo in the course of being sanctified to the performance of *any* holy duty, will prove interesting.

For the space of a week—eṭṭnâl; literally speaking, eight days, and corresponding to *in acht tagen* in German—the novitiate must remain day and night alone in the woods of the tiriêri, without a particle of clothing and with only a fire to protect him from the severity of the climate. He beats with a stone, the bark off a branch of the tûde[3] tree, which he collects. Then three times each day, morning, noon, and evening, he performs the following ceremony. Squeezing some of the juice of the bark, into a leaf-cup containing water from the stream or spring, he raises the cupfull with the right hand to his forehead, in token of respect: then lowering it to his mouth and drinking off the contents, passes the empty leaf round over his head and left shoulder, then depositing it behind his right side. This formula is repeated three times, using a fresh leaf each time. Next, he takes the remainder of the bark, and rubs his naked body all over with it, washing himself immediately in the fresh water. On the eighth day he is competent to assume charge of his office.

The week's ordeal has been extremely severe, both in point of exposure and of solitude, and one well calculated to make a suitable impression on a man who is about to undertake a solemn duty. The kâvilâl has supplied him with food from the tiriêri all this time, and there is reason for believing that the pâlâl and kâvilâl see that the novitiate does not slur the proper performance of the rites.

The Todas have no distinctive word to express purification, but describe the effect by saying sari[4] uddi, 'he is right,' by the process.

[3] Tûde, tûre, zhûre, tûrr|u = *a thicket of small shrubs.* Tamil. [POPE.]
[4] Sari. In Drâvidian çari = *right.* [POPE.]

Nº 15

AUTOTYPE, LONDON

THE TÛDE OR SACRED BUSH.

WEAPONS, BOW & ARROW, USED AT WEDDINGS & FUNERALS.

IMITATION BUFFALO HORNS.

Though the proper meaning of the word tûde, is simply a bush; yet taken in connection with its use for sanctifying purposes, it may be held to imply that it is *the* bush above all others. It is a very common little tree on these hills, fragile, and by all accounts, possessing no remarkable properties in flower, seed, or sap. I am indebted to the courtesy of Lieutenant-Colonel Beddome, Conservator of Forests, for its botanic names, viz., *Meliosma simplicifolia*, alias *Millingtonia.*

Dr. Hooker, Director of the Kew Gardens, has obliged me with the following valuable information as to the diffusion of the tree; a point on which I have been desirous to obtain the most reliable account, hoping that the localities might form geographical links by which the Todas might be traced to other tribes within or beyond the boundaries of Hindustan. 'The distribution of the plant,' Dr. Hooker is so good as to write, 'is Western and Eastern Himalaya, from Simla eastward. Khassia, Silhet, and Mishmi hills in Assam. From the Concan to Courtallam in the western Peninsula. It certainly does not inhabit Persia, the Caucasus, or South Russia, and probably not even Beluchistan.'

It was important to establish, if the race of which the Todas form a tribe, brought with them from Western Asia the use of the tûde, the *Millingtonia.* It would now seem probable that they brought with them, merely, the already established practice of self-purification with a sacred plant, and not finding in the country of their adoption that which they had been accustomed to use when in their own land, they elected the tûde in its place. If the views expressed in the last chapter, as to the antiquity of the rules of cattle inheritance—making the bell-cow a descendant by the female line from some remote ancestor—be considered of value, then some degree of support is also afforded to show the collateral practice of purification by the use of a sacred plant, to be also very ancient.

It would be interesting to know if other broken tribes of the pre-Âryan—Drâvidian—race, now living in various tracts

CHAP. XIV. of India, utilise this plant, whose picture is given in photograph No. 15.

The tûde is not used for any other rite or for any other purpose than the purification of candidates for holy orders.

When the aspirant has thus prepared himself for the performance of the most sacred duties a Toda has any conception of, he proceeds to the tiriêri close by, where the pâlâl whom he is about to relieve, awaits his arrival. I was told by my Toda friend, that he enters on his new avocations without further ceremony. Simply, the sacred relics and the bell-cows are pointed out to him, and his duties explained.

# CHAPTER XV.

## PRIESTLY DUTIES.

*Pâlâl's daily routine—Salutes the sacred Herd—Milks the Cattle—Libations to the Bell-gods—Names of Toda Gods—Does the conception of invisible Gods arise from deficient organ of Form?—Todas revere Light, not Fire—Who is the Kâvilâl?—Pâlâl demonstrates that he is never touched—Milk held in religious regard—Pâlâl collects Kûtu for his Mand.*



THE daily routine of the pâlâl's mysterious office was described to me nearly in the following words. 'On rising in the morning, I wash face, hands, and teeth, with the left hand.' In daily human life he had invariably used the right hand for this purpose; such being the custom with all Orientals certainly, who, eating with their fingers, find it necessary to reserve the right hand for that especial object. But remember the pâlâl is now a God, and to the pure all things are pure—fact!

'Then entering the inner room—ulg ârsh—of the house,' which is reserved for dairy purposes, the outer room—porram âlg ârsh—being the pâlâl's sleeping apartment, 'I make a leaf-lamp, into which I put clarified butter and 5 wicks, thus,' spreading out his fingers. I could not ascertain if the number 5 is essential, but it appeared to me to be so. 'The lamp is put into a niche in the wall, opposite the bells, which hang on the separate prongs of a stick thrust into the thatch of the roof. And I light in silence, nor salute either light—belak—or relics—maṇi.'

'Having taken up my wand and honnu or milk-pail, which

CHAP. XV.

is a bamboo joint, used as a pail to contain milk, 'I go out to my buffalos. They are all expecting to be milked, and turn towards me as I stand at the gate of the pen. I salute them by holding the wand in the right hand, with the honnu hanging from the fingers of the same hand. I bring the whole to my forehead.' Here rising, with stick in hand and my penknife thrust between his fingers, he enacted the pantomime of saluting the sacred herd. Moving his body on his legs as a pivot, he turned slowly from right to left in silence, describing a small arc of a circle, as if to include the whole of a herd standing crowded in the fold before him. He did so without bowing, keeping his body nearly erect throughout, and without speaking.

Noticing his silence, he replied to my enquiry, 'I do not, like the common people in the Mands, say danenma, mokh ultama, and all the rest of it. No, and I don't say nin arzbini.'[1] He is now a God, and quite the superior of any buffalo.

'I alone, or if the drove is large, assisted by a fellow-pâlâl, milk the cattle—the kâvilâl may not do so—lodging the honnus of milk in the dairy.

'On entering the inner room of the dairy, I go up to the bells, and dipping my hand into the milk'—here makes a little cup of the top joints of his fingers—'pour a few drops on each bell three times, muttering with each libation the names of the following Gods:—

| | |
|---|---|
| Ânmungâno | Godingâtho |
| Beligoshu | Dekulâria |

Kazudâva.'

The pâlâl being himself a God may with propriety mention the names of his *fellow-Gods*, a license which is permitted to no one else to do.

[1] Nin arzbini = *I adore thee.* See Chapter XVII., on the êtud Mand, for the application of these words.

No. 17

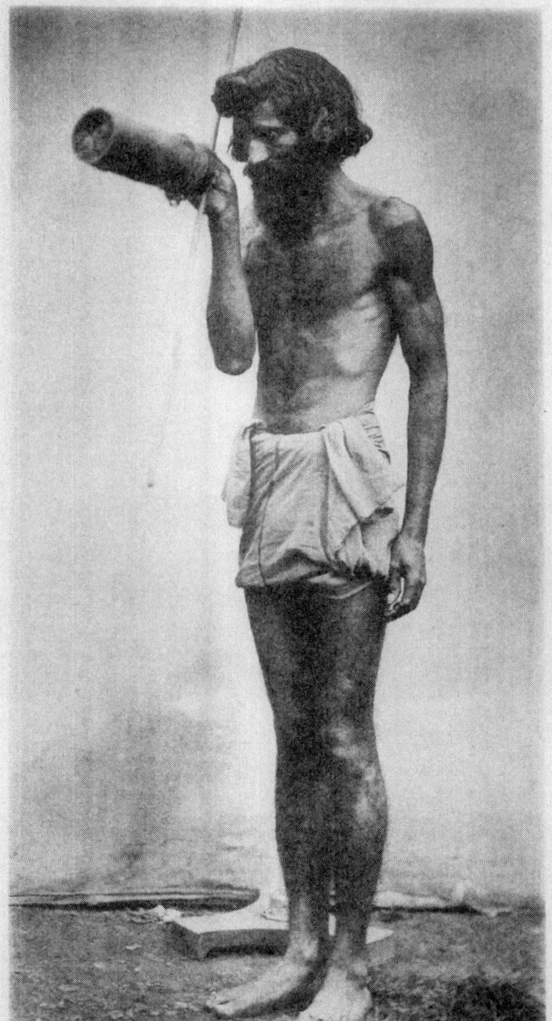

AUTOTYPE, LONDON

THE PÂLÂL SALUTES THE SACRED CATTLE.

'These are good Gods, Gods of the whole Toda tribe, and not Gods of my tiriêri only. I have never seen them. They are invisible, but ever present with us.'

Can it be possible that the invisible—shapeless—nature of Toda Gods, is a conception occasioned by the deficient organ of Form, which I have already noted as being a cranial peculiarity of this people? Was the faculty small with the Jews also?

'I then proceed to make nei from the previous day's milk. After which, I prepare my own and the kâvilâl's food. The last thing at night is to replenish the lamp.'

There were three bell-gods in my informant's tiriêri. He said that in some there were two, in another only one; but in none more than three. Axes for cutting fuel are kept by the kâvilâl in his own house in the tiriêri, apart from the dairy. They are tabued to other people, and for other purposes.

I was careful to enquire from this man if the people in saluting the sun and moon, and he in placing lights in the tiriêri, worshipped light—belak, or fire—diṭth. The reply was satisfactory; he distinctly repudiated the notion of the adoration of fire.

It has been stated that the pâlâl may not be touched by anyone on earth, save by a pâlâl, during the period of his priesthood, not even by the kâvilâl. It will be seen by what follows, that the kâvilâl also, though not to be compared with his master in point of sanctity—one indeed being a God, whilst the other is only a man—yet shares the exclusiveness of his life. He too has been sanctified by his influence of the tûde, and lives apart from the world: yet his office is of an inferior degree. He devotes his life to the duties of herding the cattle on the hill-sides, cutting firewood, et cetera: but he may not milk the cows, nor touch the relics, or approach within several paces of the pâlâl. Thus whilst he is an associate in the austere privations of the life to which he has devoted himself, yet does not participate in the glory of the office.

CHAP. XV.

Curious to form an opinion as to whether in the unheeded seclusion of their sanctuary, these recluses preserved themselves as untainted by contact with man as I had been told, I ventured to express to the pâlâl a doubt as to the possibility of his giving his servant daily food, and of selling the produce of his dairy, without touching anyone. He at once said he would show me.

He asked for three somethings—anythings: looked up to the trees for suitable leaves. What does the gentleman drink from? I gave him three tumblers, with the bright and sparkling appearance of which he appeared gratified: something worthy of the subject. Much pleased: now he could show: couldn't he just show? Sitting himself with one glass in hand, on a low wall, to represent the tûar of the tiriêri, on which he pictured himself squatting as he had so often done during the last fifteen years, he placed the second glass on the ground immediately below him, near which a Toda companion, impersonating the kâvilâl, stood waiting. Another Toda was sent to a distance to act the part of a purchaser with a third glass, which having set on the ground, he retired a few paces. Now feigning, the pâlâl poured his nei from the first to the second tumbler, which the kâvilâl then carried off, pouring its contents into the third tumbler. As the kâvilâl stepped back with the money which he picked up off the ground, the purchaser came forward and took away the glass full of nei. 'See,' he said, 'am I not paid for my nei without being touched?'

This impromptu pantomime was acted with so much justice and gravity, and all three men, though not pâlâls, understood their several parts so thoroughly, I could no longer doubt that the persons of these holy men were inviolable. I obtained also a glimpse—the truth of which further observation has tended to confirm—how the rites and ceremonies of an unlettered race may be transmitted almost unchanged from generation to generation. Publicity, combined with the identity of character which forms the marked peculiarity of extremely primitive races, and common interests, are the watchwords. The whole tribe is of one mind, and as unchangeable in disposition as a herd of dumb animals.

A certain amount of superstitious, or shall we say religious, regard is paid to the article *milk*, and in a less degree to the honnu which holds it. Until of late years, milk would never be adulterated. The honnu is tabued for ordinary purposes; indeed the people do not like it to be taken up carelessly; preferring that it be not touched at all. In this sensitiveness, one notices the feeling which has no doubt participated in forming some of the caste rules of the Âryas. As might be anticipated, the milk from the sacred herd is held in still greater reverence; the holy men of the tiriêri may consume as much of it as they please, but what is over *must be made into nei* before being sold; it must not leave the tiriêri in its natural form.

'The nei which we don't eat ourselves, I sell to the Badagas, who in return supply me and my family with grain, clothes, and a little money.' Very little of the last commodity probably. Thus as we observe, the inducement to become a pâlâl, over and above the glory of position, is the profit from the sale of nei of the sacred drove. A very neat perquisite for 'the Sons of God,' with which to repair broken fortunes.

The pâlâl rarely leaves the tiriêri Mand, but he occasionally visits the Badagas villages; obliging the people, through influence of his supposed powers of witchcraft, and the great sanctity attaching to his person, to comply with his demands for little luxuries of food, and for the grain due to his tiriêri as kûtu. He has nothing whatever to do with births, marriages, or deaths, though he is sometimes consulted for the adjustment of disputes.

# CHAPTER XVI.

## THE TIRIÊRI.[1]

*A Tiriêri Mand described—Names of Tiriêri—We visit the Tiriêri and see the Bell-gods—The holy Domain—The Priests are away—Who erected these upright Stones?—The Priests return—A Bargain struck —'Gods of our Fathers'—'These be your Gods'!!*

CHAP. XVI.

A tiriêri Mand, which is the residence of the pâlâl and kâvilâl, consists of two houses; the one a dairy or pâlthchi, in which the pâlâl lives and makes his nei, the other a house for the kâvilâl and his implements for cutting fuel. The two houses are a little apart, and separated by the tûars which surround them. A cattle pen, also encompassed by its wall or hedge, occupies a position close by. The site is invariably a spot secluded by natural advantages from contact with the outer world, and having the usual adjuncts of water, grazing and wood land.

There are at the present time, five tiriêris belonging to the tribe—there have been more—whose names are as follows;—

| Pûrth | Kudar |
|---|---|
| Mâr | Markush |

Puzhash.

And exactly in the same manner as I have explained in Chapter VI. that ordinary Mands have their duplicates and even triplicates, so these tiriêri Mands have also their corresponding sites to which the little colonies move at certain seasons, for the sake of fresh pasturage.

[1] The derivation of the word has been given in note 3 of Chapter XIII., on the Bell-gods.

No. 18

AUTOTYPE, LONDON.

THE TIRIÊRI. THE 'HOLY PLACE' OR TODA SANCTUM.

"HERE LIVE THE GODS OF OUR FATHERS"

Having ascertained that the tiriêri, with its sacred herd and its maṇi dêr, was indeed the mainspring of the entire religious faith and social system of the Todas, it became a matter of great moment to ascertain by personal inspection the secrets of its penetralia. Our *ex*-pâlâl had indeed with great apparent sincerity divulged the whole of the hidden mysteries, even to the extent of naming the Gods of his forefathers; names held in great veneration: when spoken, only pronounced in an under-tone: and which no European, and probably no native beyond the tribe, had ever previously been allowed to hear. Here would be the test of his veracity both on this subject and in other cognate matters on which we had consulted him.

We must see the inside of a tiriêri: we must view the relics, the Gods. Such was the programme: and money would of course perform the work of the magic words 'open sesame.' Calling therefore at our friend's Mand, we readily induced him to accompany us to view his old tiriêri. 'But you must not go close to the dairy' he said. Oh no!

We strolled along the pretty slopes of the verdant hills together, and he guided us over the squashy bogs, and through the ever-silent woods: and again out on the green wild, and through further nestling woods, with the cheery spring sun overhead; all in the direction of his tiriêri.

No one to overhear us out on this prairie! Now is the time! 'Bültaben'—such was his mundane name—'we want to go into the dairy of the tiriêri. You are an old pâlâl. Here is money.' 'Just to peep in at the door from a distance?' he asked. 'No, but to look at the relics in the inner room.' He stopped short, tucked his stick under one arm, and pressing the tips of all his fingers to his eyes, exclaimed, 'May both my eyes drop from their sockets, but I cannot do such a thing.' After a pause, 'The Gods would vacate the tiriêri Mand if anyone unsanctified entered it, and its pâlâl would be ruined.'

This was awkward. Another suggestion: Let us see the relics. Let the pâlâl bring them outside that we may view them. We won't go near.' Ah! that is feasible! The bargain is struck forthwith.

On we went again, much refreshed by our success, cross-questioning our guide on points of religion till he was fuddled.

'On he fares and to the border comes.'

Rising to the ridge of a prolonged knoll, he stopped and pointed below: 'There!'

Down we go into the sacred hollow. The solemn Toda, still more grave, some enthusiasm kindling his dark eye as he looks across at the place where for half a lifetime he had been a God. Over some little burns, past a group of sacred calves, looking in their dirt and stolid impudence, anything but reverential towards the *ex*-pâlâl—they were of this year's growth, and did not recognise him—up again out of the hollow: when, as we near the rounded crest of a long hillock, we find ourselves opposite two neat, but undersized houses, with a dilapidated buffalo pen. 'The tiriêri Mand! Don't go near!' So, like shying horses we circle round the spot, till we reach the ridge.

We are at the sanctuary, and in the middle of the holy domain. The pâlâls and kâvilâls are out. We will sit down and note the place till they return.

A pure green cameo of wide extent! the edge formed by an amphitheatre of hill, crowning

'with her enclosure green
As with a rural mound, the champain head.'

The arena filled with ceaseless undulations of grazing land; winding through which, a noble stream, and a score of sparkling rivulets cascading down the distant hills. A long tongue of grass land projects from one side of the hilly margin into the weald. At the root of the tongue, a wood; on the margin of which the sanctuary, near which we sit, 'taking notes.'

Wood, water, herbage, in combination with a seclusion so complete, as to include a deep sense of perpetuity. Surprising rest and peaceful beauty!

Except the single notes of birds, rich-sounding in the vibrations of the deep wood: the distant nervous warble of the lark overhead, and the hum of the busy bee in its hurry, not a single sound is to be heard over the whole wide expanse. The tiriêri cattle are browsing far away in the surrounding hollows: or like specks, may be seen dotting the sides of the distant hills.

The vertical sun is omnipresent. The holy men, I have said, were away.

Out on the extreme west is the single Makurti Peak,[2] 'where the sun goes down.' Beyond is amnôr.

How near simple appositeness approaches to taste, where the country is lovely and the subject purely bucolic! Do I confuse the sense, with taste for scenery, or have I hitherto done the Toda intellect an injustice? Such are my reflections as I note this perfectly selected site. When I now remember that the funeral-Mands—of which we shall shortly read—which I have seen, are certainly free from marked beauty, I must at least acknowledge their appreciation in the advantage and suitability of locality to be a perfect talent. Had the Toda really a love for the beautiful apart from utility, would he not have some words in his language, or a flower about his house to express the taste?

Looking at the superb glow with which the sun lights up equatorial landscapes, one ceases to wonder at, but indeed admires the instinct which leads those born and bred under its influence, to worship *light*.

Pâlâls have not returned. No occupation then but to bully our Toda. This is done till he tries to escape questions by feigning sleepiness. Keep him in motion! 'Who erected those two stones?' 'The pâlâls, who tired of their solitude, raised them to while away time.' Never! The man is sleepy! Todas bring two large rocks about four feet long each, up a steep hill, without an object! Never! Practical, lazy, Toda!

[2] See note 2 of Chapter V.

CHAP. XVI.

Archæologists have observed on such stones, which are to be frequently seen on these hills, and have asserted that they are worshipped by the Todas as lingoits. Whatever the origin of these stones, one thing is absolutely certain; that the Todas do not regard them in any way.

'They come,' said he at last, pointing to the hills near us. Sure enough, four little figures—two clothed in black—are approaching in the jerky step of men descending a steep incline, and at intervals—no touching allowed—'Listen! O listen!' shouts our conductor over the intervening hollow. They all stop. 'Two gentlemen have come to see you: let the kâvilâls remain behind, and you come o-o-o-o-on.' Sly fox, our Toda! There are to be no witnesses!

In the space of a few minutes, two gentlemen in black mantles—lamp-black and mustard-oil—with wands in their hands, keeping step as they walked,[3] had come up to about ten yards of us. We all sit down inside the circle of our own shadows.

Time is valuable; for the kâvilâls are waiting; so the interview is short. We are not to touch: merely to look at the maṇi from a distance. We are not to approach the dairy: pâlâls and kâvilâls to be paid.

There is no delay, no holy dilatoriness in bringing out 'the Gods of their fathers.' If we could have watched the pâlâls with our eyes, we must have seen them bound in through the outer door of the dairy, scramble through the inner small one, and wrench off the treasures; for in less than a quarter of a minute, they were standing before us holding their Gods in their hands.

Two buffalo-bells—konku—apparently of copper with some brass, dented and old: might be of any age; one about 5 inches diameter and 6 inches high, the other a little less.

[3] This is not the first time I had noticed Todas keeping step in walking. A most unusual sight in India, even amongst trained native soldiers off parade.

An axe, a sort of hatchet-knife, and a small knife. These latter certainly did not appear old; they were kept tolerably bright, and did not look worn, either by use or from the effects of polishing. The two last had wooden handles. 'These be your Gods'!

In reply to the enquiry, if the bells had clappers, the answer was instantaneous, energetic and simultaneous; that they had not clappers: if they had, they would have been cattle-bells—konku—but these were Gods—Dêr. The question must have been asked before.

No. 19.

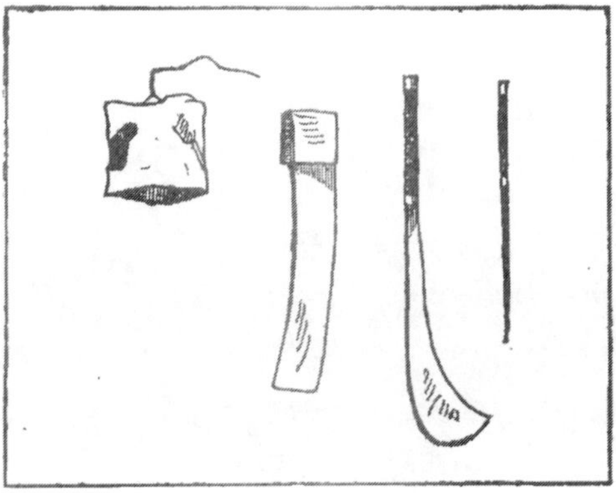

RELIC GODS—MAṆI DẸR.

*'Gods of our Fathers.'*

> . . . . Of thee
> Therefore entreat I, Father, to declare
> If I may gain such favour, as to gaze
> Upon thine image by no covering veil'd.
> DANTE, *Paradiso.*

It should be remarked that the Toda name for a bell, is konku—deep-sounding—whilst that of the common cow-bell of the district, now worn by village cattle on certain occasions, is called getti—a small tinkling thing. Hence I deduce from the sounds and sizes, that these holy bells are really national relics.

'Now,' they said, 'the Gods must not be kept out any

CHAP. XVI.

longer;' which being interpreted, meant that the kâvilâls would be coming. So, having taken a sketch of them, we threw some money to the pâlâls.

'Don't tell the kâvilâls when you pass them, that you have paid us money.' I promised; at which they chuckled. 'And don't tell any one you have seen the relics.' Phew!!

## CHAPTER XVII.

### THE ÊTUD MAND.

*Customs of the Village Dairy or Pâlthchi—Duties of the Pâlkarpâl—Important difference in the duties of the Pâlâl and Pâlkarpâl—The Tarvâl—The inside of a Dairy—The Dairy of an Êtud Mand is a Shrine—The Badagas term it Mui Mand: why?—Toda form of oath.*

CHAP. XVII.

THE customs and ceremonies of the tiriêri or Toda cathedral—seat of a divine milkman, established as the medium of conveying the Gods' gift to man—are repeated, though in less awfully sacred form, in every Mand of the tribe; in the village dairy or pâlthchi.

The configuration of the dairy has already been described in Chapter VI.

Similarly as one or more nearly-naked recluses belonging to the Peiki clan, are established as pâlâls for the care of the tiriêri, assisted by their kâvilâls; so a lesser luminary, generally from the same clan, is the unclothed, ascetic, but more mildly sacred pâlkarpâl,[1] who, also living *en garçon*, but without any pretensions to God-head, presides over the dairy of each village, helped under certain circumstances by a somewhat similar character in the vorshâl.[2] Both of these men also, have been purified in that wonderful juice which qualifies to the holy offices of milking buffalos and the charge of relics.

I state that the pâlkarpâl is generally, though not always, of the Peiki clan; for as I observe, the Peikis permit the

[1] Pâlkarpâl. See note 4 of Chapter VI.
[2] See note 4 of Chapter VIII.

CHAP. XVII.

unprofitable office of kâvilâl, and that of pâlkarpâl in villages, to be performed by members of the inferior clan of Pekkan. Moreover, in the care of dairies belonging to their own clan, the Peikis seem often to be content with the services of a Pekkan. I do not feel certain of the cause of this arrangement.

It is the duty of the pâlkarpâl to milk the village cattle, and to store and partition amongst the various families of the Mand, the shares of the divine fluid and of the nei he has made therefrom.

The village pâlthchi appears not to have any lights; for the reason perhaps, that it has no relics. However that may be, the pâlkarpâl and his companion, the vorshâl, may alone penetrate even the outer room of the dairy. Men and boys freely enter so far as the precincts of the tûar, and village feasts are often given close about the outside. But the dangerous sex are not permitted, even near the wall: and in the instance of more important villages, termed êtud Mand,[3] they may not approach within about one hundred feet of it.

The duties of the pâlkarpâl in these pâlthchis are very similar to those of the pâlâl in the tiriêri. The only differences, appearing to arise from the latter acting throughout, the part of a God, the equal of his own relics, which are also Gods, and as the superior of his cattle, the gift of the Gods: whereas the former is merely a holy man engaged in the service of the Gods.

Thus, we have seen in Chapter XV. the pâlâl saluting the cattle, as a God in Toda opinion, should do—in silence. But the pâlkarpâl, in making his obeisance, does so as their servant or dependent, saying, danenma, mokh ultama, âl ultama, êr ultama, karr ultama, ellam ultama.[4] Moreover, when he carries his honnu, containing milk, into the dairy, he repeats the formula as he crawls in through the inner door.

[3] Êtud. This word seems allied to the Drâvidian root ettu or êttu, *raise—lift up*. [POPE.]

[4] See note 5 of Chapter VII.

When the pâlthchi belongs to an êtud Mand, the relics within are Dêr. And the pâlkarpâl being only a humble servant, does not presume to mention the names of these Gods, as the deified pâlâl in *his* dairy, may with the greatest propriety do. But in pouring a few drops of milk, three times on each relic, he merely mutters nin arzbini, nin arzbini, nin arzbini I adore thee, I adore thee, I adore thee. CHAP. XVII.

Mr. Metz tells me that in certain cases an additional servant, the tarvâl,[5] would sometimes be employed. His exact occupation is not understood.

Evidently there are dairies and dairies. There is the pâlthch of the unimportant village which is merely a dairy, in charge perhaps of a stripling. Such a one I have entered, and will describe. There is the dairy which is manifestly something more; that belonging to an êtud Mand. And there is the most sacred dairy of all; that which appertains to the tiriêri; the holy of holies, already described.

In all cases, whether the charge be big or small, the servants of the sacred house, are by virtue of their office, treated with respect by the people; they are spoken of in an undertone and in a reserved manner: they are saluted: neither they nor their implements may be touched.

I had made several unsuccessful efforts to penetrate the dairy of an êtud Mand, but was always discovered when seemingly on the eve of success. Taking advantage therefore of a fog I paid a visit to the pâlthchi of an ordinary Mand, which I had observed, not to be much watched, and to which a wood afforded means of secret approach. The pâlkarpâl was fortunately absent, so crawling in, I could observe at leisure. The outer room was fitted up in every way as an ordinary dwelling, suited to the simple requirements of a bachelor of the olden time; an axe for cutting wood was

[5] Tarvâl. In Tamil we have taravu = *the order of a master* or *superior*. The forms, tara, taru in all Dravidian dialects, have kindred ideas. [POPE.]

CHAP. XVII. lying in a corner, and the man's bed was on one side of the door. The door in the wooden partition wall which led to the inner room or dairy proper, was of unusually small dimensions—about a cubit high, by half a cubit broad—and blocked up with a slab of stone. This I removed, and after penetrating the dairy, closed it behind me.

I now struck a light and leisurely examined everything in roof, and on floor. The inventory was of most simple detail; viz., the usual fireplace of three small stones—one at back, and one at each side—an earthenware vessel or two, and a few honnus for holding milk. No bell, no relic, nor lights, nor niche in wall. Only a large pair of buffalo horns, made with unusual care, of bamboo bound with cane, which I found thrust into the thatch: and several smaller horns made from twigs; all of which will be found represented in photograph No. 15. Without doubt there were no stones for any other purposes than those described.

It has puzzled me much to discover, in what way, êtud Mands should be, as the meaning implies, 'great' Mands, and why their dairies should be held in more reverence, and be guarded with more care than those of ordinary villages. In a general way, they appear to be somewhat larger than usual. One can see that their droves of cattle are of more than common size. And so the impression left after a visit, is that there is something of the cathedral about the spot. These are, however, signs that such dairies are great, but do not afford the reason why they are so. And there was no one to explain. The people themselves had probably never thought of a reason; they had been satisfied with the knowledge which had grown with their growth, that it was an êtud Mand. I will now give the result of my own enquiries and speculations.

A certain number of dairies are said by the Todas to contain a kurpu[6] or relic of an ancestor; a ring for instance, a hatchet

[6] Kurpu. Drâvidian. Tamil has kuri = *indicate, point out.* Kurippu

or other imperishable article, even as is said, a bell—konku. That many of these êtud Mands contain kurpus, I have ascertained by direct enquiry. That they all do so, or are supposed by the people to do so, is my belief. Hence we see the êtud Mands are *shrines;* the shrines of a race which burns its dead.

Now the Badaga name for such a village is mui Mand.[7] And as the very intimate knowledge which this cognate tribe possesses of Toda practice, would probably cause the word mui to be descriptive; it would materially assist us in our enquiries if we knew exactly what it does mean.

It has been ascertained that the Todas often settle disputes amongst themselves at these places—the tiriêri being too sacred to be approached for such purposes—challenging one another to make good their word, by repeating it at the êtud Mand. By joining all these notes together, I can frame an explanation that appears to me quite reasonable, and in consonance with my knowledge of the people's habits and mode of thought. They evidently consider the dairies containing kurpus, or relics of their ancestors, in the light of shrines; and in consequence, the precincts and presence to be holy ground; so holy that men would be restrained from lightly uttering a falsehood at such spots.[8] Hence it is, that these 'great' Mands are used for

—verbal noun = *a sign, indication, memorial.* The Kanarese uses guri. [POPE.]

Maṇi. Sanskrit maṇi = *jewel, bell.* Used in all the Drâvidian languages. [POPE.]

Mr. Metz draws a distinction between kurpu and maṇi; the latter is specific and implies a *metal ring* or *bell.* Thus although a maṇi is with this people always a kurpu, every kurpu is not a maṇi. It may be an *axe* or *staff.*

To me it seems that the word maṇi is a refinement introduced through contact with the Hindus; giving a more distinctly religious, sacred or holy meaning to the sentiment implied in the kurpu.

[7] Mui. In old Kanarese Muyyi is *retaliation.*

Mû in Tamiḻ is *old, venerable.* [POPE.]

[8] Mr. Metz tells me that an oath is taken, by removing the mantle, and stepping over it, in the presence of the êtud Mand.

the purpose of considering matters of weight concerning a large circle of families. This belief is greatly strengthened by the knowledge that throughout the East the practice is common, to hold similar meetings at shrines of holy men; Pirs, Jogis, Fakirs, &c.

That an êtud Mand should have larger herds of cattle than ordinary, may be accounted for by the practice of the people to give cattle in fulfilment of a vow; that if so and so occurs—a son is born for instance—the gift of a cow or calf will be made to the dairy.

It is important that we arrive at some decision on the object and use of a dairy which occupies a position so manifestly conspicuous amongst their social institutions: to enable us to clear our minds as to all the components of the Toda faith. So long as we do not know what an êtud Mand is, we should always feel that some material portion of their religious system remained unexplained.

# CHAPTER XVIII.

## THE FUTURE STATE.

*Todas have no just sense of a Ruling Almighty Power—Belief in Eternity—The Natural Causes of the belief in a Future State—Future Punishment.*



THE Todas appear not to have formed even an approximately just conception of an All-mighty, All-wise, All-good Being. Though perhaps of these attributes of a Ruling Power, they appreciate the evidences of might, with most absolute certainty, for the probable reason that they cannot avoid observing the existence somewhere of a Power which influences their destinies; that has sent them buffalos to supply food, gives them children, and that kills and cures. They see also the mysterious sun and moon in daily movement over the earth, shedding their benign rays over all, as they traverse the sky. These evidences of useful and mighty *living* Power about and above them, are manifest, equally to their mental as to their ocular vision.

So far as they may be said to have a religion at all, it seems to be a growth from some confused contemplation of all these and other visible conditions. There is very little of the abstract or the unseen involved in their beliefs.

Nature has never presented to the Todas, her awful side, in visions of ice, frost, or savage storms. They are the dolichocephalic children of sunny regions,[1] to whom nature is more

[1] See Chapter IX., on the dispositions, and the natural home of the dolichocephali.

CHAP. XVIII.

often beneficent than the contrary. Hence their beliefs are pleasant rather than otherwise, and death is free from horrors.

Even when a man's breath has left his body, and the corpse yet remains with them—forming the most eventful episode in their experience—yet no power of generalising or abstract reasoning seems to come to their aid, to assist them in this their day of agony, to frame any sort of link between the expired spirit, and the Spirit which rules the darkness, in whose bosom it has been lost to sight. Their practical experience forms the fuel, which their strong sense of *perpetuity*, fanned by the visible evidences of power in all nature, kindles into flame; dictating that the curious something which has just left that body—lying so senseless without it—must have gone somewhere. And where could it have gone, but to another place just like this? Other *Todas are there*: and they could not live without milk; *therefore* buffalos are there too!

'A high degree of education must be attained,' writes Mr. Baring-Gould, 'before the notion of annihilation can be apprehended.' Again: 'Let anyone try to imagine himself extinguished—his powers of thought, his feelings, his volitions, his perceptions broken short off—and he will see how extremely difficult is the task, and how incomplete his success.'[2]

I incline greatly to the belief that the firm faith in a future state, owes its *origin* more to the domestic feelings, strengthened by the strong conservative sense provided by the organ of Concentrativeness, than to Hope, which is ordinarily considered to be its stronghold. The first combination is that which eminently distinguishes the most primitive races, whilst Hope is a religious organ whose development betokens an advance from the primæval state. A very pretty illustration of my theory is contained in the following quotation from 'Guy Mannering,' taken from Mr. Baring-Gould's work: 'Whiles I think my puir bairn's dead,'

[2] Baring-Gould. 'The Origin of Religious Belief.'

said Madge Wildfire, 'ye ken[3] very weel it's buried—but that signifies naething. I have had it on my knee a hundred times and a hundred times till that, since it was buried; and how could that be were it dead, ye ken? it's merely impossible.'

It is somewhat remarkable that the Todas should not only feel so confident in their immortality, but be without apprehension as to the future state; in the possibility that individually they may not attain to it. No such doubts arise to perplex their simple minds. Death is not a leap in the dark, but the contrary. The mode of thought—if thinking, it may be termed—by which they seem to set at rest this difficulty of more advanced and religious races, is too curious to be lost.

Their belief appears to be based on two considerations; one, what they know: the other, a sort of self-consciousness.

As regards the first, they *know* that they and their cattle were raised from the earth by the Great Unseen. This with them is a faith assured, as if the true story had been handed down from incontrovertible sources. They find themselves living, existing, breathing: they note the breath-life to leave the clay which returns to earth. But where does this breath-life go? The reply is contained in their *knowledge*. 'Tis a little sophistical perhaps, but an illogical jump is nothing with such people. They know that Todas and cattle live in amnôr; hence they are certain, with an absolute certainty, that this departed breath has gone there to join their forefathers. In this there is nothing more wonderful than that they rose from the soil! The subject is not worth thinking about! it has long been known! Thinking is difficult to the primitive mind. Best not to think!

If with all our accumulated stores of information, we find the subject of a future state but little further advanced than it was ages ago, we can sympathise with a very simple people who have so few facts to work upon, and with whom the

[3] I would invite a comparison between this word ken, and the Toda words for I see, I dream, I smell, *et cetera*, in Chapter XXIX.

CHAP. XVIII.

process of thought is little more than the instinctive stringing and restringing of those very few and very stale facts together. With a deeply domestic, excessively conservative and practical race, void of talent for generalisation, employed in working out its own problem; what could its theory of a future state be, than an exact copy of circumstances it had witnessed in this?

The self-consciousness to which I have ascribed one of the reasons for their viewing the future entirely without apprehension, appears to me to be an *intuitive but unobtrusive appreciation of the simplicity and harmlessness of their own natures:* unsensitive doubtless as to abstract right and wrong, but whose tendencies to the commission of crime are the very smallest; small indeed, in proportion to the inefficiency of their character, rather than in any ratio to moral qualities.

It is acknowledged that they commit without much remorse, as a matter almost of habit and nearly with impunity, acts which, with races that have long been exposed to the influence of a public opinion, are scouted as degraded though secret vices, but which the unrefined Toda sense does not censure as anything very heinous; rather as peccadillos punishable in a quiet way amongst themselves.

If all Toda society is unanimous in holding such acts as of small importance, where from such a race are we to meet a Toda of the unusual moral stature to consider himself alone criminal? Todas in addition to much real harmlessness of life are never troubled by moral scruples or remorseful feelings; such as would give their consciences trouble, leading to the hope of a purer future life, or one in which those who had escaped merited punishment for crimes committed in this world, would yet suffer hereafter.

If they have words for sin and hell, they have to all appearance, merely been adopted from the Hindus; the former perhaps in its milder sense, of a trespass, to supply a want, the latter to apply to other people. But Todas all go to amnôr.

# CHAPTER XIX.

## THE BOATH.

*External appearance of the Boath—Night visit—Inside of the Boath—Where are the Relics?—The Boath an exceptional curiosity—Speculations regarding it; a Bethel? connected with the Bothan?*



ON a previous visit to the village close to which this temple—one out of only three or four in the whole tribe—is situated,[1] I had been able to reconnoitre it at my leisure whilst talking to the naked vorshâl seated on the surrounding-wall.

He told us with Toda solemnity and such an air, that there were very sacred relics in it, handed down from past generations. Here a turn in the wrist of his upraised arm implied the pre-historic antiquity I was hunting for! How did he guess my secret? But he was lamentably hazy when I strove to turn his observations to practical account. Nor could I get from him a clear description, even of his daily occupations. To sit naked on the wall and look like a scarecrow was the feat he seemed to accomplish best.

'I want to go in,' I said, advancing towards the temple.

'No,' he replied, backing towards the door of the sacred edifice, and shaking the palms of both hands and outspread fingers in alarmed delirium.

'What will happen if I go in?'

'The Gods will tear you to pieces.'

He would not agree to the proposal, though backed by a little offering, so after taking a sketch I retired.

[1] At the top of the Sigôr Ghat.

CHAP. XIX.

The appearance of the building is as follows; a conical thatched roof on a circular wall of very stout planking. The wall about four cubits high. The whole edifice some fourteen or fifteen cubits tall and six cubits in diameter. At a distance of approximately six cubits, the temple is surrounded by a massive wall of uncut stone, put together without cement, two cubits broad and three in height.

I have represented in the sketch the wall as partially

No. 20.

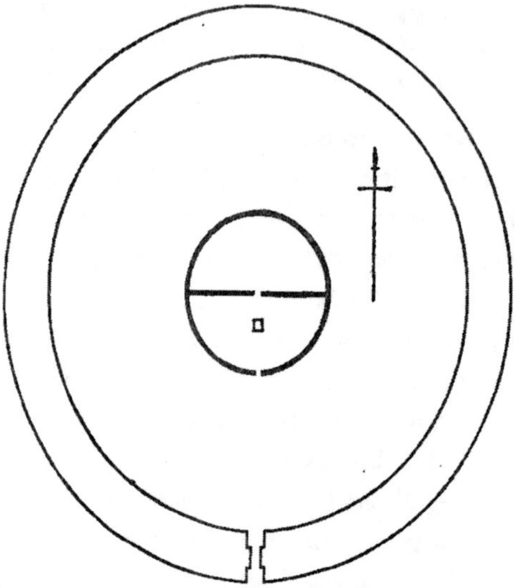

CONICAL TEMPLE—BOATH.

thrown down, with a view to displaying the entire building, but in reality the circuit of the wall is complete.

The apex of the cone is crowned with a large stone, placed there apparently with the object—however inadequate the conception—of steadying the roof, or perhaps excluding rain from that weak point.

Some days subsequent to this visit, selecting a dark night for the purpose, and accompanied by a friend—who, I had better at once state, was not the reverend companion who has

Nº 21

AUTOTYPE. LONDON

CONICAL TEMPLE.

BOATH.

been my steady associate in all innocent if somewhat inquisitorial visits—I walked over the hills to this village on burglarious intent. What should I do, I thought as I went along, if I really met a valuable relic, say some 2,000 years old, with an inscription on it? Who is it is said to have said that every man has his price? I had mine. Were I only to find a signet ring, I was ripe to commit theft in addition to the minor crime of breaking into a savage man's temple.

In this frame of mind we arrived at the spot. How nobly the little billy-cock house stood out in relief against the murky sky! The buffalos in the pen close by, were breathing hard and snorting as they caught our smell. Fastidious in them, considering that we were certainly clean, as compared with their slumbering masters and mistresses. Indeed it must have been the unusual scent that disturbed them.

All the world asleep and hushed but we two and a few fastidious cattle. Though all is quiet and our isolation absolute, we hold a preliminary survey of the premises—the vorshâl might be within—nor till we had satisfied ourselves that the only noise was of our own making, did we proceed to business.

Unpicking the stones with which, for want of lock and key, the doorway was closed, I sat prepared to enter. 'Where is the door?' asked my friend, inexperienced in Toda architecture. So he remained watching. 'Are you going into that?' I next heard from behind the tails of my coat. He must have received the response as if from a diving-bell.

The door of the temple, which by the way, faces almost due south, appears, judging by the eye, to approach in its dimensions, a cubit in height by half a cubit in breadth. Even taken angle-wise this aperture was found to constitute a close fit for full-grown men.

In we crawled, and when fairly inside, re-locked the door by blocking it up behind us: and struck a light. I do not suppose we either of us exactly knew what we had expected to

CHAP. XIX.

find; but a slight groan of disappointment, followed by rapid movements, as of rats in an empty bucket, told the melancholy tale—nothing.

The pitch darkness of the inside, and blackness of the roof and walls, absorbing nearly all the light of our candles, it was with difficulty we satisfied ourselves of the value and form of our possession.

The temple is divided by a thick wooden partition wall—which extends from the earthen floor in which it is buried, to the full height of the roof—into two compartments of equal size. There is a small doorway in this wall of the same dimensions as the first. Midway between the two doorways, at the level of the floor, is a vat or basin of about a half cubit square, made of stone.

We look through the interstices between the clumsy slabs of the dividing-wall, into the next room. That at any rate is not empty. It is the *sanctum sanctorum*, where the relics are kept.

Once more! In through the little door of the dividing wall. Quite easy now! First squat square opposite to it, like a frog. Next supple the whole body. Then go in cornerwise with *élan*! Don't attempt to rise till you are five feet off on the other side. This feat can be practised through a window-frame at ground level.

Just looking round at the little door, more in sorrow than in anger, we proceed to business. Earthenware pots, honnus, and a whirl with which to churn butter by revolving between the palms of the hands. No bell, no hatchet, neither ring nor relic of any kind, no niche for lights, no altar, no stone, no phallus or lingum. No snakes! Everyone has been telling us lies, and the world is full of sawdust!

Back through the two doors quickly, like prairie dogs. Out into the open air. The transition was as if we had been born again.

Now to philosophise. This is a very simple religious faith! How many negatives go to prove a positive! One thing is clear, every priest must be long in the back and very fond of milk! But why were the doors so unusually small, and why locked, and why these fusty lies about relics?

Some time subsequent to the events just described, an excellent opportunity occurred of making further enquiry regarding relics—the belief in which had now become much shaken—and particularly as regards those which this building had been said to contain, and whose non-discovery haunted me still.

'The people of the village say there are relics—mani—in that temple—dêrmane,[2] or gudi'[3]—I remarked as casually as I could to our old friend, the *ex*-pâlâl, 'do they bury them in the ground?'

Âha,' with a Toda grunt and shake of the head.

'Then where are they?'

Now this Toda had told us many things, and all he had said had proved to be true. Moreover neither he nor any one else had the slightest conception that a visit had been paid to the inside of the dêrmane, or that we entertained any particular interest in it. He must merely have thought to himself from the question, this is another of Paul Pry's 'I only wanted to know.'

He glanced up sideways at me, and

By his countenance
Enjoin'd me silence.

With his hand to the side of his mouth, he said in a low voice 'Under the stone on the top of the roof.'

Sold!!

I look on this dêrmane as an exceptional curiosity, possessing for our purposes an interest peculiarly its own. In the first place, it is unique in contour, though *constructed as to plan*

[2] Dêrmane = *Gods-house—residence of the Gods.*

[3] Gudi—*a temple*; a word probably borrowed from the Badagas. In Sanskrit, kudi is a *house* and a *curve*. In Telugu, it is used for a *circle* and a *temple*. In Kanarese it is a *temple*, and is written gudi. [POPE.]

CHAP. XIX.

*under the same general ideas*, and apparently for similar purposes as the dairy of a tirièri or the pâlthchi of any Mand. Then it holds a vat—which no other building does—whose use is not understood by the vorshâl in charge, and whose very existence is, I feel nearly certain, unknown to the people. If the vat was constructed for sacrificial purposes, then its use has been discontinued and forgotten, though the priest in charge is a vorshâl or sacrifice man.[4]

It is situated on an exposed site bearing the outlines of stone walls, built on a largeness of scale, and in a form, nowhere else found amongst these people—with a Kromlech and numerous Kairns dotted close about.

The specific name by which it is known—boath[5]—is peculiar, and applicable solely to that style of structure.

Now it should be borne in mind, if we would form an opinion on the origin of this edifice, that the Todas are unimaginative creatures of one idea; having one way of doing everything: intolerant of change or deviation from custom, unless for some manifestly practical advantage. How then do we find such a race in occupation of an eccentric building which does not fit in with any of its other institutions? Not a tirièri—for it is of lower grade in Toda estimation; its servant a vorshâl, not a God. Not an ordinary pâlthchi, for one of the largest size exists apart, within a few paces of it.

As there is nobody who can give an explanation of the phenomenon, I will submit a theory of my own for consideration. May the boath not be the bethel of some tribe contemporaneous with, and cognate to, the Todas, which, taking refuge like them on these hills, died out in their presence—

[4] See Note 4 of Chapter VIII.

[5] Boath. An enclosed Jain temple is basti.

It may be deemed fanciful to refer to booth or bothy. The Welsh is bwth, the Gaelic is both. This word is of very extensive use. The Tamil vîḍ and Kanarese bîḍ = *house*, may be compared.

The Todas and Drâvidians generally, have much in common with the Celtic tribes. [POPE.]

the Todas thus becoming inheritors of a curious and sacred building, possessing some relics, and possibly a herd of cattle attached? CHAP. XIX.

The point of interest in this theory consists greatly in the possibility of the original owners of this boath being the builders of the circles, Kairns or Kromlechs,[6] or the erecters of the upright stones—Genesis xxviii. 18, 19—which are all found in great abundance on these hills.

Is this form of temple or surrounding wall found elsewhere—in other parts of the world—in connection with these erections and with massive ruins? Let us read an extract from the 'Explorations in the Peninsula of Sinai,' written by the Rev. F. W. Holland, and which will be found in 'The Recovery of Jerusalem.' 'During my wanderings in 1867,' he says, 'I found that there were other ruins of a much older date: houses similar in form to the Bothan, or beehive houses in Scotland, built of rough and massive stones, about five feet high, and forty to fifty feet in circumference, with no windows, and one small door about twenty inches high. . . . These houses are generally found in groups, and near them are often seen the ruins of tombs—circles of massive stones—similar to those which in England and Scotland are called Druids' circles.'[7]

[6] See Chapter I.

[7] Wilson Warren, 'The Recovery of Jerusalem.'

# CHAPTER XX.

## THE GREEN FUNERAL.

*The two Funerals described—Last office to a dying Toda—The corpse journeys to the Kêdu Mand—The Kêdu Mand described—Obsequies—'Dust to dust'—Slaughter of Cattle—The ashes of the dead—Kotas remove the Carcasses of Cattle.*

CHAP. XX.

THE ceremonies observed on the death of a Toda may be divided into two groups; the first of which, appertaining to the funeral proper, and termed the green funeral or hase[1] kêdu,[2] is performed within a day or two after death. The second, styled the dry funeral or bara[3] kêdu, which will be described in full in the next Chapter, and is more of a commemorative nature, was formerly celebrated in the course of two or three months after the first. It was, as I understand, delayed mainly by local circumstances affecting the general interests of the community. Of late years, however, certain restrictions which the Government of Madras placed on the slaughter of cattle at the ceremonies, have caused the people to postpone these final obsequies until the death of several Todas should enable them, by combining sundry funerals, to make one great show. Hence the bara kêdu is often not effected until the lapse of a twelvemonth after death.

[1] Hase or pach or pache. Root in Drâvidian is paç = *tender, soft, raw, green.* Perhaps allied to Sansk. vaçanta = *spring.* Gaelic fas = *spring.* [POPE.]

[2] Kêdu. Tamil. Kanarese = *destruction, death.*
Telugu. Cheḍu = *perish.*
Compare Sanskrit kshi (ṇu) = *perish.* [POPE.]

[3] Bara. Tamil var. Kanarese and Telugu bar = *dry, parched, sterile, famine.* Compare Eng. bare. [POPE.]

In my desire to witness a Toda's deathbed, as well as all the ceremonies consequent thereon, I had promised a handsome present to anyone who would bring me timely information, whether by night or by day, of an approaching event; when I noticed a lad move off quietly with bright hope on his countenance, and shortly afterwards I overtook him striding over hill and dale, straight as a bird to his quarry. The reply to my enquiry where he was going was translated by the Tamil interpreter, 'Going to see somebody *too much* sick.' He was in fact on his road to some invalid Toda, whose case he thought bad.

When a man is so ill as to lead to the expectation of his early demise, he is dressed up in the ornaments and jewellery of his house, in order that he may make a respectable corpse. These he will wear until he either dies or recovers. Indeed a man who had revived from what was thought his death-bed has been observed parading about very proud and distinguished looking; wearing the finery with which he had been bedecked for his own funeral, and which he would be permitted to carry till he really departed this life.

When on the point of death, the last office his kin perform for their relative, is to give him milk, if only a drop or two, to drink. No prayer is said, nor are the Gods invoked in any way.

It is well here to observe, as reflecting on other social prejudices, that there is no religious necessity for *a son* to perform any one of the ceremonies attending on a Toda's death and funeral. The laws of Manou style the eldest son 'him who is begotten to perform the duty,' and in consequence of this absolute necessity for a son, we find amongst the Aryas a high importance set upon male progeny. The Todas, however, whilst equally craving for sons, yet do not require them for any such religious object. The pride in male children appears to be based upon less definable causes, so much so as to seem almost inherent in man.

The decorated corpse is now wrapped in a new mantle, into

CHAP. XX.

the pockets of which, food, such as roast grain, sugar, *et cetera*, and small pieces of wood are put. He is now ready for his journey to amnôr: he has food for the road.

It is a fact of interest and worth noting in connection with this narrative, that the Badagas—who have been already described as believed to be cognate to the Todas—preserve the custom common to the Greeks, of placing an *obolus* in the mouth of the dying man. So important do the Badagas consider the due performance of this last rite to the living, that they will keep a supply of this metal disc about the person in order that one may always be at hand for use on occasion. But to continue:—

The body is brought out from the little house and laid with care on the rough bier, formed with branches from the village grove.

The nearest kêdu Mand is out on a spur of that hill we see on the horizon, full six miles off. So there is no time to be lost. Good bye, dear old crone—his grandmother, and the young aunt with the new-born babe, and that sad little assembly of children, all brothers, sisters, uncles, nieces, of the dead man; some too old, others too young, all too weak, to trudge to the horizon over hill and dale.

Now his house is shut up: the little door is closed. Twigs and leaves lying scattered on the ground: a neglected grindstone leaning against the wall: a piece of forgotten matting: the cat rubbing its ill-fed body on the door panel: the pertinacious flies about the house—all conspire to tell the tale of the savage's deserted dwelling, and the drama just enacted.

The corpse is rested for a few moments on the low surrounding wall, whilst its tall bearers step into the village pathway. The little family group which is to remain, crouches weeping close by. The others are busy with their adjustments preparatory to the long walk. The whole picture is before us; primitive, simple, or savage, yet these people have a thorough human appreciation of the moment.

Raise the stretcher into the path: carry in your hands through the soft bit, pitted with buffalo hoof marks: past the slushy pound: across the little trickling burn with its fern-brake and flower-studded margin, made by Nature so unconstrained and graceful, as though she hoped, even against all hope, with untiring persistency, that the day might come when some might turn to admire her, and from contemplating the power that made those silent but appealing beauties, glean a moral lesson.

Up with the burden on your shoulders. The primitive cortège has left the Mand; the man's ancestral home, its greenwood and the rippling stream, behind. It has passed the ragged cattle pen, and the group of calves nibbling herbage in the moist lea. The well-worn village path has opened out and divided into numerous narrow cattle tracks, up some of which our small party of mourners winds from the secluded village site, to the open high ground ahead.

Strange and rarely primitive is this be-mantled, bareheaded company of men and women, boys and girls. The corpse 'wobbles' on the unequal shoulders of its four bearers, striding along so direct: pursued closely by the train of quick-stepping women, suckling infants under their mantles as they go: and by a prolonged concourse of lightly laden men, carrying fuel for the pyre or little bundles and vessels containing food: flanked by sanguine youths, who, unburdened and without a care, straggle alongside, regardless of all paths. The pace has grown too fast for sobs.

The fresh wind, through the brilliant sunshine, now blows over the wold, without moving the crisp primeval grass which crackles as they pass, but tossing about the women's curls with wanton freedom, and leading to a general rearrangement of togas.

Airily along the gentle slope of the spur extending its unbroken length gradually down to the boggy tarn ahead. We pass the half-wild herd belonging to a neighbouring Mand,

CHAP. XX.

grazing under supervision of the lank boys who now approach to view the procession. A timid cow, scenting something unwonted, looks up alarmed, wheels round suddenly and bolts: wheels again, stops, and stares from a distance. A dozen others imitate her conduct exactly. Then the whole herd advances step by step, in circling line. A word or two from the boys, and all resume grazing except one inquisitive daughter of her mother, who singly follows the procession with nose uplifted, smelling, till she finds herself isolated from her comrades—then stops and gazes. Onwards proceeds the cortège.

Across the bog by the well-known track. Up again to the high land. Along the winding crests of the smooth continuous hills. Past another Mand nestling in a sleepy hollow; its cattle-pen looking in the bird's-eye view more important than the little human habitations.

Obviously we near the kêdu Mand, for, converging towards one focus, twos and threes of invited friends are seen tracing their different courses from out secluded valleys; now seemingly close at hand as they crest the rising ground, now lost to view—till suddenly we come on them all, quietly waiting to salute the corpse as it arrives on the ground.

Here, too, a compact little body of cows, *still belonging to the deceased*, which, snorting and scrubbing against one another, hot and fly-worried, with every tail in motion, come pushing along from the dead man's village, whence they have been driven through pasture and through bog land, to perform their part in the approaching obsequies.

The kêdu Mand consists of a stone cattle-pen, and a hut of the ordinary village dairy type, which when erected for a man's rites is styled kêd nâr pâlthchi or funeral district dairy, but when for a woman is termed kêd nâr ârsh, or funeral district house.[4] Also the customary rivulet of water, the little wood

[4] Mr. Metz is my authority. The nicety of the distinction is not understood.

—somewhat shabby I notice, as if, when fuel ran short, a supply was often cut from it—and an open spot termed the âthârê.[5]

Arrived at the Mand after their hot and depressing trudge, the party deposit their various burdens; the food supply in the hut, and the bier on the ground, either inside or outside the little house, according to the state of the weather. Amidst the exchange of salutations going on all around between the different new arrivals, some engage themselves in building the pyre on the âthârê; and some of the women prepare meals inside the hut, for the large concourse of visitors, many of whom have been hurriedly summoned from long distances over the hills, and will be hungry. Others of the relatives most nearly interested, remain a lamenting group around the body.

When the funeral pile has been constructed and the last of the expected guests has arrived, a little bell—getti, not konku[6]—is hung round the necks of each of the cattle, accompanied by the words 'avan od atvo, go with him.' They are then driven in a group near to the corpse. A little hole is dug through the turf conveniently close by; from which the mourners, male and female, approaching one by one, take thrice, a handful of soil and throw it towards the buffalos: then three times more on to the prostrate body, saying 'purzh ulgama, purzh ulgama, purzh ulgama,'[7] meaning 'Let him go into the soil.' Each baby of the family had the fingers of its small hand unfurled and guided to perform this

[5] Âthârê. Âthârb. Âthârm. Perhaps from the Sanskrit ad'hâra, which is used as = *fundamental*.

The meaning would be, *the place where the final rites are performed.* [POPE.]

[6] In Chapter XVI. it was explained that getti is the ordinary existing cattle-bell of the district. I never saw a konku except as a tiriêri relic.

[7] Purzh ulgama. In Tamil puṛuthi is *dust, soil, fine earth.* This Ṛ is a strong lingual, and sounds like rlz.

Uḷ is a Drâvidian root for *in, within.* In Kanarese, oḷagê = *within.* The termination A forms the optative. [POPE.]

last rite; smiling the while, in infant wonder and approval at this new game.

The meaning of the words as, voluntarily and entirely without suggestion, explained by a Toda, is 'as we were born of the earth, we return to it.' The recumbent corpse is now raised a little in the arms of his relatives, as if to give it an air of authority. Then the cows, each with two men clinging round her horns and neck, having been dragged in succession up to their master, his dead arm is raised, and the hand made to touch the horns.

A *sacred fire* is now made by *igniting sticks by friction.*[8] The pyre is lighted. Now the corpse still in the arms of these punctilious relatives is raised over the pyre, swung lengthwise three times from side to side, then deposited—in its mantle and ornaments—on the wood, with its *face downwards*: the people crying, 'We shall kill buffalos for you.' 'You are going to amnôr.' 'May you have milk to drink.' 'May it be well with you.' 'May all thy sins go,' and so on. A lock of hair is cut off at this time.

I was careful to ascertain that the placing the body with its face downwards had not been an accidental circumstance. The people could give no reason for the act beyond their usual answer, 'It is our custom.' Nor had satirical objections to the practice of turning their friends' bodies upside down at the moment of starting for amnôr, the effect of drawing from them any excuse for, or vindication of, the apparently senseless act.

One or two cow buffalos are now despatched. The 'happy release' is performed by a single blow made on the poll of the creature's crouched head with the butt end of an axe, whilst it is held by a couple of strong men interlacing their arms over its neck and horns. As each animal falls, men, women, and children group themselves round its head, and fondle, caress,

[8] Probably by the Vorshâl. See Chapter VIII.

No. 22

AUTOTYPE, LONDON

MOURNING.

and kiss its face: then sitting in groups of pairs—both sexes indiscriminately—with the tops of their foreheads joined, give way to wailing and lamentation. A most singular and interesting spectacle, rendered more piquant and real, by the aspect of a small boy who, not finding his pair, was running about from one crying group to another, blubbering till his face was distorted and swollen, looking amongst the mantles for a spare head to rest his own against.

Thus they remain till the body has been consumed: when the lock of hair that had been cut off, together with portions of the half-burnt skull—nirrzh[9]—are collected in a piece of cloth, to be deposited in a corner of his house,[10] henceforth kept shut up, till the bara kêdu.

The silver and gold of the burnt jewellery are sought for from the ashes, but little valueless odds and ends—as knives, iron rings and other ornaments, the rings off the ends of wooden pestles—together with the ashes of the dead, are buried in the ground. The hole which contains these remains is then filled up with earth, on which water is poured. Over all a stone. The earthen vessel which held the water is broken.

Having saluted the spot where the ashes have been buried, by touching it with their foreheads, they leave the place, avoiding it henceforward, but merely on account of the painful associations connected with it. A person once dead is never *named*, though he may be made the subject of conversation.

It is a mistake to suppose these people have a feast—a jollification—after this funeral. Indeed they are as little disposed for anything of the sort as we should be in the same position. But a number of friends from a distance have to be fed, and as all are not real *mourners*, and have many of them brought excellent appetites, they eat.

[9] Nirrzh. Nîrru. = *sacred ashes, ashes.* This is at the root of it. [POPE.]

[10] Some such custom would be the origin of the Manes and Penates.

The funeral ceremonies of women and children are, I was informed, the same as for men; fewer cattle are killed, and perhaps not so large an assembly of folk are present, but in other respects they are identical.

The carcases of the slaughtered cattle are left lying on the ground. So soon as the place is clear, they will be carried off by the Kotas, who have already assembled for the sake of this meat.

Toda men sometimes shave their heads and beards as a sign of mourning, though not often. Not so those of the Peiki clan, because 'they perform sacred offices.' Women never cut their hair off.

The cremation of the body is performed with the wood of certain (seven) varieties of trees, whose names I do not know. On showing samples of them, which had been collected for me by a young man, to a pâlâl, he swept them aside with his hand, implying that, compared with the tûde, which he treated with great respect, they were as nothing.

## CHAPTER XXI.

### THE DRY FUNERAL.

*The burning of a Flute, Bow, and Arrows—The Dance—Scene with the Sacrificial Cattle—Again 'dust to dust'—Catching the Cattle—The Sacrifice—The Cattle-bell—No Priest concerned in the Ceremonies—Sprinkling of blood—Final burning of the Manes—The Kotas remove the dead Cattle.*



IF the first obsequies may be held to express feeling and mournful sentiments for the deceased as true and sound as any we exhibit in like circumstances; the ceremonies of the bara kêdu or dry funeral may with equal justice be looked on as partaking both of a propitiatory provisional nature and of a commemorative festival character—as if performed with the object of speeding the general welfare of the friend gone to the unknown country: but in a style of show and hospitality somewhat commensurate with his worldly importance.

Hence we find the Todas congregate in considerable numbers at the kêdu Mand, and display their ornaments on these occasions: feeding also a large assembly of their own and neighbouring tribes, conspicuous amongst which, the Kotas, who attend with much discordant piping or flageolet music (they are the musicians—save the mark!—of these hills). A very well-behaved multitude, but whose presence may be noted as readily by the nose as by other organs.[1]

In the very early morning of the first of a two days'

[1] One now quite understands the value of the Toda expression, 'I see with my nose.'

CHAP. XXI.

ceremonial, and long before these guests have begun to arrive, the family of the deceased have a little private ordinance of their own; in burning all his personal property, such as his stick or staff, the honnu or milk vessel, and clothes: also a *flute* or flageolet, and a model of *a bow with bamboo 'strings,' and arrows.*[2] I could not ascertain any reason whatever for this musical instrument and these spurious weapons being burnt. Be it particularly borne in mind that the Todas have no sense of music and do not possess a flute in the whole tribe: that they never hunt, and have no weapons of the chase. These toys are made by the Kotas entirely for the occasion. Thus it was, I experienced some difficulty in buying the bow, which will be found in photograph No. 15. The first question asked of the man who purchased it for me from the Kota, was 'Who is dead?'

The opening public ceremony of the day, is a kind of dance performed by from twenty to fifty men. The dance I witnessed was monotonous enough. It consisted of the body of men, keeping step whilst striding round and round like the spokes of a wheel; each spoke having three men arm in arm: and all exclaiming, rather than shouting, 'A! U! A! U!'[3] in time with their steps. I could trace nothing symbolic in the exhibition except that strange number three, which I notice in all religious matters, to be constantly appearing. It may be that the dance and shout are both merely a Toda mode of giving vent and expression to a festive state of mind.

Whilst this dance is being carried on by the men, the women prepare food in the hut described in the last Chapter, which has been repaired or renewed for this occasion. Here all the guests assemble, the two sexes sitting apart. The women of the family serve out the supplies from the diminutive door to

[2] Captain Forsyth, in his 'Highlands of Central India,' writes of the Bygas, 'their bows are made entirely of the bamboo, "string" and all.'

[3] The Toda word for *I shout,* is 'A! U! bisharthken,' or *I call out A! U!*

the men, who hand them round to all impartially. The repast over, dancing is resumed by some, whilst the younger or more active proceed to collect the cow-buffaloes that will be wanted for the morrow, and to shut them up in the pound. Meanwhile, as might be anticipated, the daughters of Eve air their finery and keep their bright eyes and teeth in practice.

The proceedings of the second day are very striking. Scene ;—The circular pen, of about thirty feet diameter, with surrounding wall, of unusual strength and neatness, about five feet high and three and a half or four feet broad, on which a dense crowd of people—Todas, Kotas, Badagas, and others—are seated, each man with staff and toga. Sun hot. Smell strong. Buzz of many voices. Squeak of many instruments. A group of buffaloes within the pound, of which, one for each dead man, wears a bell—getti, not konku—scared and desperate from the excitement of the festivity, and the alarming presence of the noisy multitude on the wall, hedging them in on every side. They make frequent timorous dashes at the wall: are as often repulsed with shouts and stick gesticulations. They crowd again, tails together, horns outwards—a habit of defence they have acquired on their hill sides to keep off wild animals: then charge the wall again, and are again repulsed. These little feints and attitudes of defence, keep up the animation of the ring till the moment has come ; when the remains of the dead, the insignificant manes—the bit of skull and lock of hair, some handfuls of ashes, a knuckle-bone or two—which have been preserved in a corner of the dwelling since the day of cremation, and now enclosed in the neat plaits of a new mantle, are laid at the gateway of the cattle pen: the ashes of the several dead whose obsequies are this day being observed, lying in the different folds of one single toga. The relatives collect around. No priest—pâlâl or kâvilâl—is present. A little hole is dug in the turf at the very opening of the pound; to which, as before described, each interested kinsman and woman, each adult and child, approaching

CHAP. XXI.

in succession, takes from it three handfuls of earth, and throws toward the group of buffaloes, who now facing the barred opening with heads down and eyes distended, stand, in the sudden and unwonted silence of this rite, apprehensive of the worst. Three more handfuls are thrown on to the mantle.

A small body of young and active men now clamber over the wall, dropping nimbly into the fold full of these scared animals. With much dexterity they seize them, singling out one at a time; two men approaching from behind either side of the head, grapple the creature's horns, and interlace their arms over its neck, so as to bring their whole weight and strength to bear, until they have the animal under control: in which work they are assisted by a third man who keeps a purchase on the extended tail, whilst others, with what appeared to me insufficient motive, belaboured its back with their sticks.

I am induced to the belief that the motive was insufficient, because these cattle would no doubt have permitted themselves to be caught far more readily without any beating. Hence I conclude that the object in maltreating the animal which is habitually used with consideration, and that knows and obeys their voice so well, must have some hidden meaning. But what that meaning may be I cannot suggest, for the people are singularly free from superstition.

It has been stated that, in former times, when less subject to the police, the animals were on these occasions, clubbed, 'not to death, but to inability to move, by a broken spine; and then left to die in agony.'[4] But, in my opinion, this account needs confirmation. Mr. Metz tells me he has seen a buffalo killed by the club which is depicted on photograph No. 15, and which they often carry at these festivals; but the deed was accidental. The fact still remains that on the occasion of funerals the Todas treat their cattle with unusual violence.

[4] Letter from the Collector of Coimbatore to the Government of Madras, in the Revenue Department, dated 1856.

When all the animals have thus been seized, and stand grouped in the pen, in separate knots, each consisting of a snorting buffalo, hard held, head and tail, by a few perspiring and breathless men, the bars of the gateway are withdrawn. One struggle more on the part of the cattle, as they pass through the gateway, to get free. Then the plunging, scuffling masses are brought down to the âthârê, where, one by one, as narrated in the last chapter, these milch cows are killed. As each is felled, and comes down on its knees, the mantle containing the ashes of the dead is laid on the ground, so that the nose of the prostrate creature may rest on the cloth, giving out its life in contact with her master's remains.

The mourners, at this time fondle the animal's face, as in the first funeral, giving way to tears with every appearance of deep and poignant grief. In their wailing, 'the expressions of sorrow,' writes Mr. Metz, 'to which they give utterance, are generally in the form of questions to (the spirit of?) the deceased; such as "Are you suffering from fever?" "Are your buffaloes thriving?" "Why did you leave us so soon?"[5] "Have you gone to amnôr?"'

Mr. Metz found that in the midst of this crying they would hold out their hands to him for a present; from which circumstance he concludes that the lamentations are uttered, not from grief, but simply pursuant to established custom. I conceive that formerly, when the obsequies took place very shortly after the green funeral, these cries were probably genuine, but that the postponement of the ceremonies of the dry funeral for the period of about a year, has no doubt injured the reality of the scene.

I have said that one buffalo for each person whose funeral is being celebrated, wears a bell—getti. This bell is not holy, but purchased in the bazaar. I could not find a reason for the practice, receiving the usual answers to my enquiry: 'It is shastr,' or 'It is our custom,' or 'Dêr or Swâmi made it so.'

[5] Often said, 'You have been but three days with us.'

CHAP. XXI.

It may be, that the bell is a religious symbol of the bell-god —konku dêr. (Note, that herds of cattle, ordinary village droves, never wear a bell.)

I was careful to ascertain if, as has been asserted, a priest superintended on these occasions. My informant, the *ex*-pâlâl, told me, 'We—the pâlâl and kâvilâl—have no duties at a kêdu, nor do we receive presents after a death. If anyone has seen us at a funeral, it is because we want to know what is going on in the district, for we live such lonely lives. But we keep at a distance, because no one may touch us.'

What I have narrated, is a just description of funeral obsequies properly executed, and as indeed, so far as adherence to form goes, they are carried out to this day. But I have ascertained, without any doubt remaining in my own mind, the truth of what Dr. Shortt has written;[6] that old and barren cows are often slain at these funerals.[7] It was formerly the custom to despatch a considerable number of the deceased's own herd for his support in amnôr. But whether the rise in value of buffaloes, or any increase of relative poverty amongst the people, has rendered them loath to deprive the living of a valuable means of sustenance; or if the fact of the Governing Power having limited the slaughter, has demoralised their minds, are points which I cannot decide. The truth remains, that whilst still believing in the necessity for providing the deceased with nutriment, they practically lessen that reduced limit, by despatching what no one knows better than they do, is actually worthless.

This early step in civilisation is, then, a pace backwards —commercial gain, by moral loss.

On the morning after the bara kêdu, before daybreak, the mantle containing the ashes is taken to the âthârê, at which the original cremation took place. Another buffalo is then killed—a male if for a Peiki or Pekkan: a female if for any of

[6] Shortt, 'Tribes on the Neilgherries.'

[7] See Chapter VII., where I write on the sources of nicknames.

No. 23

AUTOTYPE, LONDON.

MY INFORMANT.

the other three clans—and blood having been taken from the artery of one of the fore legs, at the point of junction with the body, it is sprinkled on the piece of skull preserved from cremation. Nothing is said at the time, and the Todas have no name for the ceremony beyond describing it as, bâkh nirrzhk idu, or 'put the blood to the ashes.' The mantle and its contents are now completely burnt.[8]

In none of the ceremonies described, have I seen any active acknowledgment of the existence of a God.

The main object of the festivities appears to be to gratify a pious desire to further the material welfare of their friend in amnôr, and to bow him out of this world with ceremony and honour. The whole is a grave, practical affair, in which their natural fondness for a prolonged sensation, their domestic and also their wasteful dispositions are all thoroughly gratified. He has gone to amnôr. Send one or two cows at once, at time of death—with more, with plenty, to follow. They are as realistic in this matter as the ancient Britons, who used to give *post-obits* payable in the next world. When asked what became of infants who died, they said, 'Those who have gone before, take care of them.' Their little programme is cut and dry, and the people, harmless race, are quite comfortable in their belief.

If the hut erected for these obsequies was made for a woman, it is now burnt. If for a man, it is not touched.[9]

The Kotas remove the carcases.

[8] Mr. Metz very kindly gave me the information contained in this paragraph. I believe it likely that the personal property; flute, bow and arrows, are also burnt at this time, and not prior to the festivities. The circumstances narrated are correct, though perhaps their sequence is not so. It is not easy to obtain absolutely reliable information from these untutored people: and I did not witness either of the two ceremonies myself.

[9] Mr. Metz authorises this statement.

# CHAPTER XXII.

## RELIGIOUS CULTURE.

*Toda Religion, a development from a Material Nucleus—The Milk-giver an object of Deep Reverence—Milkmen are Priests, then Gods—Todas have a bias in favour of Light as the Manifestation of Divinity—Not Idolatrous—Do not make offerings to a God—Believe in Transmigration—Callous on Demonolatry—Influenced in religious matters by other Races—Todas of Turanian stage of culture.*

CHAP. XXII.

WHAT we have seen in Toda rites and ceremonies, is little else than the arrangements which a pastoral and communistic people have made for the provision and care of an article of food, doubtless at one time essential, not merely for due sustenance, but to their very existence in the land. These customs having through the course of ages so mellowed as to have acquired all the effect and influence of sanctity, we find ourselves now in the interesting position of actual witnesses to the growth of the earliest germs of religious belief and observance, as they develop in the mind of primitive man from the material nucleus whence they originated.

We note that stage, when the cow, the milk-giver and support on which the people have depended almost from all time, has grown from an object of the greatest solicitude, to become one of deep reverence, and—so far as they have yet learnt to express themselves—of worship. The flesh is not eaten. Its milk is almost sacred. The chattels of early herds—the cow-bell in particular—have matured into Gods, and dairies bear the conception of temples.

We find that common milkmen have, by virtue of the

sacred nature of such office, advanced in popular estimation until they are viewed in the aspect of priests. The high priest, from being a servant of certain Gods, has become confused with Godhead itself. A family styling itself 'sons of the Gods,' has developed—though without arrogation to caste pretensions—into a Levitical clan, inheritors of the highest priestly office; its males being prepared and chastened thereto in sacred groves, by the use of a plant set apart for the purpose, and by abstinence from sensual pleasures; the females of the entire tribe, being not only excluded from participation in such duties, but debarred approach to all holy precincts.

These points appear to me to embrace the whole of what may be held to be Toda—performed—religion unadulterated.

They acknowledge the existence of Gods, *perhaps* even of a Supreme God—Ûsuru[1] Swâmi—but their ideas on the subject are quite undeveloped. I think I trace in them a partiality to the regard of *light*—apart from fire—as *par excellence*, the manifestation of divinity. Their beliefs, whatever they may be, are so little attended with formal signs of adoration, that we cannot, with any degree of confidence, assert this or that to be their creed. Still I believe I have grounds for the opinion that these people have a strong bias in favour of *light*;[2] the natural bent of their mind being such, that if any other race would work out for them the idea, connecting Ûsuru Swâmi with some such attribute of divinity as light, they could soon be brought to exalt Bêl into 'a king above all gods:' the more readily if deference to the cow was inculcated with such a teaching.

I submit the suggestion as one having a possible value in determining the ethnic affinities of the Toda race: and as

[1] See note 3 of Chapter XII.

[2] Note the Toda words in Chapter XXIX., showing how frequently the word 'bel' occurs, even in my small vocabulary; see *dawn*, *light*, *silver*, *bird*, *white*. Also, the names of men, and of Gods, given in previous Chapters.

CHAP. XXII.

pointing to an interesting stage in Turanian progress; that, whence various ancient creeds have sprung and ramified.

The Toda religion has not the slightest sympathy with idolatry, nor does it pay attention to natural objects, as trees or rivers: to birds, beasts, or reptiles: nor to the elements. No offerings to a God, whether of flesh—human or animal—or fruit of the soil, are made: no human victims and no self-torture. It is not that they have risen above such prejudices; they seem to me rather, not to have attained the stage when religious observances commence. Circumcision is not performed. The memory of forefathers is piously regarded, but the feeling has not expanded through veneration, into any form of hero-worship.

They believe in transmigration, but whether of soul or body probably few have formed very distinct ideas. The funeral service seems to favour the idea that the transition of the soul is the dogma which, though unexpressed, lies like an instinct in their minds: coupled with the idea that the soul is a living solid, a real duplicate Toda requiring food. But the whole scheme of their observances is so illogical, that it is impossible to deduce therefrom any clear definition of a creed.

Endeavour has been made in Chapters VIII. and IX. to convey, in brief terms, the reasons for my confidence, that sobriety, and general abstinence from exciting meat diet, are largely natural to this people. The practice certainly forms at present no part of their religious observance.

I would place the state of their belief in witchcraft and the work of demons and other unseen agencies, somewhat on a parallel with that of their knowledge of Divine work. Neither one nor the other, troubles them much. Perhaps I may best define the relative feeling, by saying, that they fear the former and hope most of the latter. Though they do, to a certain extent, practise demonolatry, they do not do so with the enthusiasm of other primitive races of South India. Indeed I had not one opportunity of witnessing feats of exorcism.

I incline to the belief that in any matters of religion beyond what I have described, they have been influenced through the proximity of cognate races, who themselves, again, have at different periods, been variously Hinduized or inoculated with the strange customs of other tribes in India, cognate or otherwise. Thus, through the Âryas, the Toda sense of adoration has been educated; more Gods have been introduced than he knows what to do with: and his natural love of relics has been intensified and improved. From being at first memorials of cattle herds, the relics have grown to be venerated souvenirs of ancestors. On the other hand, the mildness and contentedness of the tribe, have—so I think—led them to drop or to avoid much of the demonolatrous habit of other members of that Drâvidian race to which they belong. Certainly any superior ideas; any notions of the soul, or of sin, and all forms of invocation in prayer, small as even collectively they may appear to be, bear the appearance of their having come to them through the instrumentality of the Âryas; partly, no doubt, from Brahmanical sources: in part perhaps, in course of some very early contiguity, antecedent to the migration of either race, from a common cradle land, into India. Even the waste of good meat is to my mind suggestive of similar influences.

I will conclude this chapter in the words of Mr. Baring-Gould, which, applied to the Turanian state of progress, are equally descriptive of Toda culture. 'Impressed with a vague and child-like sense of the mysterious, it has not advanced into the idealising stage. God to the nomads of Northern Asia, is awful, undefined. They feel His presence about them, above them, and, with dazzled and bewildered mind, seek to know nothing more.' [3]

[3] Baring-Gould, 'The Origin and Development of Religious Belief.'

## CHAPTER XXIII.

### INFANTICIDE.

*Infanticide probably, at some time, practised by every Race—Primeval man's early difficulties—His Invention for restricting the Expansion of his Race—Infanticide perhaps marks a Stage in human Progress—The ancient Britons infanticidal—Infanticide of primitive Races a work of Love—Infanticide may be extinct, whilst Statistics imply its Continuance—A dynamical problem solved by the Todas—Infanticide the crime of weak Races, of Dolichocephali.*

CHAP. XXIII.

THE more closely we enquire into the origin or causes of infanticide—writing of the practice, not in the light of a vulgar crime, to be ranked with murder, but as a national remedy for tiding over family difficulties—the more certainly will it be proved that it bears an antiquity as great, and a freshness in its latest instances as modern, as every other malpractice which owes inducements in its commission to the suggestions of weak dispositions, or to good though mistaken motives.

We read of the custom prevailing, under one pretext or another, among savage or primitive people, in the earliest narratives that have been chronicled in writing. We hear of it also in classic times as the common habit of nations then setting examples of civilisation. It is not only the modern practice of this representative of a prehistoric race, but it is the present custom of other tribes and nationalities—both those, possibly cognate to the Todas, and some which, occupying tracts in distant parts of the world, must have been distinct from them through long ages of time.

Probably, no nation can justly escape the charge of being

descended of infanticidal ancestors, if only the vast antiquity and the vast helplessness of the human race be duly considered.

Primeval man, in the earliest stage of a silvan life, would have depended for his very existence on such natural products of the land as he could readily obtain by means of his hands, aided by simple auxiliaries, as sticks and stones. Berries, roots and sprouts, insects and small vermin would have formed the first diet of omnivorous man. In due course, and under the demand on his intelligence for the support of an ever-increasing brood, he would have added variety and value to his food by hunting and fishing. But many generations would have lived and died, and long ages may have elapsed, ere the climax of husbandry had been attained, and man learnt to domesticate an animal and subsist on its milk.

Meanwhile the rude, untaught ancestor, relying upon natural sources, was the sport of vicissitudes of climate. Bad seasons destroyed the fruit on the trees, and dried up the herbage and springs. Birds and beasts competed with him for the food that remained. Families of man, herds of animals, flocks of birds, all acting under pressure of the identical necessity, would, up to a certain point, now act alike. The first impulse would be, to spread, to migrate. These separated families formed fresh nuclei, whence, at an accelerated rate of progress, tribes would expand on all sides. Nature would repeat herself. Migrations of whole tribes would succeed; and again the spectre of ever-increasing families, and no food.

Even though man migrated ever so slowly, the condition of change implies exposure, failure of supplies, and wars with tribes whose estates were encroached upon. Hampered by the weak, the aged, and deformed—supported through his humanity—and by the sex which, in the midst of all these difficulties, still devoted much time to bringing new members into a world already too full, our forefathers were fairly brought to bay.

In animal nature there are processes at work, tending to

CHAP. XXIII.

preserve some relation between the number of mouths to be filled and the amount of food available; and if only sufficient time be allowed for them to work, an equipoise is certainly established, in a way which we are accustomed to term 'naturally.' Not so with primitive man. Not being sufficiently prudent to abstain from marriage, he is constantly face to face with starvation.

One of the early proofs of untutored man's superiority over the animal, was supplied in the scheme he now devised to prevent a recurrence of famine. Migrations had failed; had probably even aggravated the difficulties he was ordinarily exposed to. The pace was growing too fast; human mouths were multiplying more rapidly than the human intellect could discover means of providing them with food. He noted that it was in this expanding habit of his people, and in the number of unproductive members, lay the danger to his race of dying from starvation: and he entertained no such hope that Nature could by any means be made to render more provision than what with ceaseless gleaning he had hitherto taken from her.

It must have been then; with hope gone, and annihilation staring him in the face, that he applied his incipient talent to the invention of *an artifice for restricting the expansive capacities of his race.* He little knew the dangerous nature of the stake he played for life, 'rushing in where angels fear to tread.' But in those cases where families did not suffer extermination by the drastic process which had in good faith been designed to save them, there time was gained, for man's child-like brain in its torpid evolution, to devise additional methods of gaining a living.

Thus, as I believe, infanticide of the nature described—true native of climes most favourable to human growth: true offspring of undeveloped races—is an institution which, like others we now heartily condemn, has in its time served a useful and practical end. A protest against the unaided and helpless condition in which they found themselves in the world; infanticide was probably the wisest because the only possible course for our barbarous forefathers to pursue. It perhaps even marks a necessary stage of human progress.

It is a custom of primitive races to consider on matters of grave tribal importance, in meetings of Elders—styled by the Todas kûtacâram. Such an august assembly would probably have decided whether, under certain such circumstances as we have been reviewing, the national course should take the direction of destroying the sick, the aged, or infants.

Herodotus describes, in an amusing manner, of some barbarous race, how a *young man*, sentenced to death because he was *sickly*, protested, and in vain, that he was in good health.

Ancient history tells us that in some at least of the States of Ancient Greece, the destruction of *both sexes*, born *weak* or *deformed*, was either commanded or allowed.

Amongst some living savages it is the practice to despatch the *aged* as they become feeble—all for the general good.

The systematic *infanticide* of *girls* is the remaining and most common alternative. I shall be able to show, in course of the chapters on the subject of polyandry, that some tribes of the ancient Britons practised female infanticide.

In proportion as nations advance in civilisation, property and wealth acquiring enhanced importance in public estimation, other and more complex considerations take the place of, or are superadded to, the list of original simple motives for limiting the size of families. But with them we have not in this little volume, any immediate concern, beyond suggesting the possibility that advanced races which largely practise female infanticide, may be, and probably are direct descendants of infanticidal ancestors—the typic cranial form remaining, though doubtless, somewhat developed—the aboriginal practice not having completely died out, but only changed in the direction and force of its current. In perfectly primitive races, their whole habit being simple, and the connection between

CHAP. XXIII.

their motives and their action proximate and uninvolved, we have the ready means afforded us of tracing, by a comparatively short and easy road, up to first causes, and thus of acquiring an insight into human impulse, which may prove serviceable even in judging of more complicated races, and must ever be interesting to obtain.

Fortunately for the preservation of the human race, which must otherwise have become extinct, primitive tribes are greatly attached to their children. We may safely assume, therefore, in the absence of evidence to the contrary, that where wholesale destruction of progeny by the parents themselves, is looked on as an obligation which has devolved on them in order to save their race from destruction—where in fact, it is largely a work of love—there the act would be performed without needless violence. In those tribes where children are killed in a heartless manner; whether by prolonged neglect or in some actively cruel method, we shall probably not be far wrong in ascribing such action to selfish, ignoble motives.

The following is the interesting evidence of an aged Toda, who speaks of what has been enacted under his own eyes. I give the narration very nearly in his own words;—

'I was a little boy when Mr. Sullivan[1] visited these mountains. In those days it was the custom to kill children; but the practice has long died out, and now one never hears of it.

'I don't know whether it was wrong or not to kill them, but we were very poor, and could not support our children. Now every one has a mantle—putkuli—but formerly there was only one for the whole family, and he who had to go out took the mantle; the rest remaining naked at home: naked all but the loin-cloth—kûvn.

[1] Mentioned in Chapter VIII., Note 3. The English officer who first mounted the Nilagiri plateau, and visited the homes of the Todas. Events of Toda importance all date from the visit of Sulaivan. Dore, as we quote the Christian era.

'We did not kill them to please any God, but because it was our custom.

'The mother never nursed the child—no, never! and the parents did not kill it. How could we do so! Do you think we could kill it ourselves!

'Those tell lies who say we laid it down before the opening of the buffalo pen, so that it might be run over and killed by the animals![2] We never did such things! and it is all nonsense, that we drowned it in buffalo's milk!'[3]

'Boys were never killed—only girls; not those who were sickly and deformed—*that would be a sin*—papum; but when we had one girl,[4] or in some families two girls, those that followed were killed.

'This is the way it was done. An old woman—kelachi[5]—used to take the child immediately it was born, and close its nostrils, ears, and mouth, with cloth thus'—here pantomimic action. 'It would shortly droop its head and go to sleep. We then *buried* it in the ground.[6] The kelachi got a present of four annas[7] for the deed.

'I don't know if the infants thus killed, go to amnôr. Who can tell such a thing!'

[2] I find the following passage in a letter from the Collector of Coimbatore, dated 25th June, 1856, to the address of the Secretary to the Government of Fort St. George, very kindly placed at my disposal by the Revenue Department, Madras; 'The mode of destroying the infant, if a female, is by exposing it the next morning at the door of the cattle kraal; when first opened, the whole herd, half wild, rush over and annihilate the wretched infant—the Todas never lifting their own hand against it.'

[3] This response had reference to a report then current, of this second mode of destroying children.

[4] The truth of this statement is confirmed by a letter from Mr. J. Sullivan, Collector of Coimbatore, dated 5th July, 1820, to the Secretary to the Governor of Fort St. George.

[5] Also means 'a female friend.' See Chapter VII., Note 1.

[6] It will be remembered that Todas *burn* their dead. By burying these infants, can it be, that the people thought they had got rid of them *for ever and ever*? Hence my question, to which the next paragraph forms a reply.

[7] Four annas is equal to sixpence of English money.

CHAP. XXIII.

I am well convinced that the old man spoke the strict truth in describing the practice of infanticide as a thing of the past; basing my belief, on the general appearance of things, rather than on statistics. (1.) If the custom still prevailed, the circumstance could not have remained hidden from the people of neighbouring tribes, with whom a very close degree of intimacy is maintained: and its commission forming a topic of conversation in their bazaars and meetings, the news would in due course certainly have reached our ears. (2.) The people sitting before us, in course of close examination as to the number and condition of their families, would undoubtedly have evinced by manner or voice, if at any time, we were approaching a dreaded and secret subject. (3.) Two, three, and even four living daughters were met with in families: and I may add, the girls looked in very good condition and as well cared for, as the rest of the household.

In the year 1822—or 48 years prior to the date of my census—the Government of Madras put a pressure on the Todas, in order to impel them to forsake their murderous practice.[8] But no statistics exist, and none can now be formed, that will afford us means of judging the actual state of the habit, anterior to that date.

In a previous chapter of this book—in that treating on the Census—the average age at which Toda women commence to bear children, is noted as 17 years. Those women therefore, who are 48 + 17 = 65 years old, must be the earliest who show the effect of the Government's repressive action. Hence it is, that we must look to the information regarding births and deaths which has been afforded by the mothers, rating from

[8] Owing to a deficiency in the records of the Madras Government, we do not know how infanticide was actually stopped; but the orders given in its letter of 21st July, 1820, were to frustrate the practice 'by all means of encouragement and persuasion.' In carrying these orders into effect, I believe that the persuasion employed was of an impressive character.

## Table No. VIII.

*Compiled from 'Statistics of Toda Families,' Table No.* IV., *in order to ascertain the progress made towards checking Infanticide. Arranged according to the 'present ages of Wives.'*

| Present Ages of Wives | No. on the List | Detail: Alive M. | Detail: Alive F. | Detail: Dead M. | Detail: Dead F. | Detail: Born M. | Detail: Born F. | Abstract, Progeny: Alive M. | Alive F. | Dead M. | Dead F. | Born M. | Born F. | Proportion of females to 100 males: A. | D. | B. | Remarks |
|---|---|---|---|---|---|---|---|---|---|---|---|---|---|---|---|---|---|
| 1 | 2 | 3 | 4 | 5 | 6 | 7 | 8 | 9 | 10 | 11 | 12 | 13 | 14 | 15 | 16 | 17 | 18 |
| 65 | 4 | 2 | 2 | 2 | 2 | 4 | 4 | | | | | | | | | | No families have been omitted, in extracting from 'Statistics of Toda Families,' except those whose returns appear to be doubtful, or are valueless to the subject under review. |
| 65 | 53 | 2 | 2 | 5 | 1 | 7 | 3 | | | | | | | | | | |
| 60 | 5 | 3 | 2 | 0 | 0 | 3 | 2 | 14 | 7 | 9 | 8 | 23 | 15 | 50 | 88·9 | 65·2 | |
| 60 | 6 | 4 | 0 | 0 | 2 | 4 | 2 | | | | | | | | | | |
| 60 | 28 | 3 | 1 | 2 | 3 | 5 | 4 | | | | | | | | | | |
| 55 | 27 | 1 | 2 | 3 | 0 | 4 | 2 | | | | | | | | | | |
| 55 | 43 | 4 | 1 | 2 | 2 | 6 | 3 | | | | | | | | | | |
| 55 | 49 | 3 | 1 | 1 | 0 | 4 | 1 | 17 | 9 | 9 | 5 | 26 | 14 | 52·9 | 55·6 | 53·8 | |
| 50 | 8 | 3 | 2 | 2 | 2 | 5 | 4 | | | | | | | | | | |
| 50 | 21 | 2 | 1 | 1 | 1 | 3 | 2 | | | | | | | | | | |
| 50 | 42 | 4 | 2 | 0 | 0 | 4 | 2 | | | | | | | | | | |
| 45 | 22 | 3 | 2 | 1 | 2 | 4 | 4 | | | | | | | | | | |
| 45 | 36 | 3 | 3 | 1 | 1 | 4 | 4 | | | | | | | | | | |
| 45 | 37 | 3 | 3 | 2 | 1 | 5 | 4 | | | | | | | | | | |
| 45 | 45 | 1 | 1 | 2 | 0 | 3 | 1 | | | | | | | | | | |
| 42 | 23 | 2 | 2 | 2 | 0 | 4 | 2 | 18 | 20 | 12 | 5 | 30 | 25 | 111·1 | 41·7 | 83·3 | |
| 42 | 54 | 0 | 1 | 0 | 0 | 0 | 1 | | | | | | | | | | |
| 40 | 3 | 3 | 2 | 0 | 0 | 3 | 2 | | | | | | | | | | |
| 40 | 15 | 0 | 4 | 2 | 0 | 2 | 4 | | | | | | | | | | |
| 40 | 44 | 3 | 2 | 2 | 1 | 5 | 3 | | | | | | | | | | |
| 38 | 10 | 5 | 1 | 1 | 0 | 6 | 1 | | | | | | | | | | |
| 35 | 18 | 2 | 2 | 0 | 1 | 2 | 3 | | | | | | | | | | |
| 30 | 19 | 0 | 3 | 0 | 0 | 0 | 3 | | | | | | | | | | |
| 30 | 46 | 4 | 1 | 0 | 0 | 4 | 1 | | | | | | | | | | |
| 28 | 35 | 1 | 0 | 0 | 0 | 1 | 0 | | | | | | | | | | |
| 28 | 26 | 2 | 0 | 0 | 0 | 2 | 0 | | | | | | | | | | |
| 27 | 1 | 2 | 2 | 0 | 0 | 2 | 2 | | | | | | | | | | |
| 26 | 51 | 2 | 1 | 0 | 0 | 2 | 1 | | | | | | | | | | |
| 25 | 2 | 1 | 2 | 1 | 0 | 2 | 2 | 24 | 17 | 2 | 3 | 26 | 20 | 70·8 | 150 | 77 | |
| 25 | 38 | 1 | 1 | 0 | 0 | 1 | 1 | | | | | | | | | | |
| 25 | 40 | 1 | 1 | 0 | 1 | 1 | 2 | | | | | | | | | | |
| 24 | 11 | 0 | 1 | 0 | 0 | 0 | 1 | | | | | | | | | | |
| 24 | 29 | 0 | 1 | 0 | 0 | 0 | 1 | | | | | | | | | | |
| 22 | 16 | 1 | 0 | 0 | 0 | 1 | 0 | | | | | | | | | | |
| 20 | 24 | 1 | 1 | 0 | 0 | 1 | 1 | | | | | | | | | | |
| 20 | 55 | 1 | 0 | 0 | 0 | 1 | 0 | | | | | | | | | | |
| 18 | 14 | 0 | 0 | 0 | 1 | 0 | 1 | | | | | | | | | | |
| | | 73 | 53 | 32 | 21 | 105 | 74 | | | | | | | 72·6 | 65·6 | 70·5 | |

CHAP. XXIII. 65 years down to the youngest married women, if we would trace the abatement of infanticide.

It is much to be regretted that the statistics of Table No. 8 do not afford a record so complete as could be desired; even to the degree I had fondly calculated on their doing, in the course of our careful enquiries in the field. The instances, though certainly few in number, should distinctly have pointed to the change that was being effected in the course of forty-eight years; by enabling us to trace some sort of declining scale in the contrast of the sexes. The disproportion between males and females is indeed great in the Table, but it neither increases nor lessens in any form of sequence.

I have allowed the Table a place in these pages, despite its acknowledged deficiencies, and notwithstanding that the statistics, taken by themselves, give every appearance of the venerable practice being in full vigour, whilst I am fully convinced by the circumstantial evidences which I have given, that such is not the truth. I have done so, because it thus obtains a value, in showing that *the practice of infanticide may be extinct, whilst statistics indicate its actual prevalence*: that, in fact, the strange numerical difference in the sexes, which the census shows to amount to 25 per cent., implies with certainty, only that infanticide has *lately* been practised. If the custom were in its fullest possible force, consistent with the preservation of the race, the sexual divergence would be as great as 100 to 33·3; a proportion which allows one girl on an average, to every family—with less than which allowance, the race could not survive.

My readers will have noticed in Chapter XI. the suggestion, that a curious result of long continued infanticide, has been to create a male-producing variety of the human race.

It will be observed that in the Table, the proportion of females who have died, to 100 males, is 65·6: whilst of those alive, it is 72·6. This discrepancy bears evidence to the inaccuracy of the statistics. Judging from the circumstances attending the census, and the personal care bestowed on it, to obtain genuine results, I have every reason to think that the record of those *alive*, is as nearly correct as possible: but I have not the same confidence as regards those who had died. I attribute much of this inaccuracy to the imperfect memory of the people, in describing events long past—a person once dead, being rarely talked about—but very largely also to their habit of ignoring the gentler sex.

That such a habit should really exist, was suggested to my mind, on observing how much girls were left out of count when they described the numbers in families, and of how great importance the birth of a son was esteemed. If a Toda is asked how many children—kinmokh—he has, his reply will almost invariably be, so many sons—mokh:[9] and if further information is desired as to his daughters, one has to specify tûjmokh. On one occasion a father replied to the usual enquiry, 'I have five sons.' 'Where are they?' 'There—1, 2, 3, 4, 5.' I could only see four. Two or three times the numbers were gone over, each time the man gravely counting five, I finding only four. So, pointing to each in succession, I enumerated 1—2—3—4. Where is the fifth? 'There,' he said, pointing to his *wife*, who quietly nodded approval. It seems that the good woman had not yet given birth to the child which both parents had agreed to consider a *son*!

Viewing human action, ever as the resultant of many forces—passions, necessities, emotions, habits—pulling in divers directions, with various degrees of strength; we find that the Todas very early in the world's history, practically solved the difficult physical problem of finding the condition of equilibrium of those especial forces which affected them; how, in fact, to *stand still* in a world, the law of whose nature is that of perpetual change—a remarkable example of the

[9] Mr. Metz asserts positively that the word mokh is used by the Todas for *son*, and not for *child*. In other Drâvidian dialects it may have expanded in its application so as to mean children, both male and female.

compensatory skill of savages, which they owe greatly to their large organ of Weight.

In the description of the Toda character, founded on phrenologic basis, which I afforded in previous chapters, I have endeavoured to express, how weak they are in those groups of mental qualities which enable men to surmount difficulties in life by the force of their natural energies; how that their whole nature is built for the maintenance of the existing state of things: how free from cruelty, and how fond of children: how practical their character, though limited in range of vision: and how deficient in tenacity.

I have also tried to enable my readers to realise the early state of things; when the increase of numbers due to the luxurious nature of an equatorial climate had outstepped the supply of food: and the growth of human intellect—giving the ability to augment the supply—had failed to keep pace with the growing density of the population.

Now, resolve all these forces—the natural tendencies of primitive man, and the circumstances by which surrounded—in such direction as exactly to neutralise one another; and you work out the problem which the Todas had to solve. Only three courses were open to them: (1.) The progressive exercise of combined labour and skill. (2.) Abstinence from marriage. (3.) Destruction of children.

They tried the first, and failed. In regard to the second, Nature, who is ever careful of her own interests, was doubtless altogether too strong for them. We see they adopted the third course, but in such manner as to give their gentle natures—gentle above all to children—the least suffering, by killing the infants without pain, and before the parents had opportunity to love them.

The great similarity in the dispositions of the two sexes assures me that mothers co-operated with fathers willingly in the deed.

If the Todas had possessed a large organ of *Acquisitiveness*, the desire to have, to possess, to retain, would never have tolerated continued loss of property: but by husbanding resources, and by inspiring the remaining organism to repeated exertion, would have contrived somehow or in some way to *preserve their children.* Large Philoprogenitiveness combined with Acquisitiveness, both frustrated, would have caused them madly to *covet* children. The burden of their daily cry would have been

> Give me children, or else I die.

With such organisation it would have been impossible to live without young, and the equilibrium which they formed, would have included the *preservation* of their progeny. The equipoise would probably have been produced, primarily by the hoarding of food, in the manner of ants. The race would have been great in the preservation of meat, and the formation of beaver-like dams for the storage of water.

But if their heads had also been gifted with large organs of Constructiveness, Secretiveness, Destructiveness, and Combativeness; had they, in fact, been *brachycephalic*, their innate ingenuity and vigour, would, by enabling them to overcome difficulties, have obviated even the necessity to consider the matter of infanticide. *The tribe would not have been infanticidal.*

We see then, that the wholesale *infanticide, of primitive races* is not the brutal evidence of an aggressive savage vigour, but the contrary. It is the retrograde step which ignorant *tribes of weak and amiable dispositions took to escape the natural consequences of their own helplessness.* They may be recognised at a glance, by the long narrow dolichocephalic head, formed as if a vertical slice had been cut off from either side.

In process of time, as the cranium of early man expands, from the narrow to the broad type, his disposition changes; he may become cannibal, but he ceases to kill infants from the motives, and in the gentle manner described in this chapter.

The Toda's conservative sense—quite bestial in its universality—must have been much gratified at the success of his practical scheme; little suspecting, and caring still less, that when, by this infanticide, he had stopped the expanding power of his race, he had also, in removing one of the greatest incentives to labour that Nature has presented to us, intercepted national progress and development.

# CHAPTER XXIV.

## POLYANDRY.

*Polyandry defined—Instances in various parts of the world of Polyandry—Among the Celtic Britons—Laws of Inheritance—Re-marriage of Widows—Disgrace of being Childless—Desire for Children.*



THE polyandrous state is that form of polygamy which, as practised by the Todas, may both correctly and concisely be described as being the *lawful marriage of one woman with several men, either brothers or near relations.*

We must not allow our conception of savage matrimony—no matter what its form—to be cramped by comparing it too rigidly by our experiences of the 'holy state' in civilised life. Remember that barbarians, in the very nature and degree of their social condition, live in most primitive form. Their houses are crowded to excess: their clothes are scant: their ceremonies, free of all symbol, inference, or poetry, are bald, simple and direct. Toda marriage, strange as its nature may appear to be, nevertheless merits honour equally with those other and better understood forms of matrimony, commonly contracted by primitive or even semi-barbarous races.

From the days of our childhood we have been educated to the spectacle of the Turk and his score of wives—perhaps, rather respecting the awful man, for his prowess in ruling such a household of women and children. We know, also, that his form of polygamy is the ancient habit of many existing nations, as it was of races which have long since passed away: and that the practice has, within the memory of the present generation, been revived in a modern Christian community.

The Toda woman is restricted by the force of circumstances, to consort with from four to five husbands. Her marriage is also quite respectable; and in point of antiquity, it probably 'whips creation.' She weds for life, 'for better, for worse;' and the married couple give actual security for good behaviour.

That this practice is neither a modern creation nor peculiar to the Todas alone, history and works of modern travel afford ample evidence. It will amply suffice for our purpose to quote a few instances.

The Bible, in making frequent mention of customs of the barbarians—in the midst of whom we find the Jews, on their first rising to notice, embedded—strictly analogous to those which obtain amongst the Todas, in respect to matrimony; leads us irresistibly to the conclusion that polyandry was, in those early days, an old and well-established institution in the world. And that such is really the truth, will become more and more evident, as from time to time, in the course of these pages, I have recourse to Scripture in drawing attention to ancient usage. Indeed the strong feeling I entertain, that in the Todas, we have actually a living specimen of some of these races, renders the reference to the historical evidence of the Bible, the more fascinating, as it is important.

Polyandry was a recognised institution[1] amongst the famous Aryas—the race to which we English, in common with most civilised nations, have lately found ourselves to be allied by ties of language, and perhaps of consanguinity.

It is still practised by portions of that race, now settled in the Western Himalayas.

It has been noted as a custom of the ancient Medes and Getes.

Cæsar's description of the mode of matrimonial alliance,

[1] Talboys-Wheeler, 'History of India.'

which our own British forefathers in Celtic days—before the nation had become English through suffusion of Teutonic blood—used to form, has been read by every school-boy. 'It was common,' writes Cæsar, 'for a number of brothers or other near relations to use their wives promiscuously.'[2] It is not perhaps, quite pleasant to be told that such was the custom of our own ancestors, and efforts have in consequence been made to throw doubt on the correctness of the statement; but that it was indeed the habit of the Celtic portion of the inhabitants, I see no cause for doubting. If, as I believe to be the case, the custom of the ancient Britons, and of the Todas, is in this respect, identical, any light which these pages may bring to bear upon the curious and ancient practice, cannot fail to be accepted with greatly enhanced interest.

Polyandry prevails also amongst tribes now occupying divergent tracts of the Indian Peninsula, but which, speaking various dialects of the same Drâvidian language, which is the mother-tongue of our Todas, were manifestly at one time, close neighbours—viz. in the mountains of Ceylon, and along the Southern Ghats.

It exists at this day amongst the Kalmuks, and has only just died out with the last of the Tasmanians.

It is known to be the practice of 'some families of the Iroquois.'[3]

We shall be better placed, to understand all the conditions of this venerable institution, on perusing the following few simple customs—partaking of the full force of laws—in regard to the management and inheritance of property; such as land, cattle, food and chattels, which obtain amongst the Todas;—

I. It has already been told that the tribe is divided into clans—kôleh.[4]

[2] J. Cæsar, 'De Bello Gallico.'

[3] Lubbock, 'The Origin of Civilization and Primitive Condition of Man.'

[4] Kôleh is a Drâvidian—Kanarese—word, which, though used by the

CHAP. XXIV.

II. Each clan has grazing and forest land of its own, which is divided between the villages of the clan, each village being situated in its own land.

III. Each village is the abode of a family or intimately related portion of a clan, whose cattle are herded together.

IV. Whilst the land is in each case, the property of the village itself, and cannot be alienated or sold, with or without the consent of the occupants;[5] the cattle which graze on it, are the private property of individuals, being males.

V. The milk of the entire herd is lodged in the pâlthchi, or village dairy, from which each person, male and female, receives for his or her daily consumption;[6] the unconsumed balance being divided, as personal and saleable property, amongst the male members of all ages, in proportion to the number of cattle which each possesses in the herd.

VI. The grain food collected in the form of kûtu,[7] from the Badagas, is divided amongst the community.

VII. No females, whether married or single, possess property: but, under all circumstances of life, are supported by their male relations; being fed from the common stock.

VIII. When a father dies, his personal property is divided equally among all the sons. If the deceased, being an elder brother, should have no sons, his next brother inherits the property.

IX. All children of both sexes, belong to the father's family: and inheritance runs through the male line only. Thus (1) if a widow should re-marry, her sons by both marriages, have claims on their respective father's property. (2) If a widower marries again, his property will be inherited by his sons of both marriages, equally. (3) If one or more women are in common to several men, *each* husband considers *all* the

Badagas, is, curiously enough, not employed by the Todas, who have *no word* for clan.

[5] Mr. J. Breeks, late Commissioner of the Neilgherries.

[6] See Chapter XVII. for the management of the dairy.

[7] See Chapter VIII. on the custom of collecting kûtu.

No. 24

AUTOTYPE. LONDON.

PENTIRÊM

A MAIDEN OF 14 YEARS.

children as his—though each woman is mother only to her own—and each male child is an heir to the property of all of the fathers.

X. In order to avoid the complications that would arise, in the matter of food and the guardianship of property, from the re-marriage of widows, if they entered other families, taking their children with them; either a brother or other near relation of her deceased husband, takes her to wife. She 'remains in the family.' Such is Toda expression.

The following was early Semitic custom (*see* Deuteronomy xxv. 5): 'If brethren dwell together, and one of them die, and have no child, the wife of the dead shall not marry without unto a stranger; her husband's brother'—or 'next kinsman,' says a marginal note—'shall go in unto her, and take her to him to wife, and perform the duty of an husband's brother[8] unto her.' This practice, is either pure polyandry, or it pertains to that extreme communistic state of society, to which, as I shall shortly demonstrate, polyandry belongs.

I met on one occasion, the instance of a man who had just separated from a very good-looking young wife of about fourteen years of age, in order that he might marry his elder brother's widow. It was looked on as a matter of course that the widow should 'remain in the family:' and the retention of two wives, in a community where the women are considerably in the minority, is out of the question. The girl had immediately espoused another; for until children have been born, the Todas do not mind the marriage of a widow out of the family.

These and other instances of the grave, practical, and undeviating nature of this curious people, made a great impression on me at the time.

Perhaps the feeling which engrosses the Toda mind more

[8] To raise up seed unto the brother.

CHAP. XXIV.

than any other, and may be termed his ruling passion, is that of *necessity for* children.

The first instance which came to light of the serious—everything with the Toda is taken *au sérieux*—nature of this topic, was when the women of a certain village had collected round us, in obedience to summons; one was noticed sitting conspicuously apart, giving the impression that she was in some way tabued. 'What is the matter with her? Is she sick?' 'No.' 'Mourning?' 'No, not that.' 'She is a barudi'[9] they said quietly, and in the pitying tone in which one would apply the word 'crazy.' A handsome woman of forty, with the eyes and nose of a hawk. She had committed no fault; had added several boys and girls to the population. She was not ill, nor deformed, or sulky. She was merely a barudi, a widow. Now, it is a reproach to be a widow, unless quite old: or to be childless; the word barudi, in the Toda language, bearing the triple meaning of old woman, widow, and barren woman. This person, we have seen, was neither old nor sterile, yet as a widow who should be, but was not, producing children, she was put to shame.

To be a baruda, or widower, is equally a term of reproach for men.

Another illustration. We met with two brothers—men past sixty years of age, whose joint wife had died. In order to avoid the disgrace of being styled baruda, as well, doubtless, as to obtain the services of some one who could cook their meals, they had forthwith married again. But being elderly gentlemen, joint fathers of nine children, including twins, and not caring for further additions to their family, they had selected to be their joint wife, a woman of fifty, who, having been *discarded as sterile*, was then living a single and neglected life.

I have ascertained positively, that so great is the disgrace

[9] The derivation of this word has already been given in Chapter VII., Note 15.

attached to the epithets baruda and barudi, as applied to young married people, the husband would connive at any steps his wife might take to obtain children. The way in which my informant described what would be done in these circumstances, leaves no doubt in my mind of the truth of what I have written.

The Bible affords many instances of the display amongst primitive tribes of this craving for progeny, and of the reproach attaching to sterility. In Genesis xvi., 2—5, we find Sarai prefers that her husband Abram should have children by her maid, rather than there should be none in the house. We meet with a similar occurrence, narrated too with a clearness that leaves no doubt as to the intention, in Genesis xxx., 1—4, in the case of Rachel, the wife of Jacob. Again in 1 Samuel i. The book of Genesis, xxxviii., 26, gives another instance, and another motive.

Of this desire for progeny I have seen many examples amongst the Todas, so strongly marked, but to all appearances apart from the sense of personal ambition, and separate from any demands of religion[10] or requirements for support in old age, as to give the impression that it was the primitive faculty of Philoprogenitiveness, acting so insensibly, naturally, as to have the character more of a plain instinct, than of an intelligent human feeling.

There is something very affecting in the spectacle which these people present; so like animals in their primitive notions; closing in round upon one another, huddling together, and breeding with such a zeal as if they feared to lose their hold on the world. Yet, even, murdering many, that many might survive the dreaded danger.

[10] This peculiarity has already been noticed in Chapter XX.

# CHAPTER XXV.

## POLYANDRY—MARRIAGE.

*Betrothal—Peculiar nature of Dowry—Ask Papa—'Wilt thou have this man?'—The Wedding Ring—Plurality of Husbands—Confusion of Progeny—Toda expressions for Marriage—The Bow and Arrow in Weddings.*

CHAP. XXV.

THE betrothal of the sexes in marriage is arranged in this fashion. The father or other male guardian of the lad—or the young man himself if of age and in a position to negociate his own affairs—seeks an interview with the male protector of the girl whom he desires to wed. If his project be encouraged, nothing remains in the form of preliminaries but to discuss the amount of endowment—kēikuli[1]—to be given. This is never paid in cash. Money is a very scarce article in the jungles; money may be, will be spent: and land not being transferable property, as we saw in the last Chapter, whilst kine affords the means of immediate support for a family, and is inheritable, the conference must of necessity be almost entirely restricted to determining the number of cattle—buffalos—of which the kēikuli shall consist; which, although it varies to a certain extent, lies commonly between one and four in number.

We imagine the young man to say, 'I will give you two buffalos as kēikuli for your daughter.' Here we note that owing to female infanticide, girls are in great demand; hence

[1] Kēikuli or kekhuli. Kai = *hand.* Koli = *what is received.* Drâvidian root, kol = *receive.*

Another possible derivation is kukh = *woman.* Vilai = *price.* Kaikuli = *wages.* [POPE.]

the dowry is received, not given, by the damsel's parents. 'Ask me never so much dowry and gift, and I will give according as ye shall say unto me: but give me the damsel to wife.' Genesis xxxiv., 12. The girl's father may reply, 'We are all relations. I don't want your property. You have proved your sincerity. I will give you in exchange one, two, three, or four buffalos.' This return present, may be more or it may be less than that offered by the wooer. Such, as I am assured by my friend, Mr. Metz, is actual Toda method of managing these affairs.

I am not prepared to supply a reason for this custom. It may be a survival of some more ancient practice, or it may be a method suggested by self respect. The girl has been asked in marriage. She is not to be had for nothing. The young man is in earnest, and it is going to be a wedding and no mistake.

We notice that the transaction is not the payment so much as the exchange of dowers. Seemingly it is a worthless arrangement, binding on neither party. But worked in a simple way by simple minds, it appears to be held as a test of honesty of intention. And—as we shall shortly have opportunity of observing—becomes a security for good behaviour, by affording the means for punishing breaches of matrimonial compact.

When the bargain has been struck, the damsel's father intimates his formal consent to the marriage by placing his foot on his son-in-law's head, after the mode described in Chapter IV., saying, 'I give'—tashken. Affairs may now be held to have reached that stage on the road to matrimonial happiness, somewhat corresponding to the point in the negociation of French marriages, when the only remaining step to be taken, consists in consulting the young lady's sentiments on the proposed union.

The dowry is now due from the bridegroom, and he may not recede from his part of his compact; that is to say, if the

CHAP. XXV.

girl accepts him, he must marry her. The power of taking or rejecting this man who aspires to be her future lord being still hers, the opportunity of judging for herself, how far he is to her taste, is now afforded her. Most practical and sensible race!

In the absence of all rites and ceremonies, but with the approval of parents, and in full cognisance of the village community of relatives, these young people are now held to be a married pair, on trial for a day and night. An entire house—eight feet square—is given up to them, and in this they live with closed door during the short period of probation, food being passed in to them by the girl's mother. The damsel is required to make up her mind on the expiry of this brief honeymoon, either to accept or reject her suitor. If she refuse the man, he goes away the subject of depreciatory remarks. If, on the contrary, she should tell her mother that she will have him, the pair are now held to be man and wife.[2] Neither he nor she can recede from their bargain without punishment; which would take the form of a fine of some portion of the curious dower, if referred to a tribunal of Elders—kûtacaram.

The husband now gives his wife a necklace,[3] of value according to his means—unmarried girls do not wear necklaces—and sets her up with a new mantle. The bride may receive from affectionate parents little trifles towards beginning to keep house. I tried to ascertain what would be a welcome present on such occasions, but found that after my informant had mentioned a brass cup and plate he stumbled so much, I feel quite within the bounds of safety if I throw in a pair of brass armlets or silver ear-rings.

The wife now either accompanies her husband to his own house, or they both remain in her father's village, according

[2] Literally Âl = '*husband*' or '*man.*' Kâtvoti = '*wife*' or '*she who is bound to me.*' See derivation in Chapter VII., Note 8.

[3] Among some of the tribes in South India, marriage is ratified by tying a thread or thin slip of bark round the neck. This practice shows the origin of the Toda custom.

as may be most convenient to them. In either case, the marriage both in name and in fact, is identical.

It is the custom for the husband to give a feast to his nearest relatives on such a joyous occasion.

It will be seen that up to this stage, the woman is married with her own consent to one man—he who pays the dowry, or gives security to society for his own good behaviour. But now, if the husband has brothers or very near relatives, all living together, they may each, if both she and he consent, participate in the right to be considered her husband also, on making up a share of the dowry that has been paid. In fact it was formerly their almost universal custom—in the days when women were more scarce than they are now—for *a family of near relations to live together in one mand, having wife, children and cattle all in common.*

Now if we consider that one or more brothers may each become the husbands of separate wives by virtue of having each paid a dower, and that younger brothers as they grow to age of maturity, and other brothers as they become widowed, may each, either take separate wives or purchase shares in those already in the family, we can at once understand that any degree of complication in perfectly lawful wedded life, may be met with, from the sample of the single man living with a single wife, to that of the group of relatives married to a group of wives. We begin to see also why tribes following polyandrous habits, endeavour to prevent further complications by making widows 'remain in the family.'

All the children of these very promiscuous unions are held to be brothers and sisters. And as, as is manifest, a generation or two of such marriages must produce inextricable confusion in relationships, so we find that the Todas, who like nothing so much as reducing things to simple formulæ, rather ignore the whole subject, terming them anatama.[4] They will

[4] See Note 19 of Chapter VII.

CHAP. XXV.

describe the connection between such brothers as follows: 'Their fathers are brothers-in-law: their mothers being sisters, they are brothers.' An uncle is styled 'my little father'; most significant.

The marriage system I have described is elastic. It is capable of being modified in its internal working without change in the actual principle. Thus, when women are scarce, several men have to be content with one wife between them. But as women become more numerous, a greater proportion of men are able to procure a wife a-piece. This condition of permanent routine is supremely satisfying to the Toda mind.

The general expression for marriage is represented by the word kûdiken — I join.[5] Thus, 'Beliani is married to Nastufi' would be translated Beliani Nastufig kûdthchi, or they are joined to one another. But in addressing a man with the casual question of, 'Are you married?' the ordinary way of putting it, would be to say, 'Is there a son?'—Mokh vathchya? He would reply, Ha, mokh vathchi, 'Yes, there is a son:' or if married, but childless, he would detail, Ân kukh kûdthbini, mokh illade—'I joined a woman, a son is not.'

Similarly, the enquiry made of a woman would be, Belthta gavthchya?—'Is the neck-ring tied?'[6]

Mr. Metz has been so good as to describe for me a singular custom connected with weddings, which he learnt subsequently to my having left the Nilagiris: of which no sort of explanation can be supplied by the Todas.

When the wife has gone seven months with her first child, she retires with her husband alone, to the depths of the village wood, where at the foot of some tree she places a

[5] I am not certain that in the word 'join,' we have got the most primitive meaning of kûdiken. The Hindustani word kûdna, and its Sanskrit root kurdd = *play*, might be compared.

[6] For the modes in which husbands and wives address one another, see Chapter VII.

No. 25

AUTOTYPE, LONDON.

NASTUFI

"THE LITTLE SAVAGE"

A MARRIED GIRL OF 16 YEARS.

No. 26

AUTOTYPE, LONDON.

BELIANI.

lamp. Kneeling before the light, she receives from her husband a bow and arrow, made by him,[7] which she salutes by lowering her forehead to them. Taking up the weapons, she asks, 'What is the name of your bow?'—each clan apparently having a different name for its bow. He tells her the name, Kurkutvashk or Virzhvashk, or any other. Question and answer are repeated three times. The wife then deposits the bow and arrow at the foot of the tree. The pair remain at the spot without shelter but that of the tree overhead, all night, eating a meal that evening, and another in the morning, before return to the village.

This looks very much like the perpetuation of a custom inherited from some past condition of life, when Todas carried weapons. But its object, and the reason for postponing the ceremony for some months after marriage, is not easy to comprehend. Perhaps, in a communistic era, possibly antecedent to polyandry—see Chapter XXVII.—it may have implied an acknowledgment of paternity, and of the obligation on the part of the father, to provide food for the coming family.

[7] It will be remembered that the weapons used at funerals are made by the Kotas.

## CHAPTER XXVI.

### POLYANDRY—MORALITY.

*Fickleness not necessarily an attribute of Barbarous Man—Use of the Dower—Dowry sometimes not paid—What then?—Women's Influence—Divorces are rare—Company behaviour very fair—No bachelors—Ultra Communistic—Not much known of Private Practices—No Foreign Blood apparent.*

CHAP. XXVI.

THESE people have been described by travellers, as grossly inconstant in their married life; men and women leaving and even exchanging wives or husbands in fickleness, much as the whim seizes them.

Indeed it appears a common opinion that fickleness is, in a remarkable degree, the attribute of barbarous man. He is either expected to display the inconstancy of an amorous people, full of fire and wild savage license: or perhaps the softer, childlike instability of a race of Arcadian simplicity, and romantic habit: but fickleness in some form or other, as the notable peculiarity of his primitive institutions. On the contrary; whatever may be his moral condition, behold a singularly calm, collected and unimaginative body, acting invariably with a dry practical object.

Let us examine then, the condition of one of *the first steps towards organisation, which society owes to the introduction of polyandry:* and if in this early stage we still find much that appears immoral, let us discriminate between the lapse from a higher standard, and that which is merely a very slow rate of upward progress. Secluded and isolated from fellow man, there seems no reason why the Toda should not remain unchanged in habits, almost through all time: but in the presence of a superior civilisation, action may be observed to commence; habits improve, though perhaps only up to a certain low stage, almost insensibly, and much as a flower expands, chemically influenced in the light of the sun.

The combined institutions of the dower and inheritance, afford as strong guarantees for the stable nature of the marriage tie as any race of inferior moral culture could well give. Indeed, no social customs redound more to their credit for practical sagacity than these. The young man makes his offer of marriage, which being accepted, the bargain, so far as he is concerned, is closed, and his dowry is *held to be due.* The girl, after sufficient deliberation, accepts this man: when the father is liable for her portion, to the man who has now become her husband.

Women, as we have seen, not being able to inherit property, the husband and father of the family is alone responsible for the food supply.

If then at any time the wife should be discarded, the whole of her family would be interested in the question of 'who is to feed her,' and thus naturally as it were, become guardians of the law. Or if, on the other hand, the wife should leave her husband's protection, he would claim from her father, restitution of the dowry he had paid. Had it been their custom that women could inherit property, men might wash their hands of the duty of supporting wife and family, and women would have encouragement to separate from their husbands, taking their children with them. Of course, such simple traps for restraining the sexes, could never hold, except in conditions of much honesty and good faith. A child left to starve, or a woman to beg or earn a separate livelihood, are sights absolutely unknown in such a united community.

Instances have occurred, but are acknowledged to be rare; of the bridegroom not having found the means of fulfilling his part of the compact; not having paid the dowry, even by the time a child had been born of his marriage. Had this been a hard-working people, such a difficulty could have been surmounted by his acting as Jacob did for Rachel, whose proposition, accepted by Laban, was 'I will serve thee for seven years' for her.—Genesis xxix., 18. But no circumstance has yet induced the dolichocephalic Toda to labour.

In such a case as has been described, the marriage is simply cancelled, both parties being competent to marry again. But mark the decision as regards the child; whether son or daughter it remains the property of the father. The mother nurses and cares for it during infancy: but when it can take care of itself; when in fact it requires food from the family stock, it goes to its father's home. Here we recognise the influence of the property law. Some one must feed and clothe the child: but women have no property; hence the father must take charge of it. Such would be the judgment of the kûtacaram.

As regards the national feeling on such an affair; it would be looked on as a mishap, an unfortunate occurrence, and the defaulter would lose in public estimation. He might be fined a buffalo or two: but there the matter would end, in sedate quiet. The child born of the union would not suffer in any way; it is the son of so and so: there is the father, whose heir he is, and that, his mother.

If the Toda mode of inheriting property should give the impression that women are not of much account in the family, such a view would be quite incorrect. Woman's influence in the mand, through her husbands and children, is real. By the great tolerance and moderation of the men, aided by a very sufficient mental power and mastery of her subject, she maintains a good position in the house. It is not so much that the two sexes are equally balanced, for even if of like mental power, the muscular ability to enforce a requirement must always remain with the man, as that the women have settled into a position which gives ample scope for the practice of feminine duties, and of acquiring useful experience in the management of affairs. If the husbands should die, the widow would be fully competent to act as trustee of any cattle they may have left, and as guardian of her children, whether she married again, or maintained her single state.

In the event of a woman not bearing any children to her husband, he may marry again: but in such case he must support the first wife: and, as a matter of course, he has to pay another dower for the second.

In possession, therefore, of these evidences of wedded life, and bearing in recollection the staid nature of this singular people, I feel convinced that separation between pairs is not lightly tolerated. Easy-tempered, thoroughly communistic, and not very nice in their discrimination of the duties of husbands and wives to one another, many of the causes which lead to separations amongst civilised people, must be absent from them, and motives for divorce would not be frequent.

What an insight does the simple practice of the dower, not give into the direct nature of their minds! Both parties *promise*, and the promise is their bond! It is not that it is a conscientious people, but so guileless and free from talent for plot, and all so much alike, that seemingly they possess almost intuitive knowledge of one another's intentions. We notice the same peculiarity amongst the inferior animals, and for want of a better word, term it instinct. I have often thought that much of this instantaneous understanding we observe in animals, as well as the rapidity with which, amongst nearly pure races of man, information is disseminated, and the unity of impulse with which they work in combining for a common end, is due greatly to close similarity in cranial contour.[1] Are sly animals ever found associated in herds or troops?

[1] This peculiarity was a remarkable feature in the Indian Mutiny of the year 1857; the rebellion of a semi-barbarous race, of striking uniformity of cranial development.

CHAP. XXVI.

I confess to a feeling of great astonishment that barbarians should conduct their household arrangements with the staidness and good sense of members of the Teutonic family of nations. Yet, though free from taint of fickleness, Toda social morality can scarcely be defended. We find him bound down to keep the peace, and behave himself as a Toda should, and not throw his wife and children on the parish. But for the rest we find him still a gross savage.

In the outward behaviour of the sexes, I have been amused to notice how much the custom and etiquette observed in civilised life is derived from *their* model. I have never seen any among our list of the proprieties in the slightest degree overstepped by them in ordinary daily intercourse, except perhaps in their habit of calling a spade a spade. Modest-looking women are by no means rare. They remain habitually at home, keeping together as demure as cats. They have their own places of private resort, on which members of the opposite sex would not presume to intrude. They manage their cumbersome garments to perfection. But it must not be supposed that they are moral, or have scruples. It is the human animal in its wild state.

No unmarried class exists, to disturb society with its loves and broils. More's the pity! for that same society much needs to be startled into energy out of its hum-drum life! The warm breath of poetry and romance never passes through these people. It must long ago have been quenched with the introduction of infanticide and polyandry. Defects lie entirely the other way; it is a 'very much married' people. Every man and every woman, every lad and every girl is somebody's husband or wife; tied at the earliest possible age, and bound by grinding social law, in the bonds of unpoetic matrimony, extending almost over the entire term of adult life. Sacred characters, such as the pâlâl and pâlkarpâl, are merely husbands off duty. With the exception of a cripple girl, and of those women who, past the child-bearing age, were widows, I did not meet with a single instance of unmarried adult females. But, on the contrary, I have been able to record several examples of maids wedded in childhood, either to boys or to young men; and in one instance of a young woman of seventeen married to a boy of fourteen years.—See Table No. 9.

Although there *are* degrees of kinship, within whose limits the union of the sexes is held in actual abhorrence, yet half-brothers and sisters are not included amongst the objectionables. I judge from the internal evidence afforded by their mode of life; the size and crowded condition of their tiny houses: their natural dispositions, so gregarious and unacquisitive as to be uncontrolled by such moral doubts as a sense of personal property outraged, would prompt: the disproportion of the sexes: unlimited opportunity. These points conspire to convince with irresistible force, that here communism is in fullest operation.

Very possibly, some etiquette may be in force among them to place a certain bar on their private practices. But I have not had opportunity to ascertain absolutely the form and outline of their private domestic habits. My belief is—and in this respect Mr. Metz is in full accord with me—that every disgusting habit, which might be expected in such a state of life, is the common practice among them, but unaccompanied by much sense of impropriety.

The almost entire absence of evidence of foreign blood in their veins, is worthy of note, even if a reason may not be ascribed with any degree of confidence, to the phenomenon. Surrounded by tribes, varying much in appearance from the Todas, and from one another, and for many years in close proximity to an English settlement; yet not one single Europeanised countenance has been met amongst them, nor could I point with certainty to any faces bearing the stamp of a foreign native tribe.

CHAP. XXVI.

## Table No. IX.

*Child Marriages. Compiled from 'Statistics of Toda Families,' Table No. IV.*

| No. on the List | Calculated Ages when | | | Present Ages of | | |
|---|---|---|---|---|---|---|
| | Wives Married | Oldest Husbands married | Wives commenced child-bearing | Wives | Oldest Husbands | |
| 1 | 14 | 15 | 15 | | | |
| 2 | 13 | 16 | 14 | | | |
| 20 | 17 | 14 | — | 19 | 16 | Not with child |
| 24 | 13 | 21 | 17 | | | |
| 38 | 12 | 15 | 13 | | | |
| 39 | 10 | 19 | — | 14 | 23 | Not with child |
| 41 | 12 | 12 | — | 14 | 14 | Ditto |
| 44 | 11 | 31 | 12 | | | |
| 47 | 10 | 11 | — | 11 | 12 | Not with child |
| 48 | 9 | 12 | — | 12 | 15 | Ditto |
| 51 | 14 | 14 | 16 | | | |
| 55 | 10 | 16 | 19 | | | |

## CHAPTER XXVII.

### POLYANDRY—ITS CAUSE.

*Causes ascribed by various Authors — Savage social Custom traced — Origin of the Family—Absolute and Limited Communism—Infanticide —Unpremeditated origin of Polyandry—Phrenological description of Polyandrists—Obstacles to Change of custom—Nature may be Warped so as to place obstacles to Rapid Change in the Character of Races.*

MANY are the reasons to which this peculiar form in the union of the sexes has been ascribed. CHAP. XXVII.

Mr. Talboys-Wheeler inclines to the opinion that the custom might, amongst some races of the Âryas, have originally been induced 'at some primeval epoch,' in the course of migrations 'from their cradle in Central Asia, to seek new homes to the eastward of the Indus, and under such circumstances they would naturally bring with them as few women as possible.'[1]

Some authors entertain the impression that whatever may have actually developed the practice, as an established institution it commends itself to the suffrages of women through the influence which an enhanced value confers on them. One writer even going so far as to suggest that women are induced to perpetuate their custom of infanticide for the purpose of maintaining this influence. Others again, amongst whom are Dr. Inman,[2] and Mr. Talboys-Wheeler, attribute its perpetuation to the necessity for 'keeping the population low' by 'preventing any undue increase in the numbers of a family.'

[1] Talboys-Wheeler, 'History of India.'

[2] Inman, 'Ancient Faiths embodied in Ancient Names.'

CHAP. XXVII.

Sir John Lubbock is 'disposed to regard it as an exceptional phenomenon, arising from the paucity of females.'[3] In which opinion he is supported by Mr. Bonwick, who sees that 'in a condition of society where women are in the minority, as with the rapidly dying tribes of Australia, a system very like Indian polyandry is begotten.'[4]

None of these authors appearing quite to have traced the practice to its absolute origin: but rather to have assigned it to what is, at best, probably one of its proximate causes only, the few following pages are devoted to the endeavour to throw some further light on this somewhat obscure and very ancient custom.

It is not assuming too much, from our acquaintance with the working of nature's laws, that the numerical proportions of the sexes should be one of approximate equality. The census taken of all civilised countries, most carefully and oft repeated, assures us that nearly the same number of females are born in them as males: that nearly an equal portion die, though from different causes—women's feminine trials tending to compensate the risks to which men are exposed—and that the balance remains on the whole, nearly the same, in spite of many disturbing effects. Thus we grow convinced, that if the correlation between the sexes should grow to what we perforce view as abnormal, certain unusual—probably unnatural—influences must have been working to disturb the symmetry of their relations.

We are also agreed that the passion between the sexes, has in all ages, and under every diversity of circumstance, appeared to be nearly identical in the human race.

How then, in the presence of this natural equality and uniform sensibility of the sexes, with the positive information recorded in the last chapter, that every Toda woman

[3] Lubbock, 'The Origin of Civilisation and Primitive Condition of Man.'

[4] Bonwick, 'Daily Life and Origin of the Tasmanians.'

marries, do we come to find that this race had so arranged the proportion, that only one wife was available for several husbands?

Let us endeavour briefly to trace the growth of savage customs, from their primeval state up to the period during which polyandry, first was introduced, then became the concretion we now find it.[5] I believe the practice of communism, in its most unrestricted and therefore grossest form, to have been the basis of man's social system, when in the natural or absolutely undeveloped stage of his savage existence. I ground this conviction greatly on the experiences which have been gained of the very promiscuous customs of the Todas, as well as of primitive races all over the world: and largely, as a fair logical deduction, that I draw from a consideration of the Toda cranium; in which it is almost impossible to be otherwise than struck with the overwhelming preponderance of the entire domestic group of organs, over the moral, secretive, and acquisitive constitution; thus forming a combination of forces, which, in races living densely secluded lives, and at a period when the sexes were reared in equal numbers, must have produced an irrepressible desire to maintain everything—without reserve or restriction, coyness, or prudery—*absolutely in common* among the associated group, call it clan, kinsfolk, or tribe; terms which amongst these densely gregarious people, are nearly synonymous.

At some advanced period in human progress; when clans had increased in size, and circumstances had encouraged the creation of varieties in tribal custom: when the growth of local interests, and an active sense of mutual dependence, fostered and promoted by the warm preference which the

[5] I beg here to acknowledge the pleasure and advantage I have derived from the study of Mr. M'Lennan's work 'Primitive Marriage'; many of the ideas in which, on the primitive condition of man, believing them to be strikingly accurate, I have incorporated in various parts of this work, and especially in this chapter.

CHAP. XXVII.

sexes feel instinctively towards one another: coupled with the absorbing need of offspring, that I have already noticed —see Chapter XXIV.—as characterising the Todas, had united in centripetal action; then barbarian life would become a certain degree less promiscuous; by its primitive society converging into numerous congeries of near relations. The *family* would then be the *social unit*; maintaining still the ancient practice, of holding all property in common amongst its members.

By the continued action of such causes, the little family groups of kinsfolk would tend to still further condensation and exclusiveness. They would become smaller in their component numbers, by being more free of aliens: until at last, *the family came to be represented mainly by a knot of brothers, half-brothers, and cousins,*[6] *married to closely-related kinswomen* in nearly equal numbers; the men being the common fathers of all the progeny: each woman, however, the mother of her own children only. That these women were not only intimately connected to one another, but were often either sisters or half-sisters to their husbands, need occasion no surprise. I have most unfortunately not obtained the evidence which would warrant my asserting absolutely that such close inter-marriage was actually the custom amongst the Todas: yet when once we thoroughly realise the mode of daily life of a rude people, we can no longer doubt that such was and still is the practice of barbarous races.[7]

[6] 'My little-father's son is the same as my brother.' Toda saying. See Chapter VII.

[7] Supposing three brothers A B C married three women *a b c* in the indiscriminate fashion of the times—anterior to infanticide—and that six boys, or girls, were borne by each woman, of which two are fathered to each husband.

If the children of the unions be represented as multiples of A B C with *a b c*,

the sons of *a* may be written 2 *a* A, 2 *a* B, 2 *a* C
" *b* " 2 *b* A, 2 *b* B, 2 *b* C
" *c* " 2 *c* A, 2 *c* B, 2 *c* C

Then each of the pairs of sons would be brothers to one another, and *a* A,

We know by a perusal of Genesis xx. that Abram married his half-sister, and may presume that such was a common practice in his day.

Mr. Talboys-Wheeler remarks that the earlier Buddhist legends preserved in the Mahawansi, present a curious instance of promiscuous marriage amongst the primitive Âryas. Four brothers retire into the jungle with their five sisters, where they dwell in huts made of branches of trees, subsisting on the produce of the chase; each brother marrying one of his sisters not born of the same mother.[8]

Probably every race of man, at some period of its rise from the animal condition of *absolute communism* in which it originally revelled, has attained this stage, of *limited communism*. Gross as such condition of society may appear to be, it must still be acknowledged as an advance on the course to orderly wedlock. No form of sexual alliance is inconsistent with the theory that from this platform all the various systems of matrimony with which we are acquainted, have sprung and radiated: whilst, on the other hand, we have in the living customs of barbarous races in all quarters, evidence in its favour.

One of the early results of this limited form of communism, would be shown in the growth of a sense of parentage; arising from the recognition and acknowledgment of their children by their joint fathers: and in the desire which they would feel to protect and provide for this family, expanding into a certain rude conception of the responsibility of their position.

The known habits and sentiments now prevailing among the Todas have encouraged me in forming my impression of the characteristic conditions of primitive society. It seems necessary too that some such concretion of the social system

*b* A, *c* A, &c., would be half-brothers by the same father: *a* A, *a* B, *a* C, &c. would be half-brothers by the same mother: *a* A, *b* B, *c* C, &c., would be cousins german.

[8] Talboys-Wheeler, 'History of India,' vol. i. p. 117, foot note.

shall have been already formed, before we can fully account for systematic infanticide—as contrasted with a habit of indiscriminate and disorderly destruction of the weak of both sexes—or before we can completely understand why polyandry should emanate therefrom. *These practices seem to imply the pre-existence of a family scheme* of some sort.

Circumstances, such as I endeavoured in Chapter XXIII. to depict, drove a communistic people, to infanticide. Parents projected the scheme of destruction which eventuated in an undue proportion being maintained between the sexes. The early and *undesigned* consequence of the act being, that without actual change in social practice, the limited communism changed into what is styled polyandry, by a simple and natural process; for whereas it had been the custom for groups of brothers, half-brothers, and cousins, to unite themselves to nearly equal numbers of kinswomen, they now were restricted to the reduced allowance of one or two wives between them.

The balance of feeling, which must long have vibrated between the desire, the furore, on one side of the scale, to destroy every one of the unprofitable female sex, and on the other to retain women for female duties, would at last have created an equilibrium resting at that point where the smallest number of girls, necessary for the continuation of the species, was permitted to live. That the limit was one wife for a family of nearly-related men, shows probably, that even in those dark sad times, property had its interests to be attended to.

Many a tribe may, from too rash destruction of females, have promoted its own rapid extinction, by enfeebling its elastic power, or the capacity for overcoming such temporary reduction of its numbers, as might be induced by wars, famine, or disease. But eventually, supply and demand in the surviving tribes, balanced.

It is curious to observe, and worthy of note, that the tender feelings of parents should induce them, despite the force of tradition, to retain, in some instances, more than one daughter in a family; thus forming a small reserve of women, with which the vacancies which would arise in other families, from a deficiency in female births, or from girls not having been raised to years of maturity, find a counterpoise.

The exceptional practice of polyandry, which had, in an unpremeditated manner, thus grown, merely from the infanticide which had disturbed the natural proportion of the sexes, might be expected to retain something of the promiscuous ways, which for ages had been so much in consonance with gregarious and primitive tastes. Now that the custom of infanticide has been relinquished, and the discrepancy between the sexes, which was its immediate fruit, has become less remarkable—though very far from having vanished—I observe communism still remaining *de facto*, the loved habit of the people, whilst monogamy grows to be the national form of marriage. It may be that the Todas in this process of change, are merely *reverting* to an ancient usage—that prior to infanticide—instigated by the natural predilections of unaltered dispositions. Perhaps their habits are becoming modified by the influence of surrounding monogamic races.

I very much doubt if the custom of polyandry, taken in the ordinary acceptation of that word, viz., the union of brothers only, to one wife, can anywhere be found as the sole national form of marriage; thus assuming the airs of a respectable, even if eccentric custom; for, bearing in mind the extreme gregariousness of their dispositions, and intimacy of their lives: considering, also, the absolute necessity for every soul to marry, it is evident that the actual nature of the tie must very greatly depend on the living ratio of the sexes; which, of course, could not be maintained at one undeviating level. When the proportions balance, the savage prefers a promiscuous style: but as they widen, and the males preponderate, the practice of monogamy is seen, coexistent with that of a polyandry in which the husbands are *so-called* brothers.

CHAP. XXVII.

Whether polyandry was the anticipated effect of a preconcerted design, in which infanticide was the logical preliminary step, or whether this peculiar relation of the sexes was its unforeseen consequence; it still could not have continued in force amongst a people, unless it were in unison with many of their inherent feelings. The same, or parallel personal qualities or propensities, must have led to the perpetuation of both these eccentric customs, or one of them must have fallen into disrepute. And the discontinuance of infanticide must have eventuated in the abandonment of polyandry, in consequence of the intimate nature of the alliance existing between them.

Now if the Todas had been an exact contrast of what we know them to be; had they been a people possessing a strong sense of personal property, and of dislike to publicity: had they been warlike and quarrelsome: had they, in fact, possessed large Acquisitiveness, Secretiveness, Destructiveness, and Combativeness—had they been brachycephalic, in fact—and withal been amorous, we could readily have imagined their taking to a *polygamous* style: but it would be contrary to our actual experience of men, to suppose that with such energetic personalities, families could have continued in harmony where one woman was the common wife of many men.

I maintain therefore, that whilst a general deficiency in power of the propensities—and conspicuously so of the acquisitive organ—dictated the indolent measure of infanticide, in the very face of the counter action of large Philoprogenitiveness, as the best means of escaping annihilation, I am equally forced to the conviction, that the tameness of the same group of deficient organs, combined with the moderate expression of an amativeness not above the average, enabled polyandry to maintain its position when once established.

I have no means of ascertaining that the organs, upon whose sizes and combinations have depended the allied and inseparable practices of infanticide and polyandry, actually existed in the human crania, in the era within which these ancient institutions were introduced as panacea for the woes of suffering man. But I affirm that they do constitute the association that would in this day invent, as well as maintain, those two practices, if precisely the same necessities arose.

If this theory of the physiologic origin of these venerable institutions be correct, we have an evidence of the great immutability of those races which, keeping their genealogical purity of blood, remain also in the same unchanging circumstances of solitude and climate.

In due time; after the lapse of generations, the polyandry which had then concreted into definite form, could not easily have been disturbed, even if the desire to reform had been felt with force sufficient to secure unanimity.

Let us imagine ourselves exactly in their position; the institution of infanticide completely established. Fourteen years —or the marriageable age of girls—must have elapsed before any member could reap benefit from the joint movement. But fourteen years is a very long period, and its end so distant, that few of those whose voices had weight in council, would live to see the change effected. On the other hand, the existing state of polyandry, so far from being oppressive, has strong points of recommendation to such minds. The men probably recognise the fact that it limits the number of mouths to be filled. Nor is it unpleasant to the females; their duties are light—for women of barbarous races, extremely light—they are treated with consideration, and have marked influence in the home circle. Again, parents know that their surviving daughters are in great request: they marry off readily, and at small cost. The thorn in their rose, is the necessity for destroying their infants. This is, no doubt, a lasting pain to them.

Hence we find that before the movement can even be commenced, there is a *vis inertiæ* to be overcome, which would of

CHAP. XXVII. itself render it an extremely difficult matter for the people to effect a change in their habits, in respect to their marriage system. Moreover, as I have shown in Chapter XI., the unfortunate practice of infanticide leads ultimately to the constitutional physiologic change, in which a surplus in actual *births* is maintained in boys over girls, amongst tribes with whom it has become naturalised. Hence, as we see, *the excess of males over females, bred of infanticide, tends to preserve the system of polyandry, when infanticide itself has ceased to be a national practice.*

I may now affirm the dogma, that where the destruction of female infants is practised to excess, we must find, either that polyandry, or the practice of procuring wives from other races, tribes, or castes, is the custom. And where polyandry is met with, we may be confident that we either find female infanticide, or that it has lately and largely been practised.

It is on the conviction of the truth of this assertion, that I based the statement made in Chapter XXIII., that our British forefathers, who are known to have been polyandrous, were also infanticidal.

It has often been laid to the discredit of wild races; the apparently insuperable difficulties that oppose themselves to efforts made for their elevation from the obscene rut in which they were found, and in which they had lived for untold ages. I think the experience we have gained of the unsuspected existence of what would ordinarily be termed a 'natural' obstacle to change in Toda marriage custom, should lead us to suspect the possibility of nature being often warped by the long continuance of other bad practices, so as to place equally effective and invisible obstacles to sudden or even rapid progress in the mental or moral culture of races.

## CHAPTER XXVIII.

### SHADES OF EVENING.

*The people assemble—The cattle come home—Day's food—Prayer to the Setting Sun—The family retires to rest—Maternal aspect of Nature in Mild Climates.*

THE long day draws to a close. The party who had gone out in the morning to collect kûdu, have returned from the distant Badaga villages, apparently not very successful; for they grumble, and look suspicious and uneasy, as they throw their bundles on the ground. The women at home have long completed the performance of their women's work; the infants have been suckled over and over again, and passed from arm to arm of the girls of the family: the house floor and bed have been plastered, and the village frontage swept down water is in the vessels, and wood is in the slings. There is nothing now to do but curl their hair for the night, whilst gossiping with the visitors.



Gradually, and as the evening approaches, the people grow restless and absent-minded: stand up to look, and with hand to eyebrow, scan the broad pasture lands lying under the setting sun. Something of importance seems to be looked for. Rumour spreads, that the buffalos are coming in. The dense mass may now be seen approaching, slowly and leisurely—as well-fed animals should—and led by the more pressing milch cows, who filing through the intervening swamp, and with ears pricked forward, rise the hill where the familiar homestead lies nestled. Here the herd stops: a few, for reasons of their own,

CHAP. XXVIII.

saunter into the fold: the rest chew the cud in an indolent group outside.

The people sit about watching. And whilst some lads stand round the herd, to quiet the nervous with their voices, and to stop flirtations with their sticks, lest any disturbed cow should withhold a portion of her milk; the naked pâlkarpâl with honnus in hand, and pushing forward the mope-eyed sucking-calves, eases each mother in turn, of her oppressive load. Over all, the ripe glow of the declining sun; hallowing the innocent domestic scene which his rich beams have just ceased from glorifying.

Faces cheer up as the man returns to his dairy: and talking is resumed. We understand now their late anxiety and their present ease; the evening's *supply of food has been assured to them.*

Shortly, the mistress of the house may be observed through the little door of her cabin, squatted on the hearth inside; deftly feeding the fire in the vorshkâll, stick by stick, as she cooks the evening meal: head thrown back, eyes half-closed, with a hand outspread, warding the heat from her face. Outside, the family sit about or occupy themselves in shutting up the calves.

We note a man leaning against the village wall, mutter 'ekarvashk'—sunset. He rests his wand against the stones, and taking both arms out of his mantle, maintaining it in place with the elbows, leisurely puts feet to the ground. Bending slightly, and with joined hands to forehead, he says in a low tone, 'Êyan, appn! danenma, mokh ultama, âl ultama, êr ultama, karr ultama, ellam ultama!' Then readjusting his cloth, steps back again to his seat. He quietly watches the luminous God as it subsides in oriental glory behind the hill: then resuming the *sotto voce* conversation, enquires after the health of the new born calf, and if the mother has begun giving milk. An innocent grave smile plays on his face when told that both are doing well. 'A good cow!' he remarks, slowly nodding.

Long looked for dinner appears to be ready; for the heated woman now emerges into the open air, and the men and boys enter the hut, leaving the females to prolong the talk. When each member of the community has in turn, eaten, and the offerings to bhumi tai have been swept out of doors, the whole family in the village join grouped about in primitive dinginess, and quiet unconspicuous attitude; some under the veranda eaves, others on the tûar, or under its quiet shelter: and there rehearse the day's events. The naked pâlkarpâl also, having completed his separate cooking, squats apart upon the wall, whence he can hear the news and add his distant note to the conversation.

And thus the shades of evening close in upon them. The air grows chill, and the careful mother of the smallest, rises to take the infant she has kept under her dress, into the well baked house. She stops a moment: looks round to the sky where the blushing moon, ascending vertically through the trees in hot pursuit of the now vanished sun, illumines her womanly face. 'Swâmi, Swâmi!' she mutters, with hands to forehead, supporting the while, her young one in the bend of her arm, 'Mokh ultama, ellam ultama:' and stoops in at the little doorway. Two or three sleepy-headed children soon stagger in after her. Note the pretty daughter in her teens, plump and white teethed, with hair tightly curled, and eyes that brilliantly catch the sparkle of the moon. She has been taught to say her prayers: but unmarried and without a care, the sense of responsibility is not strong upon her; she has no child to shiver for. She gives a rather hurried salute, bringing her head down to her hands, rather than take the young arms out of their envelope in the chill: a quick 'Êyan, appn!' and in she ducks, shutting the door after her. A prolonged rustle may be heard as the brood settle themselves in the dark, to rest on the warm hearth; with a mantle on the floor and another covering all their nakedness. The healthy baby, with eyes wide open, trying in vain to penetrate the gloom, disturbs the mother on the raised bed, who is now

CHAP. XXVIII.

heard hushing and patting, hushing and patting, hushing and patting. A few nursery skirmishes, and all is still, within.

'Îrzhtâshk' says a man outside in the dark, yawning, 'it is night—bed time.' 'Îrzhtâshk' is repeated by these men of few words, rising. They separate for their different huts. Two to join our family party, stopping before the door, quietly make their short address to the moon, asking *it*[1] to be gracious, and that all may be well with the cattle and with the village. Again the door shuts. A little more settling: the snatch of a song: the low mutter of talk: the cry of the disturbed baby, and all again is hushed.

Îrzhtâshk, I iterate, and impressed with the lonely and exceptional beauty of the position, mount the hill; to see and to think. Not a sound is to be heard over the vast expanse, save the curious tick ticking of nature at work in the short grass. Overhead, the dear moon, now brilliant, pursuing her serene course in the transparent ether,

> 'this brave o'erhanging firmament, this majestic
> roof fretted with golden fire,'

illumines hill and dale, close prospect and far distant view, miles away down in the plains below: now showing the rounded outlines of tracts of forest, and the spurs of receding hills: now throwing a brilliant dart through the poor man's woods close by; bringing out each stick of the gnarled trees with the free hand of an accomplished artist, and sheening gracefully into the women's secluded bathing place: then resting firmly and fully, but softly, on the roof of his humble dwelling in the open patch of hill side—the home, the sanctum—and counting his cattle in their pen; tinting each horn and moving shiny back of the living group, the better to see them. She traverses all his free domain; the undulating pastures and the lonely tarn: examines the single tree out on the wild,

[1] Some savage races reverence the moon as a god, ever in pursuit of the sun goddess; but the Todas are very ignorant, and do not know to what sexes these luminaries belong.

under whose shelter the lads had sat last day. Such an interest she takes in all their haunts; like the moving spirit of a mother visiting her children in their sleep. A pitying look as if, though concerned but powerless to help, yet knowing their hidden future.

It is by night, and in such a climate, that nature assumes her most perfect expression as mother—bhumi tai—it is then that we note man, so like a child asleep in her bosom, throwing his cares upon her: he and his cattle and all that is most necessary, and all that is most dear; seemingly entrusting all to her in his hours of rest. All made for man's convenience and comfort! she appears to say. I have hushed him thus to sleep for ages! Daily I have lowered my pall of night over him, and have made my 'lesser light' so beautiful, he mistakes the work for its Creator! Here nature scarce acknowledges these primitives to be her failures. In the care she continues to take, she says they are my children, and of such all the world was once! They still need my care. They are human, and the germs of what is great!

Nature thus softens our feelings, and appeals to our lenient sense. You once were such as these! How forcibly do the words of Dante come up to disturb our unjust thoughts:

> A man
> Is born . . . and none is there
> . . . who doth read nor write;
> And all his inclinations and his acts,
> As far as human reason sees, are good;
> And he offendeth not in word or deed:
> But unbaptized he dies, and void of faith.
> Where is the justice that condemns him? Where
> His blame if he believeth not?—What then,
> And who art thou, that on the stool would'st sit
> To judge at distance of a thousand miles
> With the short-sighted vision of a span?[2]

ELLAM ULTAMA.

[2] Dante, 'Paradiso,' Canto xix., translated by Cary.

# A BRIEF OUTLINE

OF THE

# GRAMMAR

OF THE

# TUḌA LANGUAGE

BY THE

REV. G. U. POPE, D.D.,

FELLOW OF THE MADRAS UNIVERSITY, MEMBER OF THE GERMAN ORIENTAL SOCIETY.

*[From a collection of Tuḍa words and sentences presented by the Rev. Friedrich Metz, of the Basel Missionary Society.]*

## NOTICE.

These outlines are the result of a good deal of personal intercourse with the Tuḍas, during a residence of twelve years on the Nílagiris. With the kind assistance of the late lamented J. W. Breeks, Esq., the First Commissioner of the Nílagiris, the subject of the Tuḍa language was investigated a few years ago in connection with a small Archæological Society in Ootacamund. At the request of Colonel Marshall, I have put the results into this shape, to be printed in his work on the Tuḍas. I think that the facts of the language are here gathered together. It is becoming daily more difficult to ascertain what is originally Tuḍa and what is borrowed by that people from the later immigrants.

In one or two matters, I have ventured to differ from the Rev. Dr. Caldwell, whose Dráviḍian Grammar has invested such researches with a new interest. I advance my opinions with unfeigned diffidence. While agreeing in the main with that profound scholar, I yet think that the remarkable analogies between the Keltic and the Dráviḍian languages merit a more thorough investigation.

CHAPTER XXIX.

# OUTLINES

OF THE

# TUḌA GRAMMAR.

## I. THE ALPHABET.

§ 1. THE TUḌA LANGUAGE has no compositions, written or unwritten, not a ballad nor a scrap of anything to indicate intellectual activity. The Tuḍas, like their buffalos, are fine animals; but they are the least cultivated of the Drâviḍian races. CHAP. XXIX.

No trace remains of the employment by them of any written character: it is probable, therefore, that they separated from the other Drâviḍians before the 'ur-sprache' of those tribes was reduced to writing.

§ 2. This language, of which but a very scanty fragment remains in use, has more sounds than any other Drâviḍian dialect, and some of these are peculiar to it, seeming to have been modified by the position and habits of the tribe.

The Tuḍas chiefly converse in the open air, calling to each other from one breezy hill-top to another. Their speech sounds like Old Kanarese spoken in the teeth of a gale of wind.

CHAP. XXIX.

§ 3. The vowels are:

| SHORT. | LONG. |
|---|---|
| 1. **a**, as in 'America.' Ex. **atham**, *he.* | 6. **â**, as **aw**, in 'bawl.' Ex. **âḷ**, *a man.* |
| 2. **i**, as in 'pin.' Ex. **nim**, *your.* | 7. **î**, as in 'pique.' Ex. **nî**, *thou.* |
| 3. **u**, as in 'Co̱o̱k.' Ex. **ulg**, *within.* | 8. **û**, as in 'Scho̱o̱l.' Ex. **mûdu**, *three.* |
| 4. **e**, as in 'hem.' Ex. **yenak**, *to me.* | 9. **ê**, as **a** in 'pale.' Ex. **êt**, *why?* |
| 5. **o**, as in 'opinion.' Ex. **kor**, *cold.* | 10. **ô**, as in 'opium.' Ex. **ôm**, *we.* |

Some of these are occasionally modified; thus,

**ö** sounds as in German, or as **eu** in French, in 'fleur.'

Ex. **tökh**, *female.*

**ü**, as in German, or as **u** in French, in 'pur.'

Ex. **ütsh**, *five.*

**u**, at the end of a word, has a very fine sound, approaching to an **i**. The Drâviḍian 'half **u**.'

**a**, in the last syllable of a word, sounds like a very short **e**.

**ô** and **â** are almost always interchangeable: thus, the Kanarese *kâl* is in Tuḍa **kôl**.

§ 4. The Consonants are:

1. **k**, as in 'kalendar.' Ex. **âḍken**, *I play.*
2. **g**, as in 'gun.' Ex. **avaḷg**, *to her.*
3. **k'h**, as in 'blockhead.' Ex. **mokh**, *a son.*
4. **g'h**, as in 'loghouse.' Ex. any final **g** may be aspirated.
5. **j**, as in 'jam.' Ex. **majjal**, *yellow.*
6. **ch**, as in 'chin.' Ex. **chen**, *red.*
7. **t**, as in 'ten.' Ex. **terigi**, *again.*
8. **th**, as in 'this.' Ex. **atham**, *he.*
9. **th**, as in 'thin.' Ex. **nilthken**, *I stand.*
10. **d**, as in 'dog.' Ex. **nâd**, *wet.*
11. **ṭ**, lingual. Ex. **muṭṭiken**, *I feel.*
12. **ḍ**, lingual. Ex. **kûḍa**, *together.*
13. **p**, as in 'pen.' Ex. **pui**, *strike.*

| | |
|---|---|
| 14. **f**, as in 'fun.' | Ex. **pûf**, *an insect.* |
| 15. **b**, as in 'bull.' | Ex. **boath**, *a conical temple.* |
| 16. **v**, as in 'very.' | Ex. **vêr**, *another.* |
| 17. **b'h.** | Ex. **bhût**, *a demon.* |
| 18. **m**, as in 'man.' | Ex. **âm**, *Tuesday.* |
| 19. **n**, as in 'no.' | Ex. **tani**, *Saturday.* |
| 20. **l**, hard, lingual. | Ex. **beḷḷi**, *Friday.* |
| 21. **r**, hard, lingual. | Ex. **âṛ**, *six.* |
| 22. **s.** | Ex. **âsvom**, *Sunday.* |
| 23. **sh.** | Ex. **ütsh**, *five.* |
| 24. **zh.** | Ex. **êlzh**, *seven.* |

§ 5. It is difficult to decide whether all these sounds belong to the Tuḍa itself. The aspirates especially, except **kh** and **ch**, are, it may be suspected, foreign to it.

§ 6. Some of them seem to have arisen from the lingual ṛ, which is found in all the South-Indian languages, and which existed in the oldest forms of the Drâviḍian. In Madras it is sounded **y**, and in Tinnevelly **l**. In Telugu it is softened into **r**, or changed into **t** or **d**. It is a kind of triple **r**, sounded very far back in the throat, thus seeming to be a mixture of **r**, **l**, and **z**.

It resembles the Welsh **ll**. (Comp. § 43.)

| | | | | | |
|---|---|---|---|---|---|
| Thus Kan. *êḷu* | and Tam. | êṛu, *seven*, | make | in Tuḍa | **elzh.** |
| „ *kîḷ* | „ | kîṛ, *under* | „ | „ | **kirzh.** |
| „ *burude* | „ | puṛuti, *mud* | „ | „ | **purzh.** |

§ 7. It may be stated as a rule that the Tuḍa **sh** and **zh**, (which are strong linguals) generally represent a final **l** or **ḷ** of the Kanarese:

| | | | |
|---|---|---|---|
| Old Kan. and Tam. | *pal* (*lu*) | in Tuḍa | **parsh.** |
| „ | „ *âḷi*, *âri*, circle | „ | **ârsh.** |
| „ | „ *bil* (*lu*), *vil*, a bow | „ | **virzh.** |
| „ | „ *puli*, tiger | „ | **pürsh.** |

§ 8. Sometimes **sh** is the equivalent for the other linguals; thus,

Old Kan. and Tam. *karaḍi*, a bear, is **karsh.**

CHAP. XXIX.

§ 9. The letter **f** is pronounced by the Tuḍas full and clear, while any other Drâviḍian race would pronounce 'first' as *pirsht*, the sound of sharp **f** being unknown to them; as are some other sharp sounds, such as *th* in *thin*, and *s* in *sin*.

I think the Tuḍa **f** sound has arisen, as in English, from the corruption of a guttural or lingual.

*Enough* has become with us *enuf*.

So the Tuḍa **pûf**, 'an insect,' is probably Old Kan. *purlu*.

It must, however, be stated that the words in which **f** is found are precisely those which it is most difficult to trace. Thus,

**mituf** is 'nose' (? Kan. *mitte*, 'projecting').
**mâf** is a 'Baḍagan' (? (Kan.) *mâva*, 'father-in-law,' (used as a term of respect).
or a 'deer' (? *mân*).

§ 10. The lingual ḍ of the Kan. is in Tuḍa sometimes represented by r; thus,

**nar-k-en**, 'I walk.' (Kan. root *naḍ*).
**nôr**, 'district.' (Kan. nâḍ).

§ 11. **Th** (as in *thin*) and **sh** (lingual) are often euphonically (?) inserted in Tuḍa words. This is quite a Tuḍa peculiarity.

The former sound is not at all Drâviḍian (though it is Keltic); and the latter is only found in the other D. dialects in Sanskrit derivatives.

**Sh** is, however, quite the favourite Tuḍa sound.

Thus, **nilthken**, *I stand*. (§ 26.)
K. **Nil** + temp. part. **k** + inflectionable part. **en**.

Here **th** is a mere euphonic insertion.

**Ershken**, *I am*.
R. **er** + K. + **en**.

Here, too, **sh** is probably a mere euphonic insertion.

§ 12. In Tuḍa **v** or **w** is optionally pronounced before **o** initial; thus, **vodd**=*one*; but in the compound we find **oddi-adi**=*alone* (lit. one-step); and **on** or **or** is the Drâviḍian root. So in English 'one' is pronounced 'won.' CHAP. XXIX.

The possession of this sound of **w** is one of the many noteworthy analogies between the Keltic languages and the Drâviḍian.

So **y** may, as in the other Drâv. dialects, be prefixed to any word beginning with **e**. Thus, **enak** or **yenak**=*to me.*

This, too, is found in English, and is probably due to Keltic influences: *ewe* is pronounced *yew.*

## NOUNS.

§ 13. Tuḍa nouns have no inflections for number or gender.

§ 14. The Nominative, Accusative, Vocative, and Genitive cases are alike, being the unaltered root.

§ 15. The inflectional particles in use are, (1) for the dative, **g** or **k**; (2) for the instrumental ablative and the ablative of remotion, **end** (or **edd**); and (3) for the local ablative **orzh**.

These correspond very exactly to the Old Kanarese, *ge*, *inda*, and *oḷ* (comp. § 43).

§ 16. The following is a **Paradigm** of a Tuḍa noun:

| | **âḷ**, *a man* |
|---|---|
| N. Acc. Voc. Gen. | **âḷ**, *a man* |
| Dat. | **âḷg**, *to* or *for a man* |
| Abl. (instrum. and remotion) | **âḷend** (**âḷedd**), *by* or *from a man* |
| (place) . . . | **âḷorzh**, *in a man.* |

§ 17. Since the nominative, accusative, and genitive cases are alike, it is chiefly by position that the syntax of a Tuḍa sentence is regulated. A noun immediately before a transitive verb is the object; while a noun before another noun is in the genitive case, or qualifies it like an adjective.

CHAP. XXIX.

In the latter case **ad**, the root of the epicene pronoun of the 3rd person, appears to be sometimes inserted, making what looks like a genitive case.

This resembles the Kan. usage. In that language, certain nouns add **d** to the root to form the inflectional base, which is used for any case. The Tamil adds *thu* (*th* flat) to the root to form a genitive.

§ 18. The Tuḍa pronouns are irregular, but correspond very closely to those of the other Drâviḍian dialects.

## § 19. THE PERSONAL PRONOUNS.

(1) The pronoun of the 1st person.

| | SINGULAR. | PLURAL. |
|---|---|---|
| Nom. | **ân**, *I* | **ôm**, **âm**, *we* |
| Acc. | **yen**, *me* | **yem**, **âm**, *us* |
| Gen. | **yen** ; **yen-adu**, *my*, *mine* | **yem** ; **yem-adu**, *our*, *ours* |
| Dat. | **yen-ak**, *to* or *for me* | **yem-ak**, *to* or *for us* |
| Abl. | { **yen-end** / **-edd** } *from me.* | { **yem-end**, / **âm-end**, **âm-edd** } *from us* |

NOTE.—The original form of the Drâviḍian pronoun of the 1st person is uncertain.

(1.) In the oldest dialect of Tamil and in Tulu it is *yán*, in Old Kanarese án, in Old Telugu ênu, in Malayalim nján.

(2.) The inflections of this pronoun in nearly all the cognate languages have *en* ; and in the oldest forms *y* is prefixed at pleasure to all cases beginning with *e*.

(3.) The pronoun when appended to the Drâviḍian verb in *an*, *en*, ini, eni, én.

(4.) In later Tamil Kanarese and Telugu we find forms nân, nâm, and nénu, in the Nom. Singular ; and nâm, mému in the Nom. Plural. This *n* or *m* I do not regard as primitive, since it is wanting in all the old forms. The Drâviḍian languages prefix *n* to several words which they have received from other languages. Thus the Sanskrit *yuga* is in Tamil *nugam* ; and *nangûram* is the form in which the word *anchor* has settled down in the Drâviḍian dialects. I can see how *n* might have crept in ; I cannot imagine its disappearance from every ancient dialect.

(5.) This is not the place for a full discussion of the subject ; but I would compare *ân* with the very ancient form S. *aham*.

Nor can I think it clear that ôm is not related to the Sanskrit **vayam**, or to the Greek ἡμεῖς or ἄμμες, and Védic *asmê*.

§ 20. (2) The pronoun of the 2nd person. CHAP. XXIX.

| | SINGULAR. | PLURAL. |
|---|---|---|
| Nom. Voc. | **nî** | **nim-a** |
| Acc. Gen. | **nin** | **nim** |
| Dat. | **nin-ak** | **nim-ak**<br>**nim, nim-adu** |
| Abl. | **nin-end** or **nin-edd,** *by* or *from thee*<br>**nin-orzh,** *in thee* | **nim-end, nim-edd**<br>**nim-oṛzh** |

This closely resembles the ancient Kanarese and Tamil.

I do not know whether it is of use to point out the Drâviḍian root *nil,* 'stand,' with its past part. in Kan. *ninu,* as the possible origin of this pronoun.

Here **n** is, I think, undoubtedly radical.

§ 21. The pronoun of the 3rd person in Tuḍa (which is really a demonstrative pronoun, or adjective) has the peculiarity, that like the Latin *se,* it has no inflection for gender or number.

Thus **atham**=*he, she, it, they.*

[Generally *m* is an indistinct nasal, the anuswâra of the Sanskrit.]

It is declined like àl (§ 16).

| | |
|---|---|
| N. A. G. | **atham** |
| Dat. | **athan-g** |
| Abl. | **ath-end, atham-edd, athamend**<br>**atham-orzh, ath-orzh.** |

The resemblance to S. **adas** is remarkable.

Kan. **âtanu**=he ; **adu**=it.

It will be remarked that the verbal forms of the 3rd person make no distinction of number or gender. (Comp. § 26.)

This is a remote demonstrative (ille, &c.) ; **itham** is used for the proximate (hic, &c.).

CHAP. XXIX.

Besides this oldest form the Tuḍa uses the pronouns

**avan** (ille) ; **ivan** (hic)
**aval** (illa) ; **ival** (hæc)
with their plurals
**avar** ; **ivar**, which are declined like **âl**, with the addition of a kind of genitive in *du* : avandu, &c.

Here **avan**, &c., are the remote demonstratives, and **ivan**, &c., the proximate demonstratives.

These appear to be forms recently introduced, or, it may be, reintroduced into Tuḍa from Kanarese or Tamil.

*Avandu*=avan + du, and is prefixed to a noun adjectivally, and so forms a kind of genitive case: *avandu kukh*=his wife. (§ 17.)

The use of **a** and **i** as demonstrative prefixes is thoroughly Drâviḍian.

The root of this pronoun is evidently **d**.

## § 22. TUḌA ADVERBS.

(1) Words answering to English adverbs exist in Tuḍa. Some of them are also used as nouns, some are parts of the verb.

(2) The following list includes nearly all that are in use.

| | | |
|---|---|---|
| 1. *yes* | **hâ** | These seem to be really interjections. |
| 2. *no* | **âha** | |
| 3. *here, there, where* | **ite, ate, ete** | Here the *i*, *a*, *e*, as demonstrative and interrogative particles appear. |
| 4. *why* | **ête** | T. and K. |
| 5. *how* | **yetete** | Reduplicate of ete. (3.) |
| 6. *who, what?* | **athario** | Atham=*it*, âr=*who*? ô an interrogative particle. |
| 7. *above* | **mêl, mok** | *Mêl* is Drâviḍian. Mok from Sansk. =*before*. |
| 8. *below* | **kli, erk** | Kan. keḷa, irrida. Tam. kîr, irrakka. |
| 9. *before* (place) | **mud** | Drâviḍ. *mun*, mundu. |
| *before* (time) | **much** | Kan. *munche*. |

| | | |
|---|---|---|
| 10. *behind* | **pinne** | A. Kan. *pinde.* |
| 11. *outside* | **porram** | A. Kan. pora. purram in T. |
| 12. *inside* | **ulg** | Uḷ, *within*, in the dative case. |
| 13. *much* / 14. *more* [comp. (23)=*yet much*] | **upâm** / **innupâm** | A. K. *ubbarige.* In Kan. Tam. and Tel. *up* or *ub* is a root signifying increase. Comp. Sansk. upari. |
| 15. *near* | **kekhuri** | This seems to be a corruption of Kan. *kaige* oḷ=*in hand* or *at hand.* |
| 16. *far* | **bathki** | *Badike*=near, in K. |
| 17. *also, together* | **kûḍa** | Infin. of Kûḍu, *come together.* |
| 18. *alone* | **oddi-aḍi** | Odd=one. aḍi=*step, a time.* |
| 19. *frequently* | **upâm-aḍi** | Comp. (13)=more-step. |
| 20. *soon, suddenly* | **birnd** | Kan. biri-biri (§ 34.) |
| 21. *again* | **terigi** | Kan. *tirige.* |
| 22. *enough* | **ettana** | In Tamil=*this much.* Kan. ittani=the whole. |
| 23. *yet* | **in** | Kan. *innu*, more, yet. |
| 24. *when* | **etwan** | Compare (3). |
| 25. *then* | **atwan** | |
| 26. *now* | **itwan** | |
| 27. *for ever* | **etwan-etwan** | Lit.=when- when. |
| 28. *another* | **in odd**=yet one. | |

## § 23. TUḌA ADJECTIVES.

(1) There are a few words which appear to be adjectives by nature; but the majority are merely nouns placed before other nouns to qualify or limit their meaning.

(2) The following list contains some of the adjectives now in common use.

| | | |
|---|---|---|
| 1. *good* / 2. *pretty* | **ulṭhe** | *oḷ, oḷḷi, oḷḷida*, in Kan. *thi*=*thu* or *du* or *di*, |
| | **nal** | *nal* in O. Kan., and Tam., and in the other Drâv. dialects. |
| 3. *old* | **keḷ** | *Kiṛa* in Tam., *kerr* in O. Kan. |

CHAP. XXIX.

| | | | |
|---|---|---|---|
| 4. *big* | **êt-ud** | *êtt*=elevation, in Tamil. In Kan. *êḷda*=having risen | *ud* in *êtud* and in *kirud* is evidently *atham* =it. |
| 5. *little* | **kin, kir-ud** | Tam. *çin, çirridu.* Kan. *kin, kir* | |
| 6. *hot* | **bîrsh** | Kan. *bisi, bishi, bisilu* | |
| 7. *cold* | **kor** | Drâviḍian root is *kuḷ* | |
| 8. *wet* | **nâd** | This is Kan. *nâd, nân, nând* | |
| 9. *dry* | **voṇag** | K. *oṇa, oṇagu.* In Tam. *uṇa* | This *g* or *gu* a strengthening part. in K. and T. |
| 10. *male* | **têk-an** | *an* is the Drâv. masc. term. | Here seems to be an internal modification of a root to distinguish gender. |
| 11. *female* | **tökh** | These words cannot be traced to any Drâviḍian root. *dêham*= body. *tô-gai* is a poet. word for woman | |
| 12. *white* | **bel-thi**<br>**belp** | Kan. *beḷ* | |
| 13. *red* | **chen**<br>**bâkh-gudi**<br>**kandati**<br>**kepu** | Kan. *chen*, kudi, *kanda, kempu* | |
| 14. *yellow* | **majjal** | Tam. *manjal* | |
| 15. *black, blue, green* | **kar-thti** | Kan. *kari* | |
| 16. *other* | **vêr** | Kan. *bêre.* Tam. *vêrru.* | |
| 17. *great* | **perud** | | |

(3) These roots, probably among the oldest in the language, are, with hardly an exception, common to all the Drâviḍian languages; but the peculiarities of the Kanarese are found in the Tuḍa.

§ 24. Forms answering to the comparative and superlative degrees are obtained by putting a noun in the 'ablative of remotion' before the adjective; and by prefixing the adverb *upâm*=much. CHAP. XXIX.

Thus: **athumed-kirud**, *smaller than it*
**âḷed-êtud**, *greater than a man*
**upâm-êtud**, **upâmkirud**, *greatest*, *smallest*

## § 25. THE TUḌA VERBS.

(1) The Tuḍa verb has I. an affirmative form consisting of an indicative mood and an imperative mood; II. a negative form, with the same two moods.

(2) It has two tenses: I. An indefinite tense, which is present or future; II. A past tense.

(3) There are fragments of other forms which can only be conjecturally restored.

§ 26. The verb '*to be*' is thus inflected.

Root **er**.

I. Affirmative Form.

*Indicative Mood.*

(I) Indefinite Present.

| | Singular. | Plural. |
|---|---|---|
| 1. | (**ân**) **er–sh–k–en**, *I am* | (**ôm**) **er–sh–k–imi** |
| 2. | (**nî**) **er–sh–ch–i** | (**nima**) **er–sh–ch–i** |
| 3. | (**avan**) **er–sh–ch–i** | (**avar**) **er–sh–ch–i**. |

(II) Indefinite Past.

| | Singular. | Plural. |
|---|---|---|
| 1 | (**ân**) **edd–er–sh–p–ini**, *I was* | (**ôm**) **edd–er–sh–p–imi** |
| 2 | (**nî**) } **edd–er–sh–ch–i** | (**nima**) } **edd–er–sh–ch–i** |
| 3 | (**avan**). } | (**avar**) } |

This is evidently a compound form obtained by prefixing **edd** to the present tense: **edd** being for **erd.** (§ 30.)

The 1st pers. sing. takes what seems to be an alternative form in **p-ini**: **ershpini**=**ershken.**

CHAP. XXIX.

**Sh** is the Tuḍa substitute for **k**: **shk**=**kk**
**Ch** is a softened form of **k**: so in Saxon, spæc=*speech*
sceal=*shall.*

*Imperative Mood.*

**ėru**, *be thou*
**ir-mâ**, *let it be.*

Of this **mâ** I can give no explanation.

II. NEGATIVE FORM.

(I) Indefinite Present: *I, &c., am not.*

| | SINGULAR. | PLURAL. |
|---|---|---|
| 1. | **ir-eni** | **ir-emi** |
| 2. | **ir-e** | **ir-e** |
| 3. | **ir-adi** | **ir-adi** |

(II) Indefinite Past: *I, &c., was not.*

| | | |
|---|---|---|
| 1. | **er-th-eni** | **er-th-emi** |
| 2. | **er-th-e** | **er-th-e** |
| 3. | **er-th-adi** | **er-th-adi** |

§ 27. The Verb âḍ, *dance*, is thus inflected.

I. AFFIRMATIVE FORM.

*Indicative Mood.*

(I) Indefinite Present: *I, &c., dance.*

| | SINGULAR. | PLURAL. |
|---|---|---|
| 1. | **àḍ-k-en** | **àḍ-k-emi** |
| 2. | **àḍ-ch-i** | **àḍ-ch-i** |
| 3. | **àḍ-ch-i** | **àḍ-ch-i** |

(II) Indefinite Past: *I, &c., dancea.*

| | | |
|---|---|---|
| 1. | **âḍ-th-b-ini** | **àḍ-th-b-imi** |
| 2. 3. | **àḍ-th-ch-i** | **àḍ-th-ch-i** |

*Imperative Mood.*

**pui**, *strike*!
**pui mâ**, *let him strike*!

### II. Negative Form.

*Indicative Mood.*

(I) Indefinite Present : *I, &c., dance not.*

| | Singular. | Plural. |
|---|---|---|
| 1. | **âḍ-eni** | **âḍ-emi** |
| 2. | **áḍ-e** | **áḍ-e** |
| 3. | **áḍ-adi** | **áḍ-adi** |

(II) Indefinite Past : *I, &c., danced not.*

| | | |
|---|---|---|
| 1. | **âṭa ger-th-eni** | **âṭa ger-th-emi** |
| 2. | **âṭa ger-th-e** | **âṭa ger-th-e** |
| 3. | **âṭa ger-th-adi** | **âṭa ger-th-adi** |

*Imperative Mood.*

**pui ad iru** }
**pui âṭu** } *strike not* !

N.B. Of these, one is Kan. and the other Tamil.

§ 28. It will be seen from these paradigms that the Tuḍa, like the other Drâviḍian dialects, has *temporal particles*, which are inserted between the root and the personal terminations. In the present tense affirmative the temporal particle is K, which is softened into CH (as in *Church*), before I.

In the 1st persons S. and P. a *p* or *b* (it is pronounced both ways) is occasionally found. This may have some connexion with the temporal particle found in the present, in Old Kanarese, which is DAP.

This is almost the only part of the Tuḍa language that seems to indicate great antiquity. It is, however, Old Kanarese.

In ordinary Kanarese there is scarcely a trace of the *k*, which being softened into *h*, or *v*, has finally disappeared.

In Tamil it remains in the temporal particle of the present *Kirru* or *Girru* ; in a strengthening particle *gu* added to many roots ; and in some old poetical forms, such as *çey-gu*= I will do ; *çey-gum*, we will do.

CHAP. XXIX. In Malayalim it is still found in the present of many verbs: in the form of *kunnu*.

In the old form Kanarese *bê-ku*, 'must,' it is preserved; as also in *çâ-ku*, 'it is enough.'

In Old Kanarese *kum* and *gum* may be appended to any root to form an aorist. This admits no variation for number or person. Thus *avar mâḍugum*=they do.

In the past the *temporal particle* is TH (as in *thin*). This is *d* in Kanarese.

The negative mode is obtained by joining the root to the personal termination without the intervention of any temporal particle. This is common to all the Drâviḍian languages.

§ 29. The personal terminations are for the

| | SINGULAR. | PLURAL. |
|---|---|---|
| I. Pers. | *en, eni, ini* | *imi, emi* |
| II. Pers. | *i, e* | |
| III. Pers. | *i, adi* | |

These are shortened forms of the pronouns. See §§ 19–21.

§ 30. There are also in Tuḍa traces of other verbal forms which are peculiar to the Drâviḍian family of languages.

The relative participle, or adjective form of the verb, is one of these.

*In the day when I joined*, is in Tuḍa:

> **ân kûḍid nâḷorzh**
> [*I joined day-in*].

Here *kûḍid* is in Kanarese *kûḍida*, and is called a 'relative participle,' qualifying *day*, and being equivalent to *when* (*I*) *joined*, thus including in itself the relative adverb.

So, **ân âḍid nâḷ**, *the day I danced.*
Thus **edd** is=Kan. *idda*, 'which was.' (§ 26.)

§ 31. Tuḍa also forms a verbal noun, a kind of infinitive, from verbs ending in a flat consonant by changing the flat into its corresponding sharp, as in all the other Drâviḍian languages. CHAP. XXIX.

Thus âḍ, *dance* or *play*, makes

> **âṭa**, *dancing* [Tam. aḍu, aṭṭam; Kan. áḍu, áṭa, and in Tel. the same].

The past tense of the negative form is thus:

âṭa ger-ṭh-eni
*dancing did-(not)-I.* (§ 27.)

And here (1) Is not *ger-th* singularly like the Sanskrit *krita*, done? Surely this is the KAR of the Indo-Germanic 'grund-sprache.'

(2) May this not throw light on the Tamil temporal particle *kirra*? and probably on the K. (§ 28.)

(3) Does it not seem that the negative particle in such forms is really dropped? The emphatic 'dancing-did-I' remains, and the formula of negation has perished. (Comp. Earle's Philology of the English Tongue, p. 427.)

§ 32. In examining the forms of the verb still surviving among the Tuḍas, it becomes evident that many verbal inflections have been dropped. We have, it seems, but the débris of an elaborate inflectional system. There was probably a future tense with *temporal particle* **v**, **p**, or **b**, as in Kanarese and Tamil. This has disappeared, as in Saxon, and the present (like the English indefinite present) is now used as a future with an adverb. The forms **âḍ-th-b-ini** and **er-sh-p-imi** are probably remnants of it. (§ 27.)

§ 33. An infinitive mood in **a** perhaps existed; for the adverb **kûḍa** is the infinitive of **kûḍ**, unless indeed this is a word of recent importation. (§ 22.)

§ 34. The adverb *birnd*, 'suddenly,' seems to be from a root which is found in Old Kanarese, *biri*, 'burst,' and in

CHAP. XXIX. Tamil *viṛu*, 'fall,' from which, in the latter dialect, the past adv. participle, *viṛundu*, is formed. There is, therefore, a trace of a *past adv.* part. (§ 22.)

§ 35. There is no passive inflection in Tuḍa.

§ 36. The interrogative forms are obtained by adding **â**, which, as in Tamil and in Old Kanarese, is the chief interrogative particle.

Thus *has Beḷiâni joined?* is, **Beḷiâni kûḍthiyâ?**

**E** and **ô** are also interrogative letters in Tuḍa.

§ 37. It is not easy to decide whether the Tuḍa retains any trace of a subjunctive mood.

The following sentence seems to contain something equivalent to it.

**Atham Nastufig kûḍâ vaḷi, kukh in odd âḷk ûḍthchi**
*He to Nastufi not joining (marrying) when, (the) woman yet one man has married.*
If he do not marry Nastufi, she will marry another man.

Here **kûḍâ** is apparently a negative participle qualifying the noun **vaḷi**=time (Kan. *vêḷe*).

The forms **pôk-âdi** and **pôk-ârzh** are found with the meaning *of go.* Here **âdi** and **ârzh** are joined to the root. They seem to be the Kan. **arê** or Tam. **âl.** But they are probably borrowed from Tamil.

The verbal root is the imperative of 2nd pers. sing.; thus, âḍ, *play thou.* Another form adds mâ to the root; thus, pui-mâ, *strike thou.*

§ 38. The Tuḍa has neither prepositions nor conjunctions. This want of 'link words' is an index of the entire absence of the habit of reasoning.

§ 39. By way of illustration, I added a few sentences.

## SENTENCES.

(The words are in the subjoined lists.)

(1) When I married Beḷiâni I was a widow.
**ân Beḷiânig kúḍid nâḷorzh ân barudi.**
*I to-Beḷiâni joined in-day I widow.*

(2) Is Nastufi married?
**Nastufig beḷthta gavthyâ?**
*to-Nastufi silver tied?*
**beḷthta** = *silver badge.* (In Kan. beḷḷe = *silver* + (?) tâli = *marriage token.*)
**gavthyâ** = *gavth* + à or yà.
This seems to be an adv. part. = *having tied* (§ 34), followed by the interrog. (§ 36).

(3) Is Beliâni married?
**Beḷiâni kukhag kûdṭhyâ?**
*Beḷiâni to-a woman joined?*
**kukhag.** Here *a* is inserted to connect **kukh** with its case ending *g*.

(4) Your wife walks not with my wife.
**Nin kaṭṭ-vodi-kukh yen kaṭṭ-vodi—kukh naḍevadi.**
**nade vadi** (§ 27). Kan. nade = *walk.*
*v* is a Euphonic insertion.

(5) My uncle's sons are my brothers.

| **Yen** | **perudên** | **kirudên** | **mokh** | **yen** | **aṇan** | **taman** |
|---|---|---|---|---|---|---|
| *My* | *great-father* | *little-father* | *son* | *my* | *elder-brother* | *younger-brother* |
| | | **erhschi.** | | | | |
| | | *are.* | | | | |

**yen** (§ 19) **perud, kirud** (§ 23).
**aṇan** (K. aṇa = *elder brother.* The R. seem to mean *above.*)
**taman** (K. tamma = *younger brother*).
**ên** (K. ayya = *father, priest*).
**ershchi** (§ 26).

The final **n**, as the termination of masculine nouns, here seems to be fairly in the language; but I suspect it is only an obscure nasal, not differing from the epicene ending **m** in **atham.**

CHAP. XXIX.

(6) That one's father and this one's father are brothers-in-law (relatives).

**atham ên itham ên bêâḷ**
*That father this father related-man*
**atham, itham** (§ 21)
**bêâl** (bê the root of the Kan. Impersonal verb *béku*+âḷ (§ 16)).

It will be seen that the Tuḍas now use no conjunctions, a sign of their degeneracy. 'Link words' of all kinds are wanting. In fact, Tuḍa has scarcely any 'symbolic' words, except pronouns, and the smallest possible supply of these.

(7) Beḷiâni is married, but has no son.

**Beḷiâni kukh kùḍthchi, mokh illaḍe edd**
**illade** (Kan. *illada*=what is not)
**edd**=*having been* (§ 30)

The finite verb **ershchi** is understood.

## § 40. LISTS OF WORDS.

### I. Verbal Roots.

| | | |
|---|---|---|
| 1. *am, sit* | **er** | Dr. *ir*, *urr*, *uḷ* (Sansk. RI). |
| 2. *see* | { **kân-th** / **nôḍ-th** | K. *kâṇ*. / K. *nôd*. |
| 3. *hear* | **kêḷ-th** | K. *kêḷ*. |
| 4. *feel, touch* | **muṭṭi** | K. *muṭṭ*. |
| 5. *taste* | **bâi kâṇ-th** | =see (with the) mouth. |
| 6. *smell* | **mittuf kâṇ-th** | =see (with the) nose. |
| 7. *dream* | **kanas kâṇ-th** | =I see a vision. K. *kanas*. |
| 8. *laugh* | **kar-th** | K. *chiri-chu*. |
| 9. *weep* | **âḍ** | K. *aḷu*. T. *aṛu*. (S. *açru*.) |
| 10. *sing* | **ka-th âḍ** | =I play a story. K. *kaṭhe*. S. *kathâ*. |
| 11. *shout* | **A! U! bishar-th** | =I cry A! U! K. *bicchâd*. |
| 12. *talk* | **arvorkh** | K. *alavâke*=loquacity. |
| 13. *dance, play* | **âḍ** | K. *âḍ*. |
| 14. *stand* | **nil-th** | K. *nil*. |
| 15. *walk* | **naṛ** | K. *naḍ*. |
| 16. *run* | **voḍi** | K. *ôḍ*. |
| 17. *lie down* | **vori** | probably a variation of 25. |

18. *give* — **tash** — K. *tar-u.*
19. *clean* — **ârzp** — K. *âḷdu*=to dip ; *alasu*, to rinse.
20. *bow, salute* — **kombuddi** — K. *kumbu*+iḍu.
21. *ask* — **bind er-th** — K. *bêḍ.* Tam. *vênḍ.*
22. *strike* — **pui** — K. *poḍe.* Old Kan. *poyu.*
23. *kill* — **kêḍigidviti** — K. *kêḍ*=destruction. O.K. *geidu*, made. Is **vi** a causal inflection ?
24. *die* — **kêdiverti** — (? Sansk. VRIT. Dr. padu.)
25. *sleep* — **vorikh** — K. *orag-u.*
26. *do, make* — **gei** — O. K. *gê, gei.*
27. *take* — **va-th, ba-th** — K. *hatt* or *patt.*
28. *join* — **kûḍ-th** — K. *kûḍ.*
29. *tie on* — **gav-th** — K. *kaṭṭ* (but ? *kavi*=put on).
30. *negative verb* — **il** — K. *il.*
31. *it thunders* — **yêr-th-ti** — K. *yere.*
32. *go* — **pôk** — K.

§ 41. II. NOUNS.

1. *a span* — **gên** — (Kan. *gêṇu.* Tam. *sáṇ.*)
2. *a foot* — **eddgên, aḍi** — (K. *aḍi*).
3. *a cubit* — **mlâ, mlâgei** — (K. *moḷa*).
4. *a pace* — **kandaf** — (?)

---

5. *a name* — **pêru, hesru** — (Kan.)
6. *a nickname* — **porra-hesru** — (=outside name) (Kan.)
7. *a collection* — **kûṭu** — (Kan.)
8. *medicine* — **maddu** — (K. *maddu.* Tam. *marunthu*).
9. *dowry* — **këikuli**
10. *friend* — **yenkâḷ** — (Lit.=a man to me, §§ 16, 19).
11. *old man* — **keḷâḷ** — (A. K. *keṛiva*, § 6).
12. *old woman* — **keḷachi** — (K. *keṛ.* Fem. term. *ti* or *chi* is Dr.).

---

13. *family* — **kûṭasâram** — (Sansk.)

| | | |
|---|---|---|
| 14. *relation* | **aṇatama** | (K. *ana*=elder brother; *tama*=younger brother). |
| | **pâltiâḷ** | (K. *pál*). |
| | **pâyâl** | (K. *bê*+*âḷ*). |
| 15. *ancestor* | **mûpu** | (K. *mûppu*=old). |
| 16. *clan* | (No Tuḍa word) | |
| 17. *man, person, husband* | **âl** | |
| 18. *a young man* | **varsh** | (S. *bâla*). |
| 19. *son, boy* | **mokh** | (K. *maga*); **popen.** (?) **tüj mokh**=daughter (§ 23). |
| 20. *woman, girl, daughter, wife* | **kukh** | (? Comp. S. *guhya.* Tam. *kokku, kongu.* Perhaps a depreciatory word connected with the root *kug*). |
| 21. *father* | **appn, êyan, ên** | (Kan.) |
| 22. *mother* | **avv** | (Kan. *avva*). |
| 23. *wife* | **kâṭvoti** | (Kan. *kattubaḍi* = one bound). |
| 24. *bachelor* | **mokh-varsh** | |
| 25. *child* | **kin-mokh** (m.), **tüj-mokh** (f.) (§ 23) | |
| 26. *child* (infant) | **popen** (m.) (?) **kin-minthki** (f.) | (*Kin.* § 23, *minthki* is of uncertain origin; ? *manushi*: probably a pet word). |
| 27. *twins* | **mor-mokh** | (perhaps *mor* = *marr* = other). |
| 28. *orphan* | **tobbâri** | (K. *tobbili*). |
| 29. *widower* | **baruḍa** | (A. K. *baraḍa*=empty). |
| 30. *widow* | **mudegitti, barudi** | (K. *muṇḍe*). |
| 31. *great-grandfather* | **pêvian** | **pî** or **pêvi** +21, 22 — (*pî, pêvi,* forms of *piri,* 'great.') |
| 32. *great-grandmother* | **pêviavv** | |
| 33. *grandfather* | **pîyan** | |
| 34. *grandmother* | **pîyavv** | |
| 35. *brother* (younger) | **ennorvet** | (**en**=my, **or**=one, **vet**=*petta,* which in A. K.= brought forth). |
| 36. *brother* (elder) | **ennaṇ** | (*en*+*aṇ*. Kan.). |
| 37. *brother* or *sister* (younger) | **enta** | (Lit.=that one). |

| | | |
|---|---|---|
| 38. *sister* (elder) | **en akka** | (Kan.). |
| 39. *mother-in-law, father's sister* | **mâmi** | (Kan.). |
| 40. *father-in-law, mother's brother* | **mâman** | (Kan.). |
| 41. *son's wife* | **mortwirth** | (? Tam. *maru-magaḷ*). |
| 42. *daughter's husband* | **enman mokh** | |
| 43. *father's brother* (elder) | **ennan perud** | |
| 44. *father's brother* (younger) | **ennan kirud** | |
| 45. *mother's sister* (elder) | **perud avv** | |
| 46. *mother's sister* (younger) | **kirud avv** | |
| 47. *husband's brother* (elder) | **yen âl ennan** | |
| 48. *husband's brother* (younger) | **yen âl norvet** | |
| 49. *wife's sister* (elder) | **yen kâtvoti akkan** | |
| 50. *wife's sister* (younger) | **yen kâtvoti norvet kukh** | |
| 51. *wife's brother* | **pâyâl** | |

---

| | | |
|---|---|---|
| 52. *spear* | **îṭ** | (Kan.). |
| 53. *bow* | **virzh** | (§ 7). |
| 54. *arrow* | **âbu** | (Kan., Tam., Tel., Mal. *ambu.* Here the Tuḍa has dropped *m*, and lengthened the vowel, as compensation.) |
| 55. *knife* | **tûri** | (K. *dûru*, go through). |
| 56. *club* | **kuṇḍu** | (K. *guṇḍu*). |
| 57. *net* | **balle** | (K. *bâle*). |
| 58. *axe* | **mosht** | (? A. Tam. *maṛi*). |
| 59. *hatchet* | **kûrvâl** | (K. *kûr*=sharp; *bâl-u*= knife. This is the exact Tamil; a Poligar word?). |

N. B.—No Tuḍa word for *cow*, *plough*, *sword*, or *shield*.

CHAP. XXIX.

| | | |
|---|---|---|
| 60. *buffalo* (male) | **êsht** | (*êrru*=ascend, is the Drâv. for the male of any animal). |
| 61. *buffalo* (female) | **er** | (Kan. *emme*. Tam. *erumai*. Mal. *erima*. Tel. *enumu*). |
| 62. *calf* (male) | **koan** | (Kan. *kand-u*=a calf). |
| 63. *calf* (female) | **karr** | (K. *karu*=a calf.) |
| 64. *deer* | **mâf** | (Dr. *mân*). |
| 65. *dog* | **nai** | (Kan.) |
| 66. *dog* (wild) | **chen-nai** | (Red-dog, § 23). |
| 67. *cat* | **kotti** | (Kan. *kotti*). |
| 68. *tiger* | **pürsh** | (§ 7). |
| 69. *bear* | **karsh** | (§ 8). |
| 70. *snake* | **pàb** | (Kan. *pâv-u*. Tam. *pâmb-u*. Tel. *pàm-u*). |
| 71. *mouse* | **irzh** | (Kan. *ili*=a rat). |
| 72. *bird* | **bilti** | (Kan. *beḷ* seems to be the root of it). |
| 73. *crow* | **kàk** | (Kan.). |
| 74. *sparrow* | **gubbi bilti** | (See 72. Kan. *gubbi*=sparrow). |
| 75. *fish* | **mîn** | (Kan.). |
| 76. *insect* | **pûf** | (§ 9). |
| 77. *butterfly* | **kappan** | (?). |
| 78. *louse* | **pên** | (Kan.). |
| 79. *bird's nest* | **bilt-gûdu** | (Kan.). |
| 80. *bird's egg* | **much** | (Tam. *muṭṭai*. Kan. *guḍḍu*). |

---

| | | |
|---|---|---|
| 81. *village* | **mand, madd** | (K. *mande*=herd). |
| 82. *house, room* | **ârsh** | (*âri* = ring, circular enclosure, or *arrai*=room, in Drâv.). |
| 83. *cattle-pen* | **tuel** | (Dr. *toṛu* = fold. A. K. *turu*=cow). |
| 84. *dairy* | **pâlthchi** | (*pâl*+?). |
| 85. *village-wall* | **tuar** | (Tam. *çuvar*; *ç* and *t* are interchangeable). |
| 86. *fire-place* | **vorsh, vorsh-kâll** | (K. *ole*. § 6). |
| 87. *milk-pail* | **honnu** | (? Tam. *pânê*). |
| 88. *cattle-bell* | **konku** or **kong, gette** | |
| 89. *milk* | **pâl** | (A. K. *pâl*). |

| | | | |
|---|---|---|---|
| 90. | *ghee* (clarified butter) | **nei** | (A. K. *neyi*). |
| 91. | Affixes to names of villages | **gadu, gudu,** iri, **ari** | Drâ. *kuḍi*=tenancy, habitation. **iri, ari,** from root *er*. |

| | | | |
|---|---|---|---|
| 92. | *head* | **madd** | (K. *maṇḍe*). |
| 93. | *skull* | **madd-uvar** | |
| 94. | *face* | **konmun** | |
| 95. | *eye* | **kaṇṇu** | (K.). |
| 96. | *nose* | **mituf** | (*miṭṭe*, a projection+?). |
| 97. | *mouth* | **bâi** | (K.). |
| 98. | *ear* | **kevi** | (K. *kivi*). |
| 99. | *tooth* | **parsh** | (K. *pal-lu*, § 6). |
| 100. | *hand* | **kei** | (K.). |
| 101. | *foot* | **kâl** | (K.). |
| 102. | *finger* | **beḷh** | (K. *beraḷ-u*). |
| 103. | *toe* | **kàl belh** | (=foot-finger). |
| 104. | *navel* | **pokku** | (A. Kan. *pokkuḷ-u*). |
| 105. | *blood* | **bâkh** | (?) The word means *red*; comp. *râg*. |
| 106. | *membrum virile* | **boḍḍ** | (Kan.). |
| 107. | *pudendum muliebre* | **âkukh, kuk** | (= a receptacle; comp. 20). |

| | | | |
|---|---|---|---|
| 108. | *God, Lord, High Lord* | **dêr, swâmi, ûsuru swâmi** | (K. *dêvar-u swâmi* (S.)). |
| 109. | *demon* | **bhût** | S. |
| 110. | *ghost* | **bhût** | S. |
| 111. | *idol* | (No Tuḍa word) | |
| 112. | *heaven* | **amnôr** | (? *a*=that; § 21; *nâd*=region). |
| 113. | *right* | **sari** | (Kan.) |
| 114. | *sin* | **pâpam** | (S.). |
| 115. | *life* | **dsivl** | (? S. and Dr. *jîva*: also the organs of generation in a polite way). |
| 116. | *breath* | **dîv** | |
| 117. | *relic* | **kurpu, maṇi** | (A.K. *kurupu*=sign, *maṇi* =bell. Every **maṇi** is a **kurpu**, but every **kurpu** is not a **maṇi**). |

CHAP. XXIX.

| | | | |
|---|---|---|---|
| 118. | *Toda sanctum* | **tiriêri** | (K. *tiru* = sacred, *are* = place. Comp. Saxon *dry*=a magician, druid). |
| 119. | *temple* (conical) | **boath, boa** | (? The words *booth* and *bothy* present a curious resemblance). |
| 120. | *sacred shrub* | **tûre, tûde, zhûre** | (S. *tulasi*, the 'Ocymum sanctum'). |
| 121. | *bell-god* | **maṇi-dêr, konku-dêr, get-dêr** | (Comp. 88, 108, 117). |
| 122. | *head priest* | **pâlâl** | (=milkman). |
| 123. | *sacrificing priest* | **vorshâl** | (=man of the fireplace). |
| 124. | *sacred dairyman* | **pâlkârpâl** | |
| 125. | *sacred herdsman* | **kâvilâl** | |
| 126. | *religious custom* | **shâstr** | (S.). |

---

| | | | |
|---|---|---|---|
| 127. | *a kairn* | **vinn** | (A. K. *vind-u*=a heap). |
| 128. | *a kromlech* | (No Tuḍa name) | Termed 'stonedairies' or 'little houses.' |
| 129. | *funeral* | **kêḍu** | (Kan. =destruction). |
| 130. | *place of final obsequies* | **âthârm, âthâre, âthârb** | (? S. *âdhâram*). |
| 131. | *ashes* (human) | **nîrrzh** | (Drâ. *nîrru*). |
| 132. | *ashes* | **bûdi** | (Kan. *bûdi*, from S. *vib-'hûti*). |

---

| | | | |
|---|---|---|---|
| 133. | *day of 24 hours* | **nâḷ** | (Drâ.). |
| 134. | *to-day* | **êddu** | (Kan. *ind-u*). |
| 135. | *yesterday* | **ennêr** | (Kan. *ninne.* Tam. *nêttu*). |
| 136. | *to-morrow* | **makâl** | (? + S. *kâla*=time). |
| 137. | *a week* | **eṭṭnâḷ** | (=eight days). |
| 138. | *a month* | **mûpath nâḷ** | (=thirty days). |
| 139. | *a month* | **deltu** | (? A. K. *tingaḷu*=moon). |
| 140. | *a year* | **vâr** | (K. corruption of *varusha*). |
| 141. | *dawn* | **belkâshk** | (=when the morning star is seen. Comp. 146, 153). |
| 142. | *dawn* | **êrigitâshk** | (=rising time. Comp. 146. K. *êru*=rise). |
| 143. | *sunrise* | **bîrshabât, bîrshkâshk** | (Comp. 148). |
| 144. | *noon; daytime* | **pachal** | (S. Kan. *pagal-u*). |

| | | |
|---|---|---|
| 145. *sunset* | **êkarvâshk** | (Comp. 146. ? *êgu*=go). |
| 146. *night, bedtime* | **îr, îrzh, îrzhtâshk** | (Drâv. *irulu* = darkness. *âshk* in all these words is of uncertain origin. It is probably a corruption of *kâlam* = time, and seems to be *kâshk*). |
| 147. *midnight* | **nadujâma** | (Kan.=middle watch). |
| 148. *sun* | **bîrsh** | (K. *bisul-u*). |
| 149. *moon* | **tiggalu** | (Comp. 139). [touch). |
| 150. *new moon* | **muṭṭu** | (? *muttu*=pearl ; *muṭṭu*= |
| 151. *star* | **mîn** | Dr.=the twinkler). |
| 152. *sky* | **bân** | (Kan.). |
| 153. *light* | **beḷak, beḷk** | (Kan. *beḷa-k-u*). |
| 154. *darkness* | **irzh** | (Comp. 146). |
| 155. *lightning* | **mijju** | (Kan. *minug-u*). |
| 156. *rainbow* | **kvarvarvirsh** | (Comp. 53, 159). |
| 157. *rain* | **ṃlâ** | (K. *maḷe*). |
| 158. *wind* | **kâtu** | (Tam. *kâttu*. K. *gâḷi*). |
| 159. *storm with rain* | **kvar** | (K. *kâru*=the wet season). |
| 160. *shadow* | **naḷ, nerzh** | (K. *neḷal-u, neralu*). |
| 161. *smoke* | **pokh** | (A. K. *poge*). |
| 162. *thunder* | **yerthti** | (=it thunders). |
| 163. *fire* | **nebbu, diṭth** | |
| 164. *mantle* | **putkuḷi** | (A. K. *podda-kambaḷi*=a blanket in wear). |
| 165. *cloth to pass under the legs*. The lungoti | **kûvn** | (S. *kaupîna*). |
| 166. *bracelet* | **pall, ebball** | (K. *baḷe*). |
| 167. *armlet* | **tûḷwaji** | (K. *toḷwanki*). |
| 168. *necklace* | **kavich** | (Drâv. use of S. *kavacha*). |
| 169. *neck-ring* | **belthta** | (Comp. 170). |
| 170. *finger-ring* | **belth** | (Comp. 102, prob. from *baḷe*=a fillet. The Kan. roots *baḷ, beḷ*). |
| 171. *ear-ring* (silver) | **kev-belth** | (=ear-ring). |
| 172. *ear-ring* (gold) | **dsin, dseṭṭi** | K. *chinna*=gold). |
| 173. *tattoo marks* | **gurtu** | (K. *kuruh-u* ; *gurtu*) |

CHAP. XXIX.

| | | |
|---|---|---|
| 174. *hill* | **diṭu** | (K. *ṭiṭṭa*). |
| 175. *valley* | **kḷi** | (K. *kîḷ*). |
| 176. *river* | **par** | (A. K. *pari-yu*, flow). |
| 177. *forest* | **koar, mên** | (K. *kâḍ-u* ; *mara*). |
| 178. *tree, wood* | **mên** | (K. *mara*). |
| 179. *bush* | **tapi, tûre** | (Comp. 120). |
| 180. *grass* | **pullu** | (A. Kan.) |
| 181. *flower* | **pu** | (A. Kan.) |
| 182. *fruit* | **pôm** | (A.K. *paṇṇ-u*. Tam. *paṛam*. S. P'HAḶAM). |
| 183. *juice* | **kar, nîr** | (K. S. *sâra*. 184). |
| 184. *water* | **nîr** | (K. *nîru*). |
| 185. *mud* | **purzh** | (K. *burude*, § 6). |
| 186. *soil* | **mannu** | |

---

| | | |
|---|---|---|
| 187. *gold* | **dsin** | (K. *chinna*). |
| 188. *silver* | **beḷthti** | (K. *beḷḷi*). |
| 189. *iron* | **kabban** | (Kan.). |
| 190. *brass* | **tembu** | (K. *chembu*). |
| 191. *lead* | **disal** | (S. Drâv. *sîsa*). |
| 192. *stone* | **karsh** | (K. *kall-u*). |

---

| | | |
|---|---|---|
| 193. *north* / 194. *south* | The Tuḍas have no word for 'north' and 'south,' but say only 'here' and 'there'; **ite** and **ate**. | |
| 195. *east* | **kîrzh, mûralu** | (Kan. *mûda*, *kîl*). |
| 196. *west* | **blui** | =place of the sun's setting. |
| | **mok** | =above. (Tending to show that the Tuḍas originally lived on the eastern or lower side of the ghâts). |
| 197. *wet season* | **knar** | (K. *kâr*). |
| 198. *dry season* | **baram** | (Kan. *bara*, dry). |

---

Here **vom**=*vâram*. (S.)

| | | |
|---|---|---|
| 199. *Sunday* | **âsvom** | *âs* (?) |
| 200. *Monday* | **tuvom** | *tu* (?) |
| 201. *Tuesday* | **âm** | (?) |
| 202. *Wednesday* | **budavom** | *buda*=Mercury (S.) |

| | | | |
|---|---|---|---|
| 203. | *Thursday* | **tâm** | (?) |
| 204. | *Friday* | **beḷḷivom** | *beḷḷe*=silver, a name of Venus. |
| 205. | *Saturday* | **thanivom** | *thani*=*sani*. (S.) |

CHAP. XXIX.

A few of the words in this list defy all attempts to trace their origin. And this is not surprising. If in English such words as *boy*, *girl*, *dog*, and *pig*, though modern, cannot be traced, a tribe like the Tuḍas may well have invented a few terms.

§ 42. TUḌA NUMERALS.

| | |
|---|---|
| I. **vodd** | (K. *ond-u*) |
| II. **edd** | (K. *eraḍu*) |
| III. **mûdu** | (K. *mûr-u*) |
| IV. **nânku** | (K. *nâlk-u*. T. *nâng-u*) |
| V. **ûtsh** | (K. *eid-u*) |
| VI. **âr** | (K. *âru*) |
| VII. **êlzh** | (K. *êḷ-u*. T. *êṛ-u*) |
| VIII. **eṭṭ** | (K. *eṇṭ-u*. T. *eṭṭ-u*) |
| IX. **onpath** | (K. *on-batt-u*) |
| X. **pattu** | (A. K. *pattu*) |
| XII. **ponedd** | (A. K. *paneraḍ-u*) |
| XVI. **pârzh** | (A. K. *padinâr-u*) |
| XX. **êvoth** | (K. *ippattu*) |
| XXX. **mûpath** | (K. *mûvattu*) |
| XL. **nâlpath** | (K. *nâlvattu*) |
| L. **epath** | (K. *eivattu*) |
| C. **nûr** | (K. *nûru*). |

§ 43. A few subjects for discussion may be indicated here.

(1) In examining these lists I think it will become evident that the 'lingual' or 'cerebral' letters in the Drâviḍian languages are all corruptions of one letter, a kind of l. This seems to be the one Vêdic cerebral.

Kan. *maḷal-u* is Tam. *maṇal*; so
Kan. *maḷai* is Tam. *maṛai*.
Kan. *nâḍ* is Tuḍa *naṛ*.

Comp. §§ 6–8.

CHAP. XXIX.

The Drâviḍian languages had originally one cerebral, as had the Sanskrit and the Welsh.

(2) The Tuḍa *temporal particles* (§ 28) are

**k** for the *present* (**ch**, **sh**, **h**)
**th** (sharp) for the *past* (**d**)
**b** for the *future* (**p**, **v**) (only obscurely indicated).

It is perhaps in vain to form conjectures as to the origin of these, but **k** seems allied to **ge** or **ke**=do;

**th** may be connected with the root **tâ**, **dâ**, **d'hâ**=*give*, *place*, *establish*.
**b** is possibly allied to S. *b'hu* and its cognates.

(3) The Tuḍa nominal inflectional particles, or case endings, are (§§ 15–17) at the most four:

**g** (**k**); **edd** (**end**); **ad**; **orzh**.

Of these **g** I connect with **ge**=do;

**edd** (**end**=**erd**) is past of **er**=be;
**ad** (**ath**) is adj. pronoun;
**orzh** (**or**) is the root of a verb, signifying *absolute existence*.

§ 44. On the whole I venture to think that

(1) The Tuḍa is a language which was once highly inflectional; but, having lost most of its inflections, the people, who have evidently degenerated in every way as the result of isolation, have not replaced them by significant particles or auxiliaries to the same extent as the other South-Indian tribes; and the language has thus dwindled down to a mere skeleton. It now barely suffices for the purposes of a very barbarous people.

(2) The language seems to have been originally Old Kanarese, and not a distinct dialect. The Tuḍas were probably immigrants from the Kanarese country; and have dwelt on the Nîlagiris for about 800 years. Their language was Old Kanarese. A few Tamil forms were introduced by

the Poligars. Intercourse with the Baḍagars has probably modernized a few of the forms and introduced some words. Of Telugu influences I see no trace. It is true that the Tuḍa for *tree* is **mân**, and in Telugu *mânu*, while in Tam. and Kan. it is *mara*; but the soft *r* is always avoided by the Tuḍas, who turn *vâram* into *vôm*.

Nor can I trace any resemblance in Tuḍa to Malayalim, in any of the points where that dialect differs from its sisters.

NOTE. Some words have been added to the above list, since the 'outlines' left Dr. Pope's hands. If, in consequence, a few errors have crept into the Chapter, I alone must be held to be responsible for them.—W. E. M.

---

## *ADDENDA.*

(Translation of Deuteronomy, chap. xxv. 5.)

**vodd ennan athum enorvet-mokh vodd-**
*An elder-brother* (and) *his other-born* (younger brother) *in one*

**ârzulch uddâdi, vodd, âl mokḥ illâde,**
*Toda house if they are, one Toda-man a son is not,* (childless)

**kêdag-pôkadi kêdag-pôkan kâtvodi-kukh en-odd-**
*if he goes to death* (dies) *the dead-one's bound-woman* (wife) *to another*

**âlg kaṭṭaṭi, â kukh-âl, enorvet-mokh**
*man must not join, that woman's man's* (husband) *younger-brother*

**illaveniâdi, pâyâl â kukh kekhuri vorgma,**
*or if not, the brother-in-law* (near relation) *that woman near shall sleep,*

**athum kudma, kâtvodi-âlg enorvet âdi.**
*her shall join, as a wife's man's younger-brother shall he do.*

# APPENDIX

## CHAPTER IV.

*The exclamation, Tya! or Tcha!* I perused in a small pamphlet by the Rev. Mr. Downes, of the Church Missionary Society, on the customs of the Siah-posh Kafirs; which appeared in a number of the 'Pioneer' for the month of May 1873, the following passage; 'in meeting, they salute each other by saying *Too teascha,* are you come?' —(?) are you well.

---

## CHAPTER VII.

*Pernâl, the name of a Toda.* At page 349 of the Anthropological Journal for the month of January 1873, it is stated on the authority of Colonel Pearse, that the chief deity of the Malayalis—a Drâvidian Tribe of the Shevaroy Hills—is *Purinall.* The places of worship for this God, are styled, in the article quoted, hill-top temples; and are constructed of wood.

LONDON: PRINTED BY
SPOTTISWOODE AND CO., NEW-STREET SQUARE
AND PARLIAMENT STREET